'The thrilling, gripping and often painfully moving voices of those women who served alongside men in the Second World War – but were never called soldiers because they were women. Tessa Dunlop captures with verve, sensitivity and humour the indomitable spirit, the hardships and the emotion of these young women, many of them sheltered young girls, thrown overnight into the brutality of total war.'

PROFESSOR KATE WILLIAMS

'Wise, witty, compassionate and personal: Tessa Dunlop writes just the best kind of history about women.'

LUCY WORSLEY, OBE

'You'll feel the shock of finding these amazing characters are still among us – I was gripped from the first page.'

JEREMY VINE

'A fascinating and joyful read. It brushes aside simplistic myths about World War II, uncovers the forgotten stories of women who served on the front line and makes us see British women's experience of war as it must really have been – messy, intense, sometimes absurd and very often heroic.'

JONATHAN COE

'[A] moving account of 17 surviving veterans . . . Dunlop has brought the female military experience to life'

OLIVER WEBB-CARTER,

'*Army Girls* . . . is an extraordinary insight into the women who served in the Second World War.'

CLAIRE O'BOYLE, *Daily Mirror*

'A brilliant, moving and at times funny book.'

PAUL ROSS, Talk Radio

'Very compelling . . . All of the interviewees seem to be speaking from the heart'

Family Tree Magazine

'There were 290,000 women who supported the army in the ATS during the Second World War. *Army Girls* lets their voices shine through, and is the perfect tribute to the lives and achievements of these women.'

ELLA BEALES, *Aspects of History*

'It's been marvellous to read'

MICHAEL PORTILLO, The Times Radio

DR TESSA DUNLOP is a twentieth-century historian, acclaimed author (*Sunday Times* bestseller *The Century Girls* and *The Bletchley Girls*) and Royal Television Society awarded broadcaster. She was a presenter on the BBC's BAFTA-winning series *Coast*, appears on numerous history documentaries and talk shows and writes for several publications including *Mail+*, the *Guardian* and the *Spectator*. Tessa grew up in Scotland and now lives in London with her husband and their two daughters.

Tessa Dunlop

ARMY GIRLS

The secrets and stories of military service

from the final few women who fought

in World War II

HEADLINE

First published in 2021 by
HEADLINE PUBLISHING GROUP

First published in paperback in 2022 by
HEADLINE PUBLISHING GROUP

1

Please refer to page 335 for picture credits.

Cataloguing in Publication Data is available from the British Library

ISBN 978 1 4722 8211 8

Designed and typeset by EM&EN
Printed and bound in Great Britain by Clays Ltd, Elcograf S.p.A.

Headline's policy is to use papers that are natural, renewable and
recyclable products and made from wood grown in sustainable forests.
The logging and manufacturing processes are expected to conform
to the environmental regulations of the country of origin.

HEADLINE PUBLISHING GROUP
An Hachette UK Company
Carmelite House
50 Victoria Embankment
London
EC4Y 0DZ

www.headline.co.uk
www.hachette.co.uk

Preface

'The Princess was a quiet girl. She didn't put herself forward.' Gwen Evans (née Ansell) is ninety-eight years old
and served in the Auxiliary Territorial Service between
1942–6. I am writing about her in the preface of the
paperback edition of *Army Girls* because we've only just
met. Finding women in their late nineties who served
in Britain's female army in World War II comes with its
own unique set of challenges. Finding women who served
alongside HRH Princess Elizabeth in the last two months
of that conflict is harder still. Ironically both were made
much easier with the publication of this book.

Any writer will tell you that a positive response to their
work is always hugely welcome. However in November
2021, the Armistice month when *Army Girls* was published,
the sheer deluge of emails and letters I received was
both surprising and deeply moving. Sons and daughters,
nephews and nieces, friends and former military rushed to
champion their own extant or late ATS member. The book
tapped into a well of unspoken pride for a generation of
women who quietly got on with the unexpected: military
service.

Inevitably in an oral history featuring women in their
late nineties, since publication several of the original

Army Girls have 'left to meet their maker' as former private Daphne wryly puts it. In the nick of time I was able to catch and curate their memories and personal archives. Perhaps only now do I fully understand what 'living history' means. Being able to telephone Lady Martha (who recently celebrated her hundredth birthday) to double check what she wrote in a letter to her parents from a gun-site in 1943, was both a privilege and a joy.

It is this direct connection to a conflict like no other that gives our monarch Elizabeth II's extraordinary life a unique military hallmark. In the midst of her Platinum Jubilee year, we not only celebrate a queen who has reigned for a staggering seventy years but also a young princess who served king and country in World War II. More than four centuries ago it was Elizabeth I who went down in history for her rousing speech to troops in the face of the Spanish Armada: 'I know I have the body of a weak and feeble woman, but I have the heart and stomach of a king.' However, the Virgin Queen did not serve with her soldiers in uniform. That first from a female member of the royal family came much later in the form of a modest teenager, heir presumptive HRH Princess Elizabeth.

Just two months shy of war's end in March 1945 the Princess was finally permitted to join the ATS. Despite its brevity, the future Queen's military service saw her become the symbol for a generation of women who went to war in unprecedented numbers. Ever since, Her Majesty's familiar face has tied us back to the Blitz, Churchill and female service. I drew on Princess Elizabeth's military archive in the National Army Museum for this book. It makes for astonishing reading: the level of to-ing and fro-ing and bureaucratic fuss involved for one young girl to enter the ATS and learn to drive was stifling. Nothing was left to chance. Elizabeth was a pawn in a greater game and even when she was finally allowed out of Windsor Castle to train at Camberley's No.1 Motor Transport Training Centre, her experience was minutely controlled.

In the morning when the Princess arrived on site, the other girls had already been fed and drilled, and, according to Gwen, chauffeur-driven bottle green army vehicles swept up again in the evening to take Elizabeth home. Above all else, the veterans featured in this book treasure the friendships forged in their communal living quarters; the small talk, the japes and the letters home. But that rite of passage was not available to the Princess, she slept at Windsor Castle. 'I think she did have some friends. She was in a unit that was training to be officers. They were a bit separate from us but we all learnt mechanics.' Former ATS driver Gwen smiles. 'You opened up the front of a Bedford truck and put all the parts on a ground sheet. A fan belt, a carburettor, that sort of thing.' She waves her hand. 'And in front of an inspection officer you had to name all the parts and know how to put them back together again.' 'Yes, everyone.' She nods. 'Even the Princess.'

We are talking about the most famous woman in the world, revered for her longevity, her discretion and her sense of duty. I'm hungry for any detail, big or small. But Gwen, like the other Army Girls, has a more nuanced take on our sovereign's military service. HRH Elizabeth was younger than the women in this book (Gwen frequently reminds me that the Queen is two-and-a-half years her junior), and she joined the war later; a slip of a girl who squeezed into a superior officer's uniform at the last minute.

By the time Gwen arrived at Camberley for six weeks of training she'd already served in the ATS for over two years, predominantly as a shorthand typist. In comparison Elizabeth 'seemed shy and a bit unsure of herself.' Apparently the Princess 'was never pushy', quite the opposite. Freshly pressed out of her castle closet where she had been holed up with little sister Margaret while her parents picked their way across Britain's bomb sites, the future Queen lacked the easy assurance around her peers that comes with familiarity. Public messaging insisted 'The Princess is to be treated in exactly the same way as any other officer learner at the driving training centre', but that was to deny Elizabeth's exceptional position. The Princess was already accustomed to reviewing parades of uniformed troops and one day she'd be Queen and titular head of all she surveyed.

'Just as we did with the ATS commanders, we knew to respect her. It was built in. You didn't treat her differently but you just knew she was something different from you.' Gwen glides over the contradiction of royalty. 'I am a monarchist.' And to prove it she adds: 'My parents read the *Daily Mail* and it was always going over what the royals were doing.' Nowhere is that hereditary magic more important than the military, where our armed forces have always served in the name of their sovereign.

Gwen's living room is heavy with the pungent aroma of hyacinths; she closes her eyes and conjures up the past. 'We were pleased to see them. We were taught how to curtsey.' She's referring to Elizabeth's parents, King

George VI and Queen Elizabeth. They famously visited their daughter when she was doing a vehicle inspection; the photographs are legion and the Princess a composed subject. The press was a world she knew well. I wonder out loud if Elizabeth ever complained about the strictures on her army life and all the attention. Gwen looks at me and says very slowly: 'She would not have complained. None of us did.'

But at least Gwen and Elizabeth were learning to drive. 'I wanted to drive, we all wanted to drive. Once I drove a male officer to Hull and I went at 50mph. He was holding onto the sides of his seat.' Irrespective of rank or destiny, rattling Bedford trucks were joyously liberating creatures to the young female recruits at the wheel, but while Gwen carried on driving convoys and delivering troops and munitions into 1946, the Princess's military set piece was almost over before it began.

Joyce, an Army Girl and driver in this book, thinks that like her Elizabeth might've needed to sit on a cushion to reach the pedals in larger military vehicles, and former corporal Joan recalls a member of her Norfolk ATS branch who trained the Princess at Camberley. 'Irene's job was to show her what was under the bonnet of these army trucks.' Like many other female veterans she too is quick to remind me: 'The Princess had lunch every day in the Officer's Mess and went home each night.'

Elizabeth's ATS experience was so fleeting that her peers are fairly dismissive about the subject but her choreographed war was never primarily about impressing the service's rank and file. Most importantly it sent a message to the watching world that imperial Britain's fight for freedom and democracy included the military service of a young princess and heir to the throne. The war had involved everyone and so must the peace.

Joyce's fondest wartime memory was dancing the 'Lambeth Walk in a giant crocodile across Piccadilly and down the Mall on VE day. It was terrific! It was wonderful! It was as good as the pictures suggest.'* Joyce didn't need pictures; she lived it, pushing her way towards the palace and waving at a distant clutch of individuals on the balcony. 'There was Winston Churchill, the King and the Queen and of course Princess Elizabeth in her uniform. They let her out you know. She joined the crowds and probably danced down Piccadilly just like me!'

The last entry in George VI's diary that evening referred to his daughters: 'Poor Darlings, they have never had any fun yet.' The King knew just how curtailed nineteen-year-old Elizabeth's war had been – he'd instigated much of it. For many girls, the conflict pushed them out of the family home into a medley of work and play they never forgot. Not so Elizabeth. The Princess's wartime sacrifice wasn't her military service but rather the restrictions placed upon it. But if she couldn't be the same as the other ATS recruits, her training gave her invaluable credibility. For the rest of her life the Queen has tirelessly represented a generation of women who grew up in an era that demanded their military service. In extreme old age Joyce and Gwen are certain: 'She has done a wonderful job honouring the war effort', and there is not one Army Girl who disagrees.

February 2022

---

* In the book you'll discover that Joyce gave up tennis aged ninety five. In 2022 aged ninety seven she has just taken up table tennis.

Contents

Abbreviations xv
Introduction xvii
Character Cast xxvii

Part One
NOVEL WAR

1. Olivia's Drôle de Guerre 3
2. 'Flowers for the mess room' 13
3. Escape to England 27
4. 'We are standing at our posts' 34
5. Olivia's Croix de Guerre 45
6. Bombing Girls 53
7. Steel Helmets and Lipstick 64
8. Recruiting Gunner Girls 73

Part Two
A LONG WAR

9. 'YOU are wanted too!' 85
10. 'The girl behind the gunner' 97
11. 'Top Ack!' 110

12. 'Come into the army, Maud' 122

13. 'Rumours derogatory to the service' 132

14. Figureheads and Secret Work 140

15. A Reluctant Recruit 151

16. The Cookhouse – 'a woman's natural home' 159

17. Driving like a Princess 170

18. Gun-site Life 183

19. Becoming a FANY 192

20. Deadly Parlour Games 201

21. Multi-racial War 211

22. 'One can look but one must not touch!' 221

23. Boys, Girls and D-Day Landings 230

24. Operation Diver 236

Part Three
FOREIGN WAR

25. Service Overseas 249

26. Conscription Overseas 265

27. Bittersweet Victory 274

28. Germany and Beyond 284

29. Remembering the War 295

Epilogue 303

Notes 309

Bibliography 322

Acknowledgements 329

Index 337

Abbreviations

AA Command – Anti-Aircraft Command

ATS – Auxiliary Territorial Service

BAOR – British Army of the Rhine

BEF – British Expeditionary Force

BLA – British Liberation Army

CBE – Commander of the Most Excellent Order of the
  British Empire

ENSA – The Entertainments National Service Association

FANY – First Aid Nursing Yeomanry

GOC – General Officer Commanding

GL – Gun Laying

GPO – General Post Office

MBE – Member of the Most Excellent Order of the
  British Empire

MHAA – (Mixed) Heavy Anti-Aircraft

NAAFI – Navy, Army and Air Force Institutes

NAM – National Army Museum

NCO – Non-Commissioned Officer

OBE – Officer of the Most Excellent Order of the British Empire

OCTU – Officer Cadet Training Unit

OD – Order of Distinction (Jamaican Honours System)

PT – Physical Training

REME – Corps of Royal Electrical and Mechanical Engineers

RSM – Regimental Sergeant Major

SOE – Special Operations Executive

SSAF – Sections Sanitaires Automobiles Féminines

TA – Territorial Army

WAAC – Women's Auxiliary Army Corps

WAAF – Women's Auxiliary Air Force

WRAC – Women's Royal Army Corps

WRNS – Women's Royal Naval Service (also known as Wrens)

Introduction

'I just want to take a pill and make everything stop. I know I mustn't but I want to.' Daphne's had a tough year. She fell crossing the floor in early June and broke her hip. Her target was the ringing telephone (mea culpa). A stint in hospital followed and then a care home, no visitors allowed: this was no ordinary year. She's been back at home for four months, but the pain is incessant and the carers intermittent and now she has tested positive for Covid-19. 'I had a chest infection but the doctor wouldn't come out unless I took a test.' The NHS front line is staying as far away from Daphne as it can, and aged ninety-seven, she's struggling.

'I don't want you to come.'

'But I've had coronavirus recently, Daphne. I can help you.'

'Yes, but I don't want you to see me like this. I have everything laid out next door. I want you to come when I'm back to normal. I've not told you what happened after I left 65th Searchlight Company.'[1]

Returning to her restorative tonic – the war – puts the mettle back in Daphne's voice. She's rallied and is quick to remind me that she only accepts guests when her hair is freshly set and coloured (soft chestnut). 'In the army they encouraged us to take care of ourselves, that was very important.' Daphne's stayed loyal to her feminine identity and by the end of our conversation has found her military brio, insisting Covid-19 is not an excuse for lax standards.

No, Daphne didn't wield a gun, nor did she meet or physically repel a German soldier. Unlike Russia's female soldiers who, post-war, couldn't stomach the butcher's cuts in the Motherland's meat markets, Daphne didn't see blood. But she did serve. For four years she was one of 290,000 girls who supported Britain's largest military institution, the army. Daphne was a soldier, but because she was a girl they called her an auxiliary. She was full time and paid, but her military branch was always Territorial. And the Service she provided? That was for the ATS – the Auxiliary Territorial Service – separate from but essential to the functioning of the over-stretched British army.

Born feet-first in September 1938 and initially offering women little more than the opportunity to scrub and cook in khaki, by the end of the war the ATS had changed beyond recognition. This book is not a history of that exceptional service but rather the story of the few surviving women from its ranks. Their jobs spanned a wide array of trades: clerks, drivers and cooks but also interceptors, cipher and intelligence officers, teleplotters and gun-site operators. The largest military service for British women, the ATS was the umbrella organisation that incorporated the older First Aid Nursing Yeomanry (affectionately known as FANYs) and provided girl power across a vast range of fields. The women featured here return to a bygone era, when girls worked alongside the Royal Corps of Signals and the Royal Artillery, in Bletchley Park and for the Special Operations Executive, and served with the British Expeditionary Force in France and later in the British Liberation Army across occupied Europe. Daphne resists the idea of equality – 'there was absolutely no such thing then, and I don't believe in it now' – but she does admit that 'yes, I was part of a brave new world'.

In Norwich Joan has laid out her badges and medals on the nearby armchair: the France and Germany Star ('we had to apply for that one once we demobbed, it arrived in a padded box'), the Defence Medal, for non-operational military service, and the War Medal ('awarded to everyone who served full-time in the armed forces'). Beside these conventional silver and bronze accolades is Joan's ATS badge, sporting the service's three initials above crossed laurel branches. To the lay person it is just another military insignia, but embedded in this woven emblem is a history of struggle; laurels eventually replaced the demeaning roses and stalks that were the hallmark of female military service in World War I.[2] Like everything else in the women's army, the right to wear badges of rank and belonging was fought for. Joan's medals and insignia are over seventy-five years old, and they matter hugely to their centenarian owner; her abundant wartime correspondence suggests they always did. In occupied Germany by 1945 British army girls were shored up by civilian recruits. Faced with this ill disciplined influx, Joan admitted in a letter home, *'we do polish our medals!'*[3]

As a little girl Anne had prayed nightly for king and country; brought up miles away from the Metropolis in Burma, she was imbued with a steely Victorian faith in all that was good about Great Britain. Her British identity was important and as a young soldier it added gusto to the more drab and difficult aspects of drill and duty. 'I was very, very proud of having been in the army. My parents were proud of my service too. It was one of the proudest things in my life.' Later she will tell me that her younger brother Douglas was also proud of his big sister's man-sized war. I ask Anne to explain what that pride means, to break it apart so that we can all understand. 'We felt we were better than everyone else. Yes, the German army was better equipped, and the American girls had fabulous uniforms, we were so shabby! But we felt we were the best. And I was proud to belong with the best.' Not an uncritical woman, Anne concedes that this unabashed pride belongs to a different era and a different Britain. 'There are some things this country has done recently that I'm ashamed of.' But time has not dimmed Anne's very real feelings about the war. She's proud, and with good reason.

As I write we are currently in the eye of another global storm and there is perhaps no better time to revisit that idea of national solidarity, when individuals are obliged to act and think as one. The current Covid-19 crisis is in so many ways World War II's reverse; the enemy's invisible, and the national restrictions are lonely, even divisive, but the threat is real, particularly for the extreme elderly. I began this book with a cast of seventeen women, all sitting on the precipice of life with a virus swirling in their midst. I've met most of them, in gardens, across draughty thresholds and between lockdowns. I talk to the majority on the telephone, others have voice recognition email or helpful carers and children and every day I work as fast as I can, aware that at any time one might die and take her story with her to the grave. As Daphne regularly reminds me, 'I really am doing my best to stay alive for you.'

The business of survival in a pandemic is an arduous task. 'It's dreadful,' Anne concedes, 'to be alone and old.' But she understands duty, she has lived in an era when duty was the nation's watchword; the press was censored, the people were conscripted, and hundreds of thousands of her generation died. Anne's generation is once more in the firing line, but now they must be still and isolated. Pride is harder to wear in private. For the first time Anne watches Remembrance Day in November 2020 on television, rather than celebrating it with friends in her local church. It is a disappointing replacement.

There is not a woman in this book who's not proud of her military service, the wealth of memorabilia and anecdotes and association memberships is evidence of that, as are their shared stories and private moments. Many of them have subsequently met the ATS's most feted members, the late Mary Soames, née Churchill, and (joining much later in the war) our current Queen, Elizabeth II. You too will meet these headline names and discover the significance of their roles; however, even a Prime Minister's daughter and a future Queen could not dispel the ATS's enduring image problem. Joan laughs, 'We were called the officers' groundsheets.' Daphne was not amused. 'It was a nasty thing to say and most unfair as we had far fewer pregnancies than the Wrens and I know that's the case because I have read about it.' It doesn't bother Jean. 'We might have been affiliated to the ATS but we always called ourselves FANYs. We were terribly snobby, you know!'

The largest of the three female services, unlike the WRNS (Women's Royal Naval Service/Wrens) and the WAAF (Women's Auxiliary Air Force) which were regarded as comparatively innovative and modern,* the ATS never had sufficient volunteers and by 1941 the problem was acute. The publication of this book coincides with the 80th anniversary of conscription for women in December of that year. The National Service Act (No. 2) was the first time in British history that women could be directed into military service; the conundrum of how to fill the ranks of the ATS had been solved but not without considerable disquiet.† Compelling girls to serve alongside that bastion of masculinity – the army – at the height of war threatened traditional (read gendered) peacetime British values. Who were the boys fighting for if their girls were no longer at home? It was an issue that the wartime government did its best to duck, with the ATS initially roped in as temporary handmaidens in the male pursuit of war. This ambiguous status has left World War II's female soldiers with a complicated legacy.

Today's ideas and presumptions frequently jar and collide with the very distinct spheres that existed in the 1940s. In our fluid, more tolerant society 'girls' is a potentially sexiest, even pejorative label. Not so eighty years ago. Barbara talks of the anti-aircraft girls, ditto Daphne when she reminisces about her searchlight company. They were teenagers when they were recruited. Given the choice, the War Office didn't want women, it wanted girls, hence *Army Girls*, the title of this book. Conscription began for the cohort aged twenty but the bar was quickly lowered to

---

*   This was despite the negative 'never at sea' motto that hamstrung the WRNS.
†   To reduce the public fall out, conscripted women could opt to work in munitions.

nineteen. The recruitment net deliberately targeted young females, an age group identified as commitment-free, hardworking, healthy and obedient. These girls were expected to serve day and night, in all weathers, away from home and sometimes under enemy fire and overseas. The vast majority did what they were told and didn't complain.

'It was considered quite normal that we were paid less than men. That was how it was everywhere. In shops, industry and in the army.' Anne is candid. Lower pay for the same job was taken for granted (and complaining unpatriotic). Girls wrote begging letters to their parents when short of money but they didn't push for equal pay. Among themselves they tutted about the unwanted attentions of fellow soldiers, but they were careful not to offend their suitors; the sexual impropriety of 'dirty old men' towards uniformed women emerges as a theme in this book.[4] The potential for 'promiscuity' preoccupied the wartime government, who viewed it as a women's problem. Men meanwhile were focused on firing their guns, an activity in which service girls could not partake.

Apprehensive, Joan arrived as part of the British Liberation Army (BLA) in North Rhine-Westphalia in June 1945.* Her compound was surrounded by barbed wire and fraternising with Germans was strictly forbidden. A letter home captures the contradictions of 1940s warfare. *'It's strange, the men have to be armed to go out but the ATS are allowed out in pairs with no arms.'* Women were conscripted to fight, but firearms were prohibited. As part of the ATS, former domestic servant Grace served with the only British-based

---

* On 25 August 1945 the BLA in Germany became the British Army of the Rhine (BAOR).

branch of the army that saw continuous action: Anti-Aircraft (AA) Command. 'I was a gunner girl, but I didn't fire the guns, we weren't allowed to.' Under interrogation she remains loyal to the past. 'We couldn't have operated the guns, the shells were too heavy for us girls to lift.' But ask Grace what she makes of the 2018 ruling that permitted women to serve in every branch of the British army and she smiles. 'Well, let's face it, there's nothing that a woman can't do.' Times have changed, and so has Grace.

This book is not about present-day Britain, but nor can it pretend to exclusively represent the past. It is a story based on memories forged in the crucible of a war that has been recrafted for public consumption so many times its commemoration has become simplified and corrupted. Proud Anne is quite sure her generation were 'pretty run of the mill', but nowadays the few surviving British World War II veterans are introduced as heroes. Nostalgia has heightened our gratitude, and sentiment impacted on the way veterans remember their service. Letters, on the other hand, have little truck with posterity and this book is full of them. Olivia wrote to her parents from invaded France and blitzed London, ditto Joan from liberated Belgium and occupied Germany, Martha from numerous training camps and gun-sites and FANY Jean in southern Italy to her Wren sister Pat. As young adults striving to find their way amidst the boundless possibilities, obligations and uncertainties of war, their voices live on.

Millions died in a conflict where half the belligerents found themselves on the losing side. Part of a liberating army, Joan witnessed the stench of defeat first hand. Perhaps that's why the women in this book considered themselves 'lucky'. Ultimately they were all victors, and belong to a country that's become adept at celebrating its war effort (commemoration is more complicated on the Continent). For decades the hallmark of this very British war story was masculinity, but finally, with the protagonists in their twilight years, there's a growing appetite for a female version of World War II. Ninety-five-year-old Barbara has been part of that sea change. She was behind the initial push to recognise the women in Britain's war effort. 'It began as a Yorkshire campaign for the anti-aircraft girls but the press got hold of it, that's when it grew much bigger.'

In 2005 a statue was erected in Whitehall that commemorates all 'the women of World War II'. Barbara explains, 'It took eight years to find a site and cost over a million pounds. We didn't want it to be tucked away down a side alley. When it was eventually unveiled people objected. Can you believe it?' The sculptor, John Mills, was motivated by a 1940s photograph of a dancehall cloakroom and 'the concept of these women hanging up their uniforms and going back to their normal lives at the end of the war'.[5] The result is seventeen bronze headless uniforms all in a row. Former ATS driver Queen Elizabeth II formally opened the monument and fellow one-time ATS driver Barbara looked on: 'I must admit, I've always thought it was particularly ugly.'

The statue remembers the efforts of all British women during the war, but it was the prospect of female conscription into the uniformed services that unsettled the Establishment. Successive British governments had long prevaricated over the issue of women in the military and in 1938 the reluctant formation of the ATS was too little too late. The slow start for female soldiering in World

War II exacerbated the difficulty of finding extant veterans who served in the ATS before 1941, a problem for this project which deliberately tells the story of women who are still alive. Faced with the prospect of a book minus a beginning, *Army Girls* might have been a non-starter were it not for Olivia. An English girl, she too served in khaki, but for the French military not the British.

Now aged one hundred and two, she arrived in France shortly after war broke out and was awarded the Croix de Guerre for her extraordinary military service. It is Olivia's gumption that kick-starts this story. I was granted a half an hour visiting slot by her Surrey care home between waves of Covid-19. 'Why are you wearing that mask? Take it off.' These days Olivia is almost totally deaf and easily confused but 1940 remains vivid. She has been looking forward to my visit. 'I crossed France with their army when the Germans invaded.' She wasn't thinking about military service when she set off on a belated gap year in January 1940, few girls were. She laughs when I ask what she was doing in 1939. 'Flower arranging!' But beneath the insouciance is the abiding memory of her utility and derring-do. 'I was jolly lucky that I was bilingual. Very few were, you know.' Like almost every woman in this book, conflict on a giant scale gave twenty-one-year-old Olivia the chance to break away from a narrow preordained path and prove herself. 'It's a terrible thing to say but I rather enjoyed the war.'

Character Cast

in order of appearance

OLIVIA Jordan (née Matthews), born January 1919 in Sevenoaks, Kent, served with the Sections Sanitaires Automobiles Féminines (SSAF) in the French Army, 1940, and for de Gaulle's Free French in London 1940–3.

JOYCE Wilding (née Chamberlain), born September 1924 in Godstone, Surrey, served with the First Aid Nursing Yeomanry (FANY) as a transmitter hut attendant and later as a driver for the Special Operations Executive (SOE) in Oxfordshire and Essex and in Bristol for the Red Cross Ambulances, 1943–5.

ANNE Carter (née Garrad), born July 1924 in Burma (now Myanmar), was a clerk in the Auxiliary Territorial Service (ATS), 1943–6, serving in Britain, Italy and Austria and promoted to the rank of junior commander in '45.

Lady MARTHA Bruce, OBE, born November 1921 in Dunfermline, Scotland, joined the ATS rising to subaltern in (Mixed) Heavy Anti-Aircraft (MHAA) batteries on gun-sites across Britain, and later served in occupied Italy and Austria, 1941–6. Post-war she was a lieutenant colonel in the Territorial Army.

DAPHNE Attridge (née Williams), born June 1923 in Manchester, grew up in Norfolk and served with the ATS as a searchlight teleplotter with the Royal Artillery and as a teleprinter operator for the 21st Army Group, Royal Corps of Signals, 1942–6.

DIANA Lidstone (née Scott), born May 1924 in Sheffield, grew up in East Sussex and was a cook stationed in Britain serving in both the ATS, 1943–8, and the Women's Royal Army Corps, 1949–51.

BARBARA Weatherill (née Crorken), born July 1925 in Morley, Yorkshire, served in the ATS as a driver for MHAA Command gun-sites across England and a driving instructor at a Motor Transport Training Company in Wales, 1943–6.

PENNY Bailey (née Daysh), born February 1921 in North London, worked as messenger for Air Raid Precautions, 1939–42, and served as a clerk in the ATS for No.2 Command, Royal Corps of Signals, 1942–6.

VERA Waddington (née Edwards), born 1922 in Bristol, grew up in Saltash, Cornwall, where she was a domestic and a farmhand prior to joining the ATS as a predictor operator with a MHAA battery and latterly an orderly in Leicester, 1942–5.

GRACE Taylor (née Clarke), born September 1924 in Ilford, Essex, worked as a domestic before serving in the ATS, 1941–5, as a spotter, height-finder and plotter with a MHAA battery on numerous gun-sites.

JOAN Awbery (née Stittle), born September 1920 in Soham, Cambridgeshire, was a secretary and joined the ATS with the trade of clerk, 1942–6. Promoted to corporal, she was part of the British Liberation Army in Belgium and the British Army of the Rhine in Germany in 1945–6.

BERYL Manthorp, born February 1921 in Colchester, Essex, was a dance teacher in Norwich before and after serving in the ATS as a warrant officer and regimental physical training specialist on MHAA gun-sites across Britain, 1942–5.

Florence MAUD Ward (née Chadwick), born October 1919 in Stourbridge, England, was a clerk in Birmingham before joining the ATS, 1942–5, when she also served as a clerk, working predominantly in Hollymoor Military Hospital, Birmingham.

BETTY Webb, MBE (née Vine-Stevens), born May 1923 in Shropshire, England, served in the ATS and worked as an Intelligence clerk and paraphraser in Britain's Bletchley Park and the Pentagon, Washington DC, USA, reaching the rank of staff sergeant, 1941–6. She became a permanent staff officer for the Cheshire Battalion of the Territorial Army in 1959 and was their Birmingham recruiting officer between 1966–9.

NANZA Downey (née Hughes), born February 1923 in Stirlingshire, Scotland, served in the ATS working with the Royal Corps of Signals as a wireless interceptor near Harrogate, Yorkshire, 1942–5.

JEAN Argles (née Owtram), born November 1925 in Lancashire, England, served in the FANY as a code and cipher officer for SOE in Baker Street, London before postings in Cairo, Egypt and Bari, Southern Italy, 1943–5.

ENA Collymore-Woodstock, OD, MBE (née Collymore), born September 1917 in Spanish Town, Jamaica, was a clerk in the Kingston Criminal Court Office before serving in the ATS as a radar operator on MHAA gun-sites in Britain and Belgium and latterly as a clerk in the War Office, 1943–6.

Part One

NOVEL WAR

1

Olivia's Drôle de Guerre

Olivia was bored. This war malarkey was proving a little hard to take seriously. Her twenty-first birthday had been a bright light in an otherwise bleak midwinter spent 'twiddling' her thumbs. She recalls looking out of the window of Heverswood, the large family pile in Sevenoaks, Kent, and admiring the tracks left by departing cars. Neither snow nor war had deterred guests from attending her birthday celebrations and a heavy cold was not going to get in the way of a visit to France to see her 'enchanting' friend Veronique, who'd 'taken Kent by storm' the previous year. Olivia had always loved the French, but the outbreak of war postponed her long anticipated visit and in the bitter winter that followed (the coldest since 1893) her slump in morale matched theirs. Young French soldier and philosopher Jean-Paul Sartre noted of the army in early 1940, 'all the men who left with me were raring to go at the outset' but now 'they are dying of boredom'.[1] Olivia had her own philosophy. 'Determination is the answer. Determination. I was always very good at doing what I wanted to do.'[2] On 29 January 1940, one day after her birthday party, Olivia left for France.

The youngest of four sisters, she'd long felt like the 'runt' of the litter. A final push for a son and heir had resulted in yet another daughter, who was small, opinionated and not particularly pretty. 'It was a great disappointment that they didn't have a boy.' Olivia hated boarding school, resented being too young to go on the family's ski holidays and rarely saw her parents; 'Harry Bird, our gardener, was more like a father to me.' But despite these shortcomings (or perhaps because of them), she had a great appetite for life and was well placed to acquire the accomplishments that were an upper-class girl's lot. Music, tennis and riding were passions and Olivia's French governess gave her a head start on the language front, an ability that was expanded by a trip to Germany in 1936. Or was it 1937? Things are somewhat foggy now but Adolf Hitler was unforgettable. 'I was out in Munich being "finished" and we were in the same restaurant, I saw him having a cup of tea next door to me. I don't think I was politically conscious but I was very conscious of this man Hitler.'

Olivia's blasé description of Germany's controversial leader chimes with Britain's divided opinion in the 1930s. The Left were quick to shout down his fascist credentials but they didn't push for rearmament, meanwhile the Conservatives admired the Fuhrer's national assertiveness and always were more wary of Russia's communists. This muddled picture partially explains Britain's appeasement policy and is epitomised by Olivia's conclusion: 'Hitler hadn't really got going. We didn't think of him as too much of a danger, he had a little thing with the Mitford sisters.' Her brush with Germany's leader was a minor celebrity sighting and not particularly surprising given she was staying in Munich with a family that had earlier hosted the Mitford girls. These 'charming German aristocrats' understood the impending danger; 'they were dead against Hitler, they realised his dangers, you could feel how unhappy they were about his regime,' but she admits, 'they didn't ram it down our throats.' Olivia was their guest, why spoil things with politics?

She was still heavily invested in her self-proclaimed 'permanent gap year' when Hitler invaded Poland in September 1939 and pushed Britain, then France (six hours later) into war. After a five-month delay, Olivia's own wartime sojourn across the Channel began with a characteristically 'super fortnight's skiing' in Megève among friends. But elsewhere the strain of war had started taking its toll. 'The English and the French have never got on.' Olivia gives a wan smile, but in 1940 fractious relations between the two allies were no laughing matter and the Phoney War (Drôle de Guerre), a damp squib on both sides of the Channel, exacerbated tensions.* By May 1940 Britain and France had dumped their respective leaders and almost fallen out. Meanwhile Olivia's skiing trip had given way to more important matters. 'I realised I wanted to do something for England!' but as she was in France, it was the 'father of my friend Veronique, General Héring, the military governor of Paris' who facilitated her next move. In mid-February Olivia arrived in the French capital where she stayed in a student hostel, was kitted out in well-cut khaki and began training with the Sections Sanitaires Automobiles Féminines (SSAF), an elite female wing attached to the French army. Within a matter of months Olivia's skittish confession that she'd 'brooded through the beginning of the Phoney War' thinking this

---

* The Phoney War was the period before major British–French land engagement with Germany began in May 1940.

'seems rather silly, I will go to France and see what's going on' had turned into something much more serious.

A studio photograph of Olivia in her khaki cap, jacket and tie is evidence of that change. She wore her uniform well and beneath the military veneer, cherry lips and waved hair belie an adopted Parisian chic. This English girl knew how to adapt and survive – she'd learnt to the hard way. There's a story from her early teens: riding on the local cinder track Olivia was bucked from a horse and smashed her face. The injury was so bad that eventually the family contacted a pioneering plastic surgeon in London, who gave Olivia a new nose and took a skin graft from her mouth to patch over the damage – but on the day of the accident it was business as usual. Her sister's eighteenth birthday party carried on downstairs, and wounded Olivia was stitched up and somehow 'got through the evening' in a household where 'we weren't allowed to be miserable'. General Héring, her French military host, had chosen well; Olivia was a perfect, non-squeamish addition to the SSAF, a pioneering French service inspired by memories of the Great War. Mud, blood and avoidable death on their own soil led to the establishment of this feted female corps in 1940. It was a hybrid force designed to retrieve and care for the wounded through the combined roles of traditional nursing and more contemporary ambulance driving.

A Red Cross first-aid course was secondary to Olivia's training in map-reading and mechanics in the wealthy Parisian suburb Versailles. 'As I hadn't the faintest notion of how an engine worked in English, it was double Dutch to me in French.' Olivia was better at riding horses than driving cars but mastered sufficient basics to be given her own ambulance. These vehicles were the SSAF's essential weapon and generous donations its life blood. In an all-French regiment, Olivia's special status as the token English girl had not gone unnoticed and she was duly allotted a Renault ambulance gifted by the Duchess of Windsor, a diplomatic affront which still stings today. Blamed for Edward VIII's abdication, divorcee American Wallis Simpson was loathed in Britain and the couple's reputation had gone from bad to worse. Untimely fraternising with Adolf Hitler at his exclusive Bavarian retreat, including Edward's full Nazi salute, was compounded by the latter's appeasing attitude and rumours of a leaked battle plan to the German High Command. The Duchess of Windsor was the last person Olivia wanted to meet and she struggled to maintain composure when Wallis arrived to hand over the ambulance. 'My colleagues all curtsied to her. I firmly stood my ground and just shook her hand.' This was war, reputations (and gestures) mattered.

*

Clement Attlee, the self-effacing leader of the Labour Party, understood the currency of reputations: 'To win the war we want different people at the helm than those who have led us into it.' In May 1940 he launched an uncompromising attack against Neville Chamberlain's Conservative government; German ascendency in Norway had finally called time on Britain's political appeasers.[3] It was the First Lord of the Admiralty, Winston Churchill, Hitler's most vocal and consistent critic, who took the helm at the head of a new national government. A belligerent patriot, this seasoned sixty-five-year-old politician was not naive about the Allies' prospects in the spring of 1940; in his first House of Commons speech as Prime Minister he predicted 'blood, toil, tears and sweat'. But even Churchill was taken aback when, two days later, the French leader Paul Reynaud telephoned him and despairingly predicted 'we have been defeated . . . we are beaten'.

Like all the Allied commanders, Churchill was surprised by the sheer speed with which the Blitzkrieg punctured British and French defences. Panzers streamed through the Ardennes into the north-eastern corner of France and by 16 May nothing lay between the steel snake of Germans and Paris.[4] Olivia's crash course in ambulance mechanics and first aid came to an abrupt halt. 'I never took my exams.' Instead, on 30 May, an *ordre de mission* dispatched the SSAF ambulance fleet towards an advancing enemy.

> *Dear Mummy and Daddy . . . we arrived last night after a rather hair-raising journey from Paris . . . a good deal of time was spent hopping in and out of ditches when the aeroplanes came over but they didn't seem to want to waste anything on us.*

General Erwin Rommel's Panzer Division was moving so fast it overtook the retreating French, and Olivia was heading into the eye of the storm. With a leg that scarcely reached the pedal, going 'flat out' to keep up with the convoy was a challenge, but doable if she tipped forwards in her seat. Frantic days were matched by nights spent loading and unloading injured troops off trains. '*The news doesn't seem good, but let's hope we will win in the end.*' She signed off her last letter home with an optimistic flourish. After muddy intermittent breaks taking cover from German bombers they eventually arrived at '*some barracks in a heavenly old town*'.

Surrounded by undulating vineyards and equipped with an improvised evacuation hospital, Bar-le-Duc in north-east France provided a brief reprieve. There, basic food was supplemented by a local greengage conserve and measures of French wine. A photograph with a handful of uniformed girls standing and staring against the backdrop of a whitewashed barrack holds the moment. Olivia is sitting centre stage, her cap defiantly on her head, clutching a large bottle of wine and smiling for the camera. She's a foreigner in a strange land but this young female soldier exudes an extraordinary confidence. At the high noon of her war, Olivia even found time to perfect her French slang with male troops (girls in khaki worked wonders for morale).

Is this where she first became aware of the Allied retreat? When she felt scared for Dick and Raymond, her British brothers-in-law fighting in France? Where she saw her first German soldier? She can't remember, but amidst the chaos and with an ubiquitous Red Cross on her sleeve, she is certain that among the injured she nursed a couple of German prisoners. Her recollection is of gauche adolescent boys in hostile grey, the youngest just fourteen years old. What more could she do for this lad in his last hour? The reply was uncompromising: 'Thank you but there is only one thing I want and you cannot give me that.' She pressed him. 'I want my Fuhrer, *mein Fuhrer*.' The enemy had fanaticism on its side.

It was a female French officer who ordered the SSAF out of the town. Olivia was back behind the wheel, with one attendant and one casualty but this time they were heading south: France was on the move and Germany in the air. The Luftwaffe were dancing and diving in the sky, swooping into low attacks, strafing helpless victims. Trained soldiers and pitiful civilians were caught like rabbits in headlights, 'momentarily seized by the instinct to stand and watch' instead of taking cover or firing back. Olivia didn't have the luxury of either option. 'If you had injured personnel on board you had to keep driving.' Sometimes that was difficult; the roads were log-jammed. The great French Exodus had begun.

In Britain by the end of May the military focus had shifted dramatically. The Dunkirk retreat between 27 May and 4 June 1940, when 338,000 troops were rescued from France's northern coastline, has gone down in history as a victory snatched from the jaws of defeat. Britain was still in the game of war, but only just. English Olivia meanwhile was clinging to life in a French odyssey that had lost faith in its British allies and its own ability to fight back. As a flotilla of ships set sail for British shores, over six million French refugees began to pour south. Pilot and writer Antoine de Saint-Exupéry watched from the air and thought it looked as if someone had kicked a massive ant hill.[5] Olivia was in the middle of a man-made nightmare.

Roadsides were strewn with animal corpses and abandoned cars, German airborne attacks added to the panic. Olivia had no idea where she was going. Surrounded by machine gun fire and chaos she recalls a 'pathetic assortment of people fleeing'. Farm carts, old folk, pigs, dogs and the odd cow amidst a giant swell of humanity on foot. Her status as an ambulance driver afforded a level of priority and speed and a final supper (bread and chocolate) upon arrival at Dijon. There was no more sustenance for a week; adrenaline mitigated the impact of hunger and constipation. As for sanitation, Olivia won't talk about that, but adds it wasn't a French strength at the best of times. By now the SSAF girls were in the heart of France, and the numbers of broken men in Olivia's ambulance mounted; one died en route and there was a final intake from a hospital in Clermont-Ferrand. The fleet of Red Cross vehicles with their young female drivers exited the town and climbed a hill; Olivia's convoy was heading straight into a ruthless German attack on a freight train station. 'The marshalling yards were being bombed, but we had casualties on board so we couldn't get out and hide or stop. I was so frightened I started singing the Marseillaise at the top of my voice.' *Do you hear the roar of those ferocious soldiers?* Her injured men joined in. *They are coming right into your arms!* An ambulance was hit and abandoned. *To cut the throats of your sons, your comrades!*

Olivia and her cargo survived, but France was about to capitulate. World War I hero, the noble, blue-eyed Marshall Philippe Pétain, replaced Prime Minister Reynaud and on 17 June talked of his 'compassion and solicitude' for the 'unhappy refugees'.[6] Millions of French received the news of an Armistice with relief, but for Olivia it changed the game entirely.

When she 'finally arrived at a beautiful chateau in Bordeaux' Olivia was summoned by the female Commandant who explained that the French had surrendered and a new government was being set up in Vichy (where the SSAF were heading). 'Being the only English girl I was now "*de trop*" (unwelcome) and in no way could they take me with them.' The Third Republic was dead; Britain and France were no longer fighting on the same side. Despite all she'd been through, it is this time that Olivia describes as a really 'frightening experience for me'. Until now she'd been part of a regiment, wearing the same uniform, singing the same songs, driving the same ambulances, focused on the same goal: survival. Serving the French army and coming under fire was tough, terrifying even, but they'd had each other. Now Olivia had to find her way back to England, alone.

2

'Flowers for the mess room'

Olivia was by no means the only British girl serving in France. Behind the British Expeditionary Force's (BEF) lines were several thousand Auxiliary Territorial Service women. Their presence was a last minute affair; in December 1939 the ATS's first director, Dame Helen Gwynne-Vaughan, was still struggling to find a French-speaking orderly.[1] The service's stuffy ten commandments for supporting the BEF were finally drawn up in February (including 'no frills or flounces', no lipstick, no powder[2]) and it was early spring before units were posted across the Channel, by which time Olivia was already training with the French SSAF.

With headquarters in Le Mans, by May the ATS had a contingent of drivers and a dedicated team of bilingual telephonists alongside cooks and orderlies. Dame Helen noted with pride that in the Paris exchange, ATS girls went on putting calls through until the last possible moment, tumbling 'into lorries just as the Germans were marching into the other side of Paris'.[3] These service women were among the final Allied troops to leave Dunkirk at the same time as Olivia was hurtling across war-torn France but it's hard to imagine this unusual Francophile girl in the British ATS. She shakes her head when I mention its name. The largest women's military service in Britain had an unspectacular start and was unlikely to appeal to gadfly Olivia. 'No,' she insists, 'I was the French equivalent of a FANY.'

In one short sentence Olivia identifies the complexities of uniformed service for women at the beginning of World War II. Established in 1907, the First Aid Nursing Yeomanry (FANY) was an independent, socially elite, ground-breaking organisation. Or as former FANY Joyce puts it: 'a very conscientious group of helpful intelligent women, of whom most were privately educated!' She giggles. We are sitting in her West Sussex garden in the summer of 2020 and she is raking through FANY memorabilia with pink polished nails. A carefully crafted card dated 12 May 1945 catches our eye. 'Oh, that was given to me when I was a driver at Briggens House near Harlow, where they forged documents for resistance fighters.' Together we pore over the handwritten lyrics.

> . . . *the FANY are so well brought up*
> *They'd suffer no confusion*
> *But in a voice of cool disdain*
> *Would deprecate intrusion*
> *And yet the temptation's very strong*
> *In face of FANY beauty*
> *Hold on a second while I see*
> *The next time I'm on duty*

While Olivia began her war driving, Joyce ended hers behind the wheel serving in an organisation that always provoked a titter. 'Oh yes, everybody always made a joke out of the name. It was rather embarrassing! But the FANYs were impressive women and World War I was their first important event.' Joyce is one of two FANYs we will meet in this book; in their early teens at the outbreak of war, they both joined up in 1943 and ever since have retained a keen affection for their former FANY status.*

Inspired by Florence Nightingale notions of women riding out and administering aid to dying men on the battlefield, by World War I this first uniformed service for women saw FANYs on horseback give way to FANYs in khaki behind the wheels of ambulances and armoured vehicles. A subscription-only organisation (early members were expected to own and ride a horse), it remained deliberately small and selective, or 'a bit snobby' in the words of numerous ATS veterans. But there is no doubting FANY bravery.

They had an exceptional World War I with hearty women staffing a regimental aid-post right behind the front line and providing the first female ambulance convoy to officially drive for the British army.[4] This service cemented a reputation that saw the FANY front up to conflict at the end of the 1930s with a cadre of 400–500 well-trained women, a vantage point which helps explain their broad-ranging, often highly confidential and dangerous war work, the scope of which went well beyond driving.[5] But the latter is what they were best known for and Olivia is correct, her French Sections Sanitaires Automobiles Féminines had much in common with the FANY. Before the ATS had arrived on the Continent in February 1940 a convoy of ambulances with forty FANY drivers had already departed for Finland via Sweden, and in France that summer the FANY served alongside the Free Poles,

---

* Today the FANY (PRVC) is the longest standing and one of the most highly decorated of all female volunteer units.

providing them with a mobile canteen and returning to Britain after the majority of the BEF had withdrawn from Dunkirk.

Joyce muses that although the FANY began as a voluntary organisation, when she 'joined I thought of myself as part of the army and was paid'. The FANY temporarily relinquished their voluntary status in World War II, a change which necessitated their inclusion under the umbrella of the ATS. That Joyce has no recollection of this and instead identified with the army is indicative of the acrimonious relationship between the two female organisations. The FANY's anomalous position infuriated the ATS's inflexible Dame Helen, who was derided by a FANY grandee as 'the most tactless person I think I have ever had the misfortune to know'.[6] Neither side conceded ground easily, with the FANY only partially sacrificing their independent identity to the ATS and its intractable leader.

For Dame Helen, 'the very existence of the FANYs, with their tradition and panache, within her ATS' presented 'both a challenge and an affront'.[7] Certainly the much larger, more cumbersome ATS was a very different beast. Its predecessor, the Women's Auxiliary Army Corps (WAAC), also had a presence in France during World War I, which helped establish the forthright reputation of Dame Helen. She emerged in 1918 as a minor celebrity and was the first female to be awarded a military CBE, but on the whole jobs in the WAAC were menial and the project short-lived. Despite Dame Helen's best efforts and in contrast with the elite FANY, the service was disbanded after World War I.

As late as 1936 the Committee for Imperial Defence argued that a female force in peacetime was neither desirable nor necessary. Given the subject's neglect, it is perhaps no surprise that nearly twenty years after the end of World War I, when Dame Helen was almost sixty (as she noted, too old to serve), the government had no one else to turn to for help. In September 1938 she headed up a new ATS instruction school which relied on her anachronistic know-how, social network and recruitment tactics. This loyal band of country ladies masquerading as local officers and executing drill in drab khaki had limited appeal. Few working-class girls could afford to attend weekly training sessions and the elite FANY kept their distance for as long as possible. Debonair young ladies like Olivia (racy enough to get her ears pierced!) and Joyce ('I loved tennis and music') were unlikely to have much truck with the local squirearchy's efforts.

Joyce laughs at her pre-war existence: 'The awful thing is as a child, I never remember my mother doing any cooking. There were all sorts of people, a nanny, a houseman, a cook, looking back it was an extraordinary life.' With a family home in Surrey and attending the same school as the Churchill daughters, it's no coincidence that she ended up in the FANY, a service which considered itself a cut above the prosaic realities of war. Similarly, before September 1939 Olivia recalls parties (lots of them), musical quartets, house guests, ponies and tennis galore, and when Kent got tiresome there was a second home in Devon supported by a clutch of servants. The wireless with its mass-appeal messaging was abhorred. If hair-raising adventures across a foreign country suited Olivia's gusto, more socially conservative ideas of military service belonged elsewhere.

*

'My mother was the first woman to be recruited into the ATS.' It lands like a bombshell. The daughter of Mrs Garrad is sitting in front of me. 'My family were all rather imbued with the Anglican idea of duty, which has gone a bit out of fashion now.' We're talking in the sunny annex of Anne's attractive Norfolk home. Legs set square in front of her and hands on knees below a direct gaze, she admits, 'I can be intimidating.' Aged ninety-six, there's plenty of the former soldier in Anne, and when she expands on her family tree, travelling through the branches of service and devotion, she opens a window to another world.

Her Victorian-born parents were Anglican mission-aries in Burma, where Anne was born; the Garrads' marriage was a compassionate one between two equals whose Christian duties and commitment to Britain's imperial project shaped their adult lives. When Anne's father contracted sprue (a disease which required a stint in London's Tropical Diseases Hospital) the family returned to Britain in 1932. Briefly in Worcester, and then Som-erset, local vicarage life in the Mother Country replaced religious evangelism in the Empire. 'Going to church was like cleaning my teeth, preparing for Sundays was part of life.' It is fitting therefore that chorister Anne, cherub-like in a maroon gown and white bib, was in the vestry when she heard that Britain was at war. 'The service had been put back ten minutes and we all stood on tiptoe for the wireless announcement. I remember the broadcaster's centurion-like voice very much. My friend Jane fainted and we all had very very serious faces.'[8]

She couldn't profess to understand what war meant exactly, but in 1939 fifteen-year-old Anne was more famil-iar with the terminology of war than most girls of her

age. In Barrow Gurney, their Somerset home, her mother
Marjory Garrad was good friends with Mrs Gibbs, a local
aristocrat who'd been tapped up in early 1938 to become
the local county commandant for a newly formed Auxiliary Territorial Service. Charged with the appointment of
junior officers, vicar's wife Marjory was Mrs Gibb's first
port of call. 'Mum's brother had been killed in France in
the last few weeks of World War I. He'd returned from
Canada to fight for Britain, it was ghastly.' This painful
loss accentuated Marjory's desire to 'do everything within
her power to prevent a second conflict. I think the idea
was that if she had a hand in it, she could control the
horror of it.' While other mothers contented themselves
with a spot of part-time work in the Women's Voluntary
Services co-ordinating evacuees and distributing gas
masks, Marjory's previous form as a single woman who
served in the Red Cross during World War I and then
travelled alone to Burma explains her choice of a more
strident form of service. The ATS, initially designed to
provide women in a supporting structure for all three
armed forces, was established on 8 September 1938, just
a couple of weeks before Prime Minister Chamberlain's
ignominious return from Munich. Anne recalls, 'Mother
duly set off to the county town of Taunton to sign on.'[9] A
quirk of fate perhaps, but fitting nonetheless, that Marjory
Garrad was given the very first ATS 'number ever issued
in the whole country. W/1.'

Anne concedes that yes, Marjory's pioneering appointment had the blessing of her father. This was 1938, when
vicars might have expected their wives to occupy a more
backseat role. Not Reverend Garrad however, who would

soon be urging young men to leave their farms and fight for king and country. Sacrificial duty was national service in its most noble form. If Anne dreaded her father's patriotic hectoring, in equal measure she felt pride when Mrs Gibbs and her mother, county commandant and senior leader respectively, hot-footed it to London for obligatory square-bashing and a staged press photograph. Their timing was impeccable, there was an uptick of interest in the service after the Munich Crisis and Anne delights in the memory of a picture in the *Bristol Evening Post*. 'A bevy of middle-aged ladies wearing ATS armbands, twinsets and pearls and high heels, being drilled by a purple-faced sergeant major of the Guards, so we all felt in very safe hands!'[10]

Dame Helen could be reassured that recruitment went 'on apace' in Somerset, albeit within the confines of rural England's social hierarchy. 'The class system was used as a recruiting tool', of this, Anne is sure. Up and down the country reports of unlikely ladies and roaring drill sergeants – 'L-e-f-t turn!' Q-u-i-c-k march!' – had a surreal air, as journalists picked their way between describing the pantomime of posh women, addressing the country's acute military needs, and preserving the status quo. Newspapers revelled in the feminine invasion of numerous army barracks. 'Floors got an extra polish, pans got an extra scrub.' Women had 'left their maids at home' and 'brought with them flowers for the mess room and smiles for the parade ground'. But beneath the brouhaha and gloss the message was clear: 'More recruits are needed – especially women who can cook!'[11] Initially no effort was made to hide the fact that the ATS was intended as little more than the army's domestic wing, dressed up in military garb.

*

History has regarded Dame Helen's legacy with caution. A product of the old governing class, her commitment to the idea that 'patriotism is more foreseeing among educated people' today makes for uncomfortable reading.[12] It's likely that her failure to adapt to changing times contributed to Dame Helen's inability to win a parliamentary seat in the 1920s, with her later high-handed treatment of the FANY indicative of a brusque intolerance. But viewed in the narrow context of the army, this was a woman trying to push fellow women into an institution that was the very embodiment of patriarchy and hierarchy. It's small wonder she relied on old-fashioned recruiting techniques in an inter-war world where feminism had more or less fizzled out and equality didn't exist. Whatever her failings, Dame Helen was a survivor, a 'termagant' even, who didn't take no for an answer, and by July 1939 she had been appointed the ATS's first director.[13]

Like Dame Helen, Martha (Lady Martha Bruce, OBE) was and still is a product of feudal Scotland. Aged ninety-nine, this diminutive wise-owl, neatly tucked into a hooded Orkney chair, recalls her most intimate encounter with the then-director of the ATS. 'Post-war I was driving Dame Helen to a reunion event in Glasgow. She was bent forward, very arthritic, a bit like me now! I knew she was very bright, I wanted to be able to hear what she was saying, but she was so disabled that it made conversation difficult.' It was the late 1950s; Martha was a major in the Territorial Army and Dame Helen a figure she had long regarded with awe. Both women shared a passion for the military and both were pioneers in their own right but Dame Helen came first; she paved the way for Martha, who was struck by the achievements of this military director. Beyond her impact on two world wars, Martha stresses that Dame Helen was a 'full-time professor, a botanist' when university-educated women were still considered an oddity. Perhaps even now, in extreme old age, Martha feeds off her memories of this extraordinary woman. It's hard talking to a stranger in your sitting room or on the telephone about years of service long ago when you're a bit deaf and blind and tired, but just as Dame Helen turned up to a final reunion bent double, Martha always answers my questions.

Martha's own Scottish backstory is a helpful reminder of the world in which Dame Helen operated. Rising democracy and taxation had knocked the landed aristocracy, but one per cent of the population still enjoyed over half the nation's wealth.[14] Britain, particularly in rural areas, was a highly stratified society, the functioning of which, Martha concedes, depended on the heft of 'the hierarchy as it was in those days, far more than it is nowadays'. Yet although born the oldest child of Edward Bruce, the 10th Earl of Elgin, and his wife, Katherine, there are no airs and graces about Martha. In a pair of scuffed trainers and an old brown jersey, she doesn't use her title, has a track record of speaking truth to power and form when it comes to commanding respect. And her parents were exceptional, of that she is in no doubt. Much more than a product of their rank and class, the Earl and Countess of Elgin were passionately committed to their local community and country. Martha describes her father as a man whose life was split into multifarious forms of service; early on he was a commanding officer in the Territorial Army and a lieutenant colonel in France during World War I. Later the Earl of Elgin sat in the Lords pressing Scottish matters and in Scotland he was a lord-lieutenant and two times Lord High Commissioner.[*]

Martha pauses, and pats her hand gently on her knee. 'He more or less ran the county. And my mother was equally busy.' Kitty, as she was known to friends, had worked in the Foreign Office, organised the Red Cross across Fife and 'knew everyone in Scotland worth knowing'. This active life was only partially interrupted by the onset of motherhood and the demands of primogeniture – 'she could pause a bit when her third child was a boy'. Despite their commitments, Martha remembers very hands-on parents. 'Our nanny always told us we were lucky to have so much contact with our father and mother.' Younger sister Jean concurs that their childhood was an exceptional one, 'but we didn't realise it was different from everybody else's until we went to the local Brownies and discovered that the other girls' "nannies" were in fact their grannies!'

While younger brother Andrew was packed off to boarding school aged eight in preparation for Eton, the girls' education was accorded less importance. There were several governesses before Martha led the way to Downham School in Hertfordshire, a well-known destination for classy Scottish girls. She jokes that the main educational quest was to 'find a rich husband' but concedes her grades

---

[*] Lord High Commissioner to the General Assembly of the Church of Scotland

were good (the best even) and believes that schooling away from home instilled a respect for authority and discipline. Martha thrived in Downham's structured environment; she enjoyed a brief stint as head girl and was awarded a first-class guiding certificate. The latter involved a trip to Buckingham Palace and a meeting with a fellow guider and childhood acquaintance, a shy younger Princess Elizabeth. Martha is tight-lipped on this subject; personal discretion and respect for the monarchy are hallmarks of her personality.

Guiding also ran through Anne's formative years, although in Burma its precursor, the Brownies, were renamed Bluebirds for 'obvious reasons'. A trend for patriotic uniformed youth movements had seen Baden Powell's Boy Scouts take off in 1909, but the world's first Chief Scout didn't anticipate that his winning combination of physical exercise, military training and moral vigour would attract so many girls. Female scouts wriggling on their tummies and leaping over dykes were deemed wholly inappropriate, and the Girl Guides Association was quickly introduced as a replacement. The scouts' rough-and-tumble spirit and martial training were sorely missed and by the 1930s the adventure aspect of guiding had been pushed to the fore in an environment where physical exercise for girls was actively encouraged.[15] Martha's aunt, 'who practically ran the village', was a very keen guider and Anne, a Bluebird from the age of six, was soon adept at camping, lighting fires and outdoor cooking. Aged ninety-six she is still a Norfolk County Vice President of the Guide Association and, sitting alone mid-Covid-19 pandemic, explains that 'the reason why Guiding has been so successful is that we were all involved together in our activities. Humans are built to be together.'

Despite these vivid memories of communal learning and activity played out against the backdrop of encroaching war, in the late 1930s harnessing girl power was not a priority. Much to Martha's chagrin, her mother's preoccupation in the summer of 1939 was the need to present her daughter at Court. A tradition established in 1780, Queen Charlotte's Ball had long outlived its patron. Olivia, in a dress with a train, clutching an ostrich feather between white gloved fingers appears to have quite enjoyed 'coming out' in 1938, but Martha is unequivocal: 'It was the worst year of my life.' Her parents had spent considerable amounts of money acquiring a house in London, a base from which to launch their eldest daughter into society. Nor had the prospect of war put a dampener on the event, which other debutantes recall with nostalgic longing:

'I seem to remember that London was brighter and gayer that year.'

'Debs in 1939 were rather like butterflies emerging from chrysalises – with just a few brief months to flutter around before the stark reality of the war.'[16]

Martha, more comfortable in a guiding uniform than a party frock, did not want to 'flutter around'. Her mother, Kitty, on the other hand, enjoyed 'being in at the top of everything. She was much more social than I was and she liked being on gold chairs and on dance floors which I hated.' But in the summer of 1939 Martha's sister, Jean, kyboshed their mother's social ambitions. 'I came back from school with chickenpox and infected mother, who'd never had chickenpox. She was furious because it meant she couldn't chaperone Martha. I can see her now, sitting up in bed, picking off the scabs, pretending she was OK.' Martha headed south and curtsied in front of the King and Queen without the propelling force of Kitty, the Countess of Elgin. Shy but sufficiently self-possessed to manage the circuit alone, it is perhaps no coincidence that her one outstanding memory of the trip was a top-level military tip-off. 'Somebody asked me if I would like to join the ATS. But at the time I was only seventeen, so too young.' Martha went back to Downham to complete her schooling, returning to Scotland in the summer of 1940 with seven distinctions and the prospect of military service in her sights.

3

Escape to England

It was 18 June 1940 and Olivia was trapped in France, more precisely Bordeaux, which had swollen from 250,000 to nearly a million residents in a matter of weeks. The heart of the city was horribly exposed (on 20 June the Germans killed 65 people there in a bombing raid) and for a strategic port that the Nazis would occupy for the next four years the French surrender promised little reprieve. With the arrival of German soldiers imminent, British Olivia (albeit in a French uniform) was particularly vulnerable and, no longer protected by her unit, had to get out as soon as possible. 'Although, it's a funny thing, one never really despaired. If you're in that situation, you don't.'

The British legation was her first port of call, where she found a disconsolate sailor sweeping 'up the bits' after a rushed evacuation. Olivia's memories are jumbled but she recalls hearing how 'I'd missed the recent departure of possibly Churchill and certainly a man called de Gaulle by a matter of hours'. In fact Churchill did not fly into or from Bordeaux, but desperate to keep France 'side by side' with Britain, he did visit the country five times between 16 May and 13 June. Charles de Gaulle on the other hand had taken a flight from Bordeaux to London on 17 June. Olivia is certain she had no idea who 'this de Gaulle chap' was. At the time few did, even in France. However, as Churchill had identified days earlier during a final showdown with the French, this 6-foot-5-inch General was '*l'homme du destin*'.[1] Implacably opposed to France's separate peace, de Gaulle had just escaped to London and did not return to his homeland for four years. Olivia would meet him much sooner than that.

It was the solitary attendant at the legation who asked her to deliver some papers that de Gaulle had left behind. 'I shouldn't imagine they were terribly important, but they made me feel important.' And feelings were about all Olivia had left. The British man could help her no further. With no money and no flights, she was directed to an American base where they recommended neutral Spain and gave her a ticket ('I can't remember where to') but she can recall being pulled onto a train full of retreating French soldiers. Here was one of their own, and a woman too, amidst 'forty men and eight horses'. The journey was fruitful: there were exchanged stories, 'they knew about my section'; lots of kindness, 'they realised I had to get back to England'; and many stoppages that saw Olivia swap the train for a motorbike on the beach at Arcachon. She mounted this new challenge with much encouragement from her soldier friends. 'They showed me how to work it, I'd never ridden a motorbike before, but I could ride a horse . . . !' Olivia laughs. She didn't even know how to change gears, the bike got very very hot and then, the *coup de grâce*, she ran out of petrol. 'I did start feeling desperate.' It's unclear exactly where Olivia was on the south coast of France, or where she was heading. Did she ever know?

Advice came thick and fast. The uniform helped, of that she is certain. By now she had jettisoned the idea of

Spain, ('too defeatist'), ditto the prospect of Vichy France. God, no. Olivia kept her sights firmly set on England. Parked on an esplanade thick with burnt-out cars, she found a van with keys. Serendipity and a modicum of petrol took her to Bayonne, where fear and exhaustion were rewarded once more with kindness. 'A Frenchman wound down the window and said, "Do you want a lift?"' Even in confused old age, Olivia is very definite: she loves the French and in those desperate days, they loved this English girl right back.

She was given a lift to neighbouring Saint-Jean-de-Luz. A picturesque harbour, this is the only port on France's Atlantic seaboard between Arcachon and Spain and with the French Armistice deadline just two days away, it hosted an extraordinary impromptu rescue mission. Dunkirk's Operation Dynamo story is told and retold, but after the assortment of ships famously sailed to safety, there was an almighty scramble, otherwise known as Operation Aerial, to evacuate the hundreds of thousands of British and Allied troops and civilians still stranded in France. On 17 June RMS *Lancastria* was sunk off the western port of St Nazaire and thousands of children, women and men drowned[*] in the biggest British naval disaster of all time. The stakes were perilously high and as the German army surged south, the options available to Allied ships rapidly diminished. St-Jean-de-Luz, just nine miles from the frontier with fascist Spain was a last port of call. Olivia arrived in the nick of time.

'I saw an English sailor on the jetty. I was in a French uniform and had no identification but he took one look

---

[*]   Estimates range between 3,000 and 5,800 fatalities.

at me and said, "It's all right luv, I can tell yer British."'
She stuck with her new companion, who pointed her in
the direction of a British ship. Locals in their fishing boats
were rowing evacuees across the harbour and in Olivia's
case embarkation included a hairy climb up a rope ladder
(the vessel's gangplank was raised and the swell considerable). She hauled herself onto the deck and came face
to face with an intractable English officer. 'There's no
accommodation for women on this troopship.' Olivia was
a girl who generally got her way, but not on this occasion;
she had come up against the gendered rigidity of the British military. There was a real enemy that any minute now
might bomb them from the air (the Luftwaffe arrived in
St-Jean-de-Luz on 25 June) but no matter, she could not
stay on that ship.

Rather than have a woman onboard, the officer
procured a small boat to take Olivia to a nearby mine-
sweeper. She recalls a warship 'seething with humanity,
mostly Polish troops who, like me, had retreated from the
north-east to the south-west of France.' It is fitting that
this anomalous girl found her berth amidst the Polish
army. Unable to escape at Saint Nazaire, they had made
a fighting retreat to St-Jean-de-Luz and by the Armistice
deadline, 24,352 Polish troops had escaped out of France.
Many of those travelling with Olivia were injured; displaying a Red Cross on her sleeve, she administered
refreshments (dry biscuits and water) and basic first aid.
Her own onboard perks included sleeping (alone) in the
captain's cabin. Being a woman wasn't all bad.

*

On 18 June, the same day that Olivia arrived in Bordeaux, de Gaulle made a first broadcast to his fellow countrymen from a BBC studio.

> I, General de Gaulle, now in London, call on all French officers and men who are at present on British soil or may be in the future with or without their arms; I call on engineers and skilled workmen from the armaments factories who are present on British soil or may be in the future, to get in touch with me. Whatever happens, the flame of French resistance must not and shall not die.[2]

For a little-known general, this ardently patriotic Frenchman had already caused quite a stir. Arriving in London on 17 June, it was his second appearance in the British capital in less than two days. Briefly the French Minister of War (before he was sacked), on an earlier 24-hour round trip he'd proposed that Britain and France should fuse together as one country. The bold idea came to nought but de Gaulle's audacity had impressed, and when he returned to London Churchill recognised him as the head of the 'Free French' and Britain's only alternative to Vichy France.

De Gaulle's biographer Julian Jackson points out that although few people heard his first speech, the theme of which was 'France had lost a battle not a war', a Rubicon had been crossed and nothing was left to chance.[3] After four days and nights drifting precariously between the Atlantic and the English Channel, when Olivia finally arrived in Plymouth, a pamphlet was pressed into her hand. Written in French but sent from the Lord Mayor of Plymouth, Viscount Astor, the propaganda printed by the

Ministry of Information was uncompromising. France had agreed to an undignified peace with Nazi Germany, but there was another way. Churchill promised that victory for Britain would be victory for a Free France: '*Courage. Calme. Victorie. Vive la Vraie France. Vive l'Angleterre!*' Still in her uniform, Olivia had presumably been identified as a French service woman who might respond to de Gaulle's rallying cry. His name was at the bottom on the piece of paper and an address: 125 St Stephens House, Westminster, SW1.

Olivia could be forgiven for initially not paying the pamphlet much attention. Prior to her arrival, stuck out at sea endlessly scanning the horizon, she'd experienced a wonderful surprise. 'I suddenly looked up and there was Eddystone Lighthouse! I shouted, "Oh look! It's Eddystone Lighthouse!" The captain nearly murdered me. He said, "You are not supposed to know where you are!"' Gales of laughter. Olivia couldn't help herself: Eddystone Lighthouse on England's south coast had special meaning; with a large family holiday house in Thurlestone, Devon, her childhood had been spent exploring local coves and beaches with the lighthouse a beacon on dark nights. And there it was, welcoming her home. Her mother might well be holidaying in Thurlestone right now. Olivia couldn't wait to disembark and as the only English person onboard, she received preferential treatment on arrival in Plymouth. 'They let me straight off, I was so lucky.'

Bursting with anticipation, she telephoned ahead but there was no reply. 'Oh damn,' I thought. 'Maddening!' (She later discovered her mother had taken a party out on the golf course.) 'I caught the train to London instead. We arrived in the middle of the night and were sent off to Park Lane Hotel. I'd picked up a rather nice American man. (We had separate rooms so that was all right).' Olivia the French soldier was on a high. 'The next morning I rang up my father in his bank.' What news she had to tell. She was alive and safe! She had been away from home for months in besieged France, under fire and out of contact, and latterly was even reported missing. Her father, Trevor Matthews, the chairman of Grindlays Bank, accepted the call.

'Oh, we knew you'd get back all right,' came the nonchalant response.

'I was furious that was all he said. They didn't seem worried at all. I was so disappointed.'

Olivia came back down to earth with a bump. She was just a girl and girls didn't count for much in war. Over eighty years on, aged one hundred and two, she still insists, 'I was of no importance, just in the army, right down below.' In 1940 war was framed as something men undertook to protect women. Olivia, safely back in London, went to Piccadilly's upmarket Fortnum & Mason and ordered a food hamper for the displaced Polish soldiers she'd left behind. She was unlikely to receive much attention in a family where her sister's husband Dick had just been shot in the chest on the beach at Boulogne. Stretched out on the back of a door he was carried onto a ship, 'for a while his life hung in the balance'. In comparison Olivia's war was too easy to dismiss as an adventure. In London, the changed nature of conflict hadn't fully dawned on people. The recent sinking of the *Lancastria* and the death of thousands of civilians was covered up in the press; aerial warfare and bombs were indiscriminate, but in June 1940 very few had fallen on British soil.

4

'We are standing at our posts'

By the summer of 1940 the ATS's first recruit, Anne's mother, Marjory, had already left the service. Once again, her good friend Mrs Gibbs, 'a true blueblood' was behind the decision. 'Mrs Gibbs lived in this huge, huge house which, once war got underway, she handed over as a convalescent home to the army.' Mrs Gibbs was to be the governor and Marjory her Red Cross secretary. The decision is partly explained by personal loyalties and Marjory's experience as a nurse during the Great War. Once the conflict began in earnest she returned to what she knew best and where she considered herself to be most useful. In the summer of 1940 the British Expeditionary Force suffered 68,000 casualties, with over 14,000 wounded men returning to England. It was automatically presumed that women would step into wartime's idealised feminine space – nursing – and Marjory did just that.

Anne is sure that both Mrs Gibbs and her mother left the ATS after 'a long and successful recruitment campaign'. But while their Somerset regiment might have been at full capacity, by 1940 the service was already trailing two newer rivals in terms of popularity and military esteem. The Women's Royal Naval Service (WRNS) had been formed in May 1939, attached to the navy, and the

Women's Auxiliary Air Force (WAAF) emerged from a branch of the ATS in July 1939. None of the services were given much encouragement during the first two years of war, an attitude best summed up by an Air Ministry official in September 1939: 'There is no need for a recruiting drive in the case of the WAAF.'[1] However, unlike the ATS, the more compact WRNS and WAAF benefited from reputations for innovation and respect. The WAAF enjoyed the associated sheen of RAF crews and offered important jobs in the air force's communications network while Britain's seafaring history ensured the WRNS was regarded as the most socially exclusive service for women. In comparison, the army's reputation as old-fashioned, undemocratic and 'potentially horrendous' did not bode well for the popularity of its sister service, the ATS.[2]

In her departure, Anne's mother was not alone. More than 13,000 ATS members left the organisation during the first fifteen months of the war. Eager volunteers discovered that fitting thousands of women into a military machine designed for men was not simple. Commanding officers were wary of change, preferring to duck the issue of potential manpower shortages rather than take a risk with an unknown auxiliary who couldn't be disciplined under military law and wouldn't be available for operational service. More generally, the Service simply wasn't ready for large numbers of recruits, and a 'state of chaos' prevailed. In the bitter winter of 1939–40 newspapers complained about a lack of warm coats and a paucity of decent accommodation and trained officers compounded the problem. Dame Helen later conceded the ATS got off to a 'bad start'.[3]

*

The early loss of over 13,000 ATS recruits pointed to a worrying trend but not one that was immediately acted upon. Enrolled not enlisted girls could leave the service when they liked, few would judge them. At the beginning of the war *Woman's Own* preferred to remind its readers of the importance of home – 'We are standing at our posts as the men are standing at theirs'[4] – and in 1940 most girls didn't have much choice. Daphne was just sixteen and living with her mother in Norfolk when war broke out. 'I ran errands and worked in the local shop, Hockleys. It was a general store with cigarettes and sweets, oh, and a Vantas machine.' The large enamel soda fountain was under Daphne's charge. 'Fizzy drinks were a penny, but if you didn't have money you could buy a little file of tablets instead. You popped one in water and up it bubbled; they were just a ha'penny.'

Politics and worries of state rarely reached the counter, but by 1939 Daphne's Norfolk village had already undergone radical transformation. 'It was because of the aerodrome in Feltwell. The village was tiny, totally self-contained without a bus service or anything, but we had this great big aerodrome.' Norfolk's east-facing flat fields were identified as the ideal home for Britain's rapidly growing bomber squadrons in the late 1930s. The influx of men and their flying machines changed the complexion of Daphne's young life. 'As well as working at the shop, I helped at a cafe near the aerodrome in the evenings.' With neat bobbed hair, bare legs and a skirt and jersey combo, Daphne walked along the vetch-filled verge to a make-shift bungalow that doubled up as a cafe for the airmen. 'I helped out, coffees and teas, that sort of thing. And I set up a library.' It was there that she met Reg, a 'lovely, lovely man,' ten years her senior. 'I knew when war broke out because suddenly he had to give up mufti and start wearing a uniform. It was his job to maintain the bombers.' Most of all she looked forward to their snatched moments together; they held hands and laughed and he told her she was beautiful. 'I was quite pretty, I suppose.'

Daphne's story is punctuated with smiles and stern reminders; when it first appeared on the horizon, war shimmered with the paradox of foreboding and promise. Fields attached to her house played host to some of the earliest raids of the war; giant aircraft would take off and come back from Feltwell, 'so low when they flew over our house I could see the pilots' faces and their damaged beams, pockmarked with enemy fire'. Young wonder caught the moment, and Daphne can still detail the minutiae of the Vickers Wellington bombers, with guns attached nose to tail and 'thousands of pounds of bombs in their bellies'. The air shook. It wasn't common knowledge in the shop but she was aware that there'd been a first aerial attack on somewhere called Heligoland, although she didn't know the details. Daphne was focused on serving customers and keeping things just so in the shop, she polished the Vantas machine and left it to Reg to tell her what she needed to know. This was the first man she'd been really close to. 'Because you see, I didn't have a dad.'

'I'm not sure you should put in the book that my father lost all his money gambling, because everyone in our village thought that my mother was a widow.' But after some reflection she concedes that perhaps only one person remains in Feltwell for whom this information will mean anything. Daphne has long since left Norfolk but reputations matter and it was a struggle for her mother, Annie, bringing up three children alone. 'Father wrote once and said, "I know I'm not good enough for you but please come home." He wanted us back but we never returned. Mother left Manchester when she was pregnant with my brother, I was a baby and my sister a toddler. We never saw our father again.'

Daphne skirts around an early life defined by strong women: a grandmother who held the fort in Norfolk while Annie, 'a brave woman, worked up in London, in the Pontins counting house. But when Grandma died, Mother had to give up that job and come home.' To compensate for the absence of a father, Annie made sure there were men in her children's life. Uncle Will has a pipe in his hand and breeches held up with braces; the photograph is of a round friendly-face man who was something of a father figure to young Daphne. She nods and explains that she was regularly sent to stay with Uncle Will and Aunt Lucy in Welwyn Garden City. 'Mother did whatever she could to make ends meet and maintain standards.'

Before the war, Daphne spent long periods playing with their only child, William, who was just a couple of years her senior. She enjoyed summers up the trees and in the yards of Hertford's new age garden city and remembers a close-knit, affectionate family. Uncle Will would come back from a shift at the Shredded Wheat factory, and Aunt Lucy always had his dinner ready ('she might have worked in her youth, but when I knew her she kept house'). Cousin William was a sensitive boy who was very close to his mother. 'I remember him crimping her hair, they spent a lot of time together. I didn't know about such things in those days, but looking back I wonder if he might not have been homosexual. He was, how would you say, effeminate? A lovely boy.' She produces another photograph: Uncle Will and Aunt Lucy's son stares back, soft dark brows and full lips, William has the whimsical look of a movie star. Daphne draws up to the war again and that first summer of 1940. 'It was a terrible shock that he had to go into the army, but boys aged eighteen and over were conscripted. He was so sweet-looking' and not, in Daphne's mind, military material in a world where overt masculinity was the presumed marker of a good soldier. The airmen she knew at Feltwell were larger-than-life with their jaunty packs and flying suits. It felt odd to think of William camped out somewhere in France (or was it Belgium?), waiting for the Germans.

The teenage cousins exchanged letters in the spring of that year. Daphne, a terrific correspondent, sent more than she received. 'Then one day my airmail letter was returned. I didn't know what, but I knew something had happened.' Daphne stared down at the ominous unopened mail and her mother contacted Aunt Lucy. 'It turned out his parents already knew. To begin with he was missing in action but then they found out he was dead. They were so upset they hadn't told anyone.' Seventeen-year-old Daphne was sent to stay with her aunt and uncle in July 1940, 'to distract them, I suppose, to cheer them up'. Gamely she did her best, but there was a gaping hole in the house, a ghastly invisible absence from which neither parent ever recovered. 'Well, you wouldn't, would you? He was their only child. They cried a lot, every day. I don't remember them saying anything about the war. All they cared about was that they lost their lovely son.'

Thick with grief, the small house in Welwyn Garden City now felt a world away from Feltwell with its airmen and opportunities. Aunt Lucy's and Uncle Will's war was over in a country where for most people it hadn't properly started, not really. Meanwhile Daphne was already privy to two wars. A teenage bystander, she had experienced, up close and personal, the private pain that death leaves in its wake and, waiting for her back at home in Norfolk, the still shiny sharp-edged potential of aerial warfare. Germany's bombing campaign against Britain had not begun but here was a shop assistant already keyed into the conflict. And aged ninety-seven, Daphne still is. 'There is so much I can tell you. I remember everything. I was straightening my hat in the mirror, it was very early on a Sunday morning in the first months of war.' Dawn was breaking as Daphne readied for church. 'We had to go to St Nicholas as Feltwell's big church, St Mary's, couldn't be blacked out.' She was looking back at herself in the half light, satisfied with the reflection, when it began, a sudden insolent breakout across the silent dawn. Her harried mother pushed Daphne brusquely into the pantry. 'I couldn't think what was happening.' But she would discover soon enough. 'It was the ack-ack guns, that was the first time I heard them firing into the sky. The sound was extraordinary. You know what the ack-ack guns were, don't you, dear?'

*

Named after the distinct stabbing sound that ricocheted out beyond their shells, Daphne is quite certain that she heard ack-ack guns during the Phoney War. Defiant metal-mouthed interlocutors tilted into a vast expanse of sky, by the onset of war gun-site clusters were an increasingly common sight, and Norfolk's aerodromes among their key defensive locations. According to AA (Anti-Aircraft) Command's historian, 'in the five and a half years from September 1939 to May 1945 there were very few nights and days in which an AA gun was not firing at something, somewhere' in Britain.[5] It is therefore highly probable that Daphne's Sunday morning memory is accurate. But it's equally likely that the barrage she heard did not hit an enemy aircraft. With the exception of a few offshore sorties, the Luftwaffe stayed away in the first few months of war. When guns in Liverpool and Manchester identified enemy targets in November 1939, it transpired that both were firing at their own aeroplanes. In each case the target escaped unscathed, a blessing which highlighted a fault line in the service beyond aircraft recognition – the extraordinary difficulty of shooting down a fast-moving aircraft that could appear at any moment and attack any part of Britain.

In the last letter Olivia sent home to her parents from France on 30 May 1940 she wrote: '*One thing quite certain is that the morale of the air force is wonderful. I met quite a lot of them in Paris and they all said that when the volunteers were needed for a raid there were so many that they had to draw out the names from a hat . . . They all think the war will be won in the air.*' For most young men the prospect of fighting in the sky held tantalising appeal, but in equal measure standing behind a static gun and firing ammunition into the air only to watch it fall back down to earth again had little to recommend it. Between the wars fighter technology had come on in leaps and bounds while the hardware of the army's AA gunnery lagged further and further behind. Scientific advances did exist and high-tech kit, when it was available, could add to a battery's range and scope, but early raids confirmed the worst, one error between aircraft detection and the command to fire and a gun-site's efforts came to nought. It seemed little had changed since Conservative Prime Minister Stanley Baldwin's ominous observation that 'the bomber will always get through'.[6] And it was a problem compounded by a paucity of good men.

At the beginning of the war air defence expanded exponentially; sites mushroomed across Britain and the service tripled in size to over 300,000 men but as General Sir Frederick 'Tim' Alfred Pile, AA Command's resourceful leader, observed, many recruits were not worth having. The first conscripts began arriving at gun-sites by Christmas 1939 when battery commanders quickly discovered they'd been allotted the dregs of an overstretched army. Pile was unequivocal: for every 25 new recruits 'one had a withered arm, one was mentally deficient, one had no thumbs, one had a glass-eye which fell out whenever he doubled to the guns, and two were in the advanced and more obvious stages of venereal disease'.[7] A quarter of the new recruits were not fit for service. From the get-go Pile knew that women would 'perform their duties more efficiently than some of the low-category men' but he also knew the rules: ATS women were not allowed on 'operational sites' and no women in any service could occupy a combat role.

And so it was in 1940 that a 'plague' of male 'dim-wits'[8] were on the ground waiting, watching, for the arrival of the hawk-eyed Luftwaffe and the beginning of Germany's merciless bombing campaign. It was only a matter of time; any thought of a negotiated peace had been firmly rebuffed and by 18 June Churchill warned the nation: 'I expect the Battle of Britain is about to begin . . . the whole fury and might of the enemy must very soon be turned on us.'[9]

'It never occurred to me that we'd lose.' Daphne, still in Welwyn Garden City with her aunt and uncle, had a peripheral vision of what came next. 'No, I didn't always know which aeroplanes were ours, but I could see them, fighting, jabbing, shooting at each other.' She stops. 'I thought this was it, that the only thing we had to do was to win this fight in the sky and then it would all be over.' Daphne, a teenage witness waiting for a quick win, did not consider for one moment – 'never, NEVER, never' – that the war was an event she might partake in. It was still a man's game, just watching it made her tingle with 'frightened excitement. It was like something you'd never seen before. We had heard of Zeppelins and bombers but not dogfights.'

*

In 1940 Hitler had 2,670 bombers and fighters for deployment in the west, not enough for a full-scale invasion of Britain unless he could win air superiority quickly and decisively. That summer it was Britain's RAF fighter planes and their international crews that met this threat, with very little effective help from the guns on the ground. Diana, aged sixteen, was a year younger than Daphne, but based in East Sussex she had a better view. 'The sky was always so blue, it was a lovely summer.' Against this God-gifted turquoise canvas, Diana watched as men tested their mettle each against the other, in their silver-bellied darts. By mid-August German attacks on coastal ports and airfields had morphed into a massive daylight assault intended to destroy the RAF in dogfights across southern

England. 'I saw all our aircraft, Spitfires, yes, whatever they were called. Yes, and they got a German plane, one crashed not far outside Wadhurst. All the locals ran after it wanting souvenirs, something from the enemy to have forever.' The village was full of talk for days afterwards.

The pilot was taken to a prisoner-of-war camp and we saw the swastika on the side of the plane. No, I didn't think of joining one of the services then. I was looking after evacuee children for Mrs Booth. I'd been picking sweet peas for a local Chinese man but after war broke out it was all tomatoes that he grew and Mrs Booth didn't think it right for me to be wheeling a barrow all day.

Diana was adopted, or at least Mrs Booth wasn't her biological mother. Her real mother only visited once a year, in a smart suit with carefully chosen sensible presents – coloured pencils, a school satchel, that sort of thing. Regardless, Diana remembers a happy childhood. Mrs Booth looked after other people's children (not quite an orphanage, sometimes the parents worked overseas) and Diana was her oldest and her favourite charge. Even war seemed to have had its perks; from an early age Diana had learnt how to handle babies and enjoyed wheeling out the neighbour's evacuee tots in a large Silver Cross pram. Like Daphne, she was hypnotised by the Battle of Britain. Nightly she prayed for the pilots and Mr and Mrs Booth listened to Mr Churchill on the wireless. 'Never in the field of human conflict was so much owed by so many to so few.' Not once did Diana consider her role in a broader conflict. Why would she? She was just a girl.

5

Olivia's Croix de Guerre

'Well, I had an excuse to go straight around to this chap de Gaulle.' In 2008 Olivia sat down with her nephew and in a bracing fifty-minute interview told him the story of her war.[1] After the comedown of arriving back in her native England to a less than prodigious family welcome, the relief that she had one more mission is still discernible. Thanks to the papers that were handed to her in the British legation in Bordeaux and the pamphlet pressed into her palm in Plymouth replete with name and address, Olivia knew exactly what to do and where to go.

De Gaulle had been given a tiny set of Victorian offices right beside the Houses of Parliament, overlooking the Thames. This French patriot and his band of helpers had been squeezed uncompromisingly into the armpit of the British Government; it was not a comfortable fit. De Gaulle's position was both precarious and humiliating; after France's surrender, he'd experienced the indignity of returning to England as a solitary refugee seeking to establish a Free French movement on British soil. A lone operator the Foreign Office didn't trust, he relied on Churchill's support ('what could I have done without his help?') but as the champion of French resistance, he could not be seen as the puppet of the perfidious unpopular Brits.

With candour, de Gaulle later wrote 'I was starting from scratch. Not the shadow of a force or of an organisation at my side. In France, no following, no reputation. Abroad neither credit nor standing.'[2] For his extraordinary mission to succeed, de Gaulle had to establish an independent military force, a nucleus upon which to build and fight for France from the outside in. He knew there were injured and displaced French soldiers and sailors in England awaiting repatriation and French warships still as yet unclaimed. But, as a man in a foreign land with no transport and terrible English, de Gaulle urgently needed help. Olivia's timing was impeccable.

During her first appearance in his office she's certain she did not see de Gaulle. 'If I had met him, I would never have dared work for him.' Vastly tall, indefatigable and so very French, he was an intimidating prospect. But reverse that perspective and imagine Olivia: small, unassuming, self-possessed, a distinctly classy English girl still in her French uniform proffering information from distant, dangerous Bordeaux. Did she ask for a job there and then? That's what Olivia remembers. Certainly she came away with one, and more besides. 'He had no transport, so I said to my father, "This chap de Gauuulle" (she hovers pleasurably over the name) "is here now, can we lend him a car?"' The family Wolseley, complete with petrol, was duly delivered to St Stephen's House – de Gaulle had just acquired a vehicle with its very own driver-translator.

*

Olivia's memory is fading now; much of her story comes from notes, letters, memorabilia and that recorded interview. But aged one hundred and two, when she talks Olivia reveals what mattered most; like boulders in a sieve, through constant replay in her mind's eye it is the memories of the war that have endured. 'I was very lucky I could speak French. Very lucky.' Again she repeats her good fortune, 'Because, you see, I couldn't do anything else useful.' The self-deprecating loop, where above all she marvels at her own lack of utility, is a reminder of a woman's place when a patriarchal society goes to war and it is ironic given Olivia spoke German as well as French and could also drive. These skills had opened the door into another country's army, where she'd enjoyed the code of uniform, status and belonging, a symbolism that helped her clinch a second posting as one of de Gaulle's first employees in London. 'His English was terrible, quite hopeless.' She is tickled by this. 'There seemed to be very few people who could speak both languages.'

Churchill presumed that de Gaulle would be joined by other better-known French players. But in those early days when they failed to materialise, the British Prime Minister acknowledged, 'You are alone, I shall recognise you alone.'[3] Meanwhile, Olivia offered the Free French all she had: her time and her father's best car. She had returned to an England that disparaged their defeated neighbours across the Channel. 'People were very rude about the French. They reckoned that France just gave in and you know one had to be rather careful.' But de Gaulle was different. She wrote to her parents in August 1940; '*It was very thrilling last night, my man broadcasted and I went with him actually into the room while he was doing it.*' De Gaulle's first transmission had had little impact, but it established the idea that while 'France has lost the battle, she has not lost the war', a slogan which he built upon week after week in his recording sessions, when he talked directly to France, challenging and undermining the Vichy Government. Olivia was enraptured: '*They had great difficulty in making him sit still as he got very excited and insisted on gesticulating wildly.*' The BBC operators weren't accustomed to such ebullience, and the Foreign Office struggled with de Gaulle's increasingly direct attacks against Marshall Petain, fearful he might push the Vichy Government towards Germany.

Olivia was in the centre of an extraordinary French experiment. '*They may be going to make me broadcast in French next week. I said I would provided they wrote it all out for me. I don't expect it will come off.*' And outside the studio she doubled up as an able chauffeur. Attached to the French army she'd sped her way across ravaged France but her own family had not seen her do it. Back in wartime London there was something triumphantly public about her new role as de Gaulle's driver. Letters home are full of it: '*I've been doing longer runs, latterly mostly out to Odiham aerodrome where they've installed a few of our chaps.*' Firmly ensconced in her French project, and still wearing her uniform, Olivia's insider knowledge was invaluable. '*It's quite impossible finding one's way if one doesn't know the road. Let's hope it will fox the Germans as well.*' It was spring 1940 when Britain started taking the threat of German invasion seriously and duly removed all the road signs. By August 1940, when the nation's neck was tilted up towards the famous 'few' and their dogfights overhead, Olivia with her motorcar once more occupied one of the very rare mechanised routes to speed and glory available to women. She loved driving and was gutted when the Wolseley had to be returned to its owner.

> *I saw Daddy yesterday and he drove back the big car. It was*
> *kind of him letting me have it like that. I'm rather frightened*
> *I may lose my job as they can't find me a car yet. However*
> *let's hope something will turn up as I shall be miserable if*
> *it's given to someone else.*

Olivia had passed her driving test in March 1939
and although all testing (only introduced in 1934) was
suspended during the war, for the vast majority of young
girls driving a car was just a dream. Yorkshire born and
bred, ninety-five-year-old Barbara is sure of that. 'Well,
my parents didn't have a car. My dad was a police officer
in the West Riding Constabulary. He used a bike or went
by foot. I remember him learning to drive in an old Ford
in a field, but we didn't own one.' Aged fourteen when
war broke out, she spoke for much of the nation. The
motorcar was a great harbinger of change, promising
freedom and speed, but in 1939 driving was still a minority sport and petrol rationing made it more so. Tucked up
in the Dales and travelling over 17 miles twice a day in
a converted hearse, then by bus, to her grammar school,
Barbara was under no illusions as to how life-changing
automobiles could be. But driving one was unimaginable.

> To begin with the war seemed remote in the Upper
> Dales, news was a week old when we got it. That's
> right, my mother did serve in the Great War, in
> uniform for the WAAC, but it was mainly domestic
> duties, she certainly didn't drive. I'm trying to think
> if I ever saw a woman drive. I don't think so but
> there were the upper-bracket girls whose daddy had
> brought them a little car.

Olivia fell into that upper bracket but ideally she needed her family's big Wolseley for de Gaulle's growing project, not one of her family's smaller cars, although it was better than nothing.

I've got the little car up here and am at present driving the head of all the armaments and interpreting for him. It is most interesting and involves going to all sorts of odd places and one gets to know the inside of things. I'm rather miserable as I think he wants a bigger car because we sometimes have to go a long way.

In the summer of 1940 most of the women in this book were still waking up to the idea of global conflict but not twenty-one-year-old Olivia, she was already at the apex of her war story. Condemned to death *in absentia* for treason by the Vichy Government, de Gaulle was, Olivia remembers, someone 'who chose those around him carefully'. Gradually the Frenchman pulled in a team of considerable talents: among them Georges Boris, a left-wing economist and political adviser; René Cassin, a fifty-five-year-old jurist who became the legal expert; and Émile Muselier, a retired admiral who was soon head of the Free French naval forces. De Gaulle's biographer concludes that these first followers of Gaullism were 'strikingly diverse'.[4] The arrival of their British handmaiden Olivia reinforced that diversity and she did everything she could to facilitate their needs. The new head of armaments would get his car if Olivia had anything to do with it. *'I am trying my hardest to get hold of a bigger government car so as to be able to take him as it will be very interesting.'*

Olivia was an English girl in a team she tetchily referred to as *'the frogs'*. Compromised and assailed on all fronts, as one observer noted: 'for someone of de Gaulle's temperament his total dependence on Britain was intolerably difficult to bear . . . the slightest contact with friendly well-meaning people got him on the raw to such an extent that he wanted to bite.' The de Gaulle Olivia remembers was a 'shy difficult man' who kept 'himself to himself' and railed against British officials who were quick to deride him as the man with 'a head like a pineapple and hips like a woman'.[5] This discomfiture sheds light on his embrace of Olivia. Help from this young girl was no doubt easier to bear than other more compromising offers. An outsider herself, she had no rank and knew how to keep her distance. 'Communication was rather difficult because he was so tall and I was so small.' And above all else, he knew he could trust her. Like de Gaulle, Olivia had also risked her life for the Third French Republic, a feat that was formally recognised in September 1940, when her actions in France were rewarded with one of the country's greatest military honours.

> Miss Olivia Matthews, a voluntary driver, showed energy, courage and endurance worthy of the highest praise. She spared no efforts in bringing help to and evacuating sick and wounded civilians and soldiers in the most threatened areas without any thought of the danger.[6]

'The Croix de Guerre? I wondered when you were going to ask me about that,' the old woman smiles. A regimental order in French, signed off by Maxime Weygand (once the supreme commander of the French forces, then Minister of National Defence for the Vichy regime), confirmed Olivia's hero status in black and white. But today she shakes her head. 'I was of no importance whatsoever, I just went along with everybody else.' Praise is still hard to hear, as it was then. But if her parents had been slow to comprehend the magnitude of her actions, the arrival of a French medal changed their minds. Olivia beseeched them:

> *My dear Mummy,*
>   *Do stop writing to people about the C de G. It's SO embarrassing having to write back, especially to Mrs Willis who I haven't seen for such ages.*

Her former headmistress Mrs Willis was overjoyed with the news, gushing to her mother: '*It is wonderful about Olivia – but we all thought she would do something if an opportunity arose, didn't we? I can just see her facing German soldiers and tackling impossible problems.*' The local Sevenoaks paper was equally enamoured with their unlikely hero; the headline lauded 'Brasted Resident Awarded French Croix de Guerre'.[7] However, the article closes not on Olivia's feats but instead on those of her injured brother-in-law Dick Hubbard, 'who was badly wounded at Boulogne'. A clue perhaps as to why she consistently repeats in old age, 'I was quite hopeless, right down there, not important at all.' In 1940s Britain, no matter what their achievements, girls came second.

6

Bombing Girls

'We used to be saying, "I wonder who got it. I wonder who got it last night."' That was quite a common phrase when they were bombing.' Penny was the oldest of four children; they all lived together in Haringey, North London. 'Dad was just a bricklayer, he worked locally and Mum looked after us kids.' Ninety-nine years old, Penny stands up and, with the exquisite poise of a lifelong ballroom dancer, walks across the room. 'There are pictures somewhere of the area and what it looked like.' Having failed to achieve air superiority in the Battle of Britain, and suffering heavier losses than the RAF, by the beginning of September 1940 the German High Command switched tactics and prioritised the systematic bombing of British cities, with London their main target. Searchlights, sirens and bomb blasts stalked the lives of Londoners for months on end, Penny's included.

In many ways she was more prepared for the fallout than most. Leaving school at fourteen, Penny had attended a Pitman night school and acquired basic secretarial skills. Her parents paid (they wanted the best for their eldest: '"You're only a penny's worth," that's what Dad used to joke, cos I was so small!'). 'I got a job with the ARP in their office. I wasn't a volunteer, no, it was a paid position.' By January 1938, the Air Raid Precautions Act compelled all local authorities to create their own ARP services and so it was that newly qualified Penny got a job as a telephonist at the heart of pre-war planning. To begin with the focus was on the distribution of precautionary leaflets and air raid shelters.

'My dad was pretty handy, he dug our Anderson shelter into the back garden. And my younger brother and sister were sent away, I remember that. But it didn't last long. They came back pretty quick, before the bombing began.' For Penny the beginning of the war had a dream-like quality, with a paid job in a brand-new telephone exchange, and a boyfriend who looked great in uniform. 'Ronald joined the Royal Navy, we'd been sweethearts since fourteen.' Penny and Ronald were a shiny young couple on the cusp of life. 'I thought it was grand he was doing his bit. You see my dad had won the Military Medal in the First World War for bringing someone back over the top so I supported Ronald when he became a submariner.' Penny understood the curated language of conflict with its heroes and medals; she entertained no doubts, looked forward to her letters from Ronald and initially enjoyed her work with the ARP.

What began as an operation full of eager volunteers and workers 'getting a bit fed up' waiting 'for something to happen' changed dramatically in September 1940.[1] Overnight, lines were bombed and communications cut; young lads ran messages in their Scouting uniforms, older boys in the Auxiliary Fire Service didn't come home for days on end. Penny was masterful at coordinating her part of the capital, keeping her cool and connecting the calls. But the novelty soon wore off adrenalised shift work with no end in sight and home times of meagre rations and a cold bunker never designed to be slept in. 'I got fed up with the bombing, going up and down the shelters. It was no life.' She spent her nights pressed up, hugger-mugger, against her younger siblings, her mother's worried face turned away. 'The neighbour said we could join him in his shelter, he had more space because his family had gone away, but we preferred it all together.'

Before the war mass psychological trauma from aerial attack had been predicted, and in 1938 a committee of psychiatrists suggested that overhead bombing would cause three times as many mental as physical casualties. The morale of a nation was at stake. Hitler was banking on that when he switched the thrust of his bombing campaign from industry and airfields to Britain's urban underbellies and Churchill understood the intent behind 'these cruel, wanton, indiscriminate bombings of London'.[2] Night time raids replaced daytime sorties, and for fifty-seven consecutive nights the bombers returned again and again. Penny, strained at work and burdened by her mother's worry, increasingly loathed the Blitz; it curdled any small comfort that home previously offered.

'The waiting was perhaps the worst of it, and then there was the shaking, it was frightening.' Penny's sentiment was widespread; Churchill's youngest daughter, Mary, would later declare that although there were other anxious times, in 1940 'never again, I think did one feel one could scarcely breathe. We got through the days living from news bulletin to news bulletin and reading what each one might bring.'[3] If, previously, war had reinforced gender division, with uniformed masculinity idealised as the nation's saviour, air raids and indiscriminate bombs drastically dissolved the myth that there was a division between battle zone and home front. Women and children were victims too. Penny worked all hours, pitching in, plugging away on those telephone lines, hiding in the shelter, but she couldn't shift a feeling of frustration and helplessness. Smashing in on her life, a once distance conflict had become her war and she wanted to do something about it.

She wasn't alone. During that winter of 1940–1 the vast majority of young girls still lived at home. They were observers in a war that was blowing up around them, in the newspapers, on the streets, in their own houses and beyond the capital, right across the country. 'We took the cat and the dog and the bird, we'd all go down the shelter. I shouldn't be here to tell the tale, me mum was screaming at us.' It's August 2020 and Vera is sitting in her front room in Leicester scrolling through memories; eighty years ago this second daughter of six children had never been further than Plymouth. 'I used to pick and pack the tomatoes ready for market and sometimes the boss would say, "You have to come with me today to Plymouth to sell the goods," and we'd go in the van, or on the train across the River Tamar.' Then back home Vera would come, over the stile and up the lane, down the hill, a mile or more, back to her mother and life in Saltash, their small Cornish village.

'You mark my words, there'll be another war,' Vera's father thundered across the breakfast table. He read the *Daily Mail* and was primed for what came next; he almost looked forward to it. Mr Edwards hadn't had good work since the Great War, a caretaker role in a school couldn't compete with a former life in the navy. 'In 1939 Dad was called up again to train with the lads at Devonport.' A spring in his step, Mr Edwards returned to barrack life and Vera's ma stayed home with her sprawling offspring. 'She'd yell up the stairs, "It's Moaning Minnie," that's what she called the siren, Plymouth got it bad in early 1941 so we heard it a lot, that Moaning Minnie.' Vera remembers prepping for the shelter – small eats, comforting knick-knacks, warm clothes – rueing the prospect of spending another night with her siblings in a damp hole at the bottom of the garden. 'Well, there we were that night and it was ever so quiet, so my sister Dorothy and I said "Mum we're going back up the house, we've gotta go to work in the morning."'

'You're not going back to bed, you'll stay here! They'll be back, you mark my words!'

Vera and Dorothy, recalcitrant teenagers, railed against this maternal imposition. 'We got out the shelter and went to bed. And then the bomb dropped just at the back of us!'

Vera's still surprised – it's 2020 and she's shouting in her front room; back then the limp Union Jack in her glass cabinet meant something. 'The blast blew all the windows out. It killed old Mrs Johnson at the back of us. Mr and Mrs Johnson, they got a direct hit, she didn't stand a chance. I went to school with their Aubrey.' Vera and Dorothy had defied their mother and it nearly cost them their lives. 'The paving stone was kicked up over the house and landed in the front garden, if it had come through the roof . . .' Their mother refused to remove the slab of stone protruding from the grass; it stayed there for years afterwards, a reminder of the near miss and the two sisters' unforgettable defiance.

Vera was shaken. After a night of no sleep she was up early the next morning, heading back to the market garden where ordinarily she took a breakfast of hot shredded wheat and a fry of eggs and bacon. But not that day.

> As I was going up the lane I was sure I 'eard *da da da da*. A dogfight going on above me, machine guns, our fighters with the Germans. I was frightened, I turned tail and ran all the way home and Mother, when she saw me, she said, 'What you doing back 'ere!' I said, 'I is frightened,' but she made me go back to work so that is what I did.

Eighteen-year-old Vera confronted her fear and walked back to work; as she picked her way across the familiar fields she thought, 'It's no good staying here. I'm going to fight back.' The war had cracked open the world and Vera wanted her part in it. 'I thought I'd like to do something else, there was not a lot going on in Saltash.'

*

Older, wealthy, independent; Olivia was plugged into a new life with the Free French in the centre of London when the Blitz came raining down. She wrote to her parents: '*We had a terrific incendiary raid the night before I left and I had a priceless time putting out a whole lot on the roof opposite with a wavy navy [Royal Navy Reserve], the commissionaire, a cockney Tommy and a doctor.*' Living alone in her sister's empty Westminster flat next door to de Gaulle's offices, Olivia thrived on a merry-go-round of danger.

> *We saw the roof blazing and snatched up the sandbags under the lamp-posts, of course the premises concerned were locked*

*so the wavy navy ran at the windows with his boots and just
as we'd broken the window nicely the owner turned up with
the key to the door. We rushed up nine flights of stairs drag-
ging the sandbags . . . Once up there we put out the fire and
then had to do some roof-top stunts to get to another which
was blazing on the opposite roof.*

In her triumphant letter Olivia, who would later admit
that the Blitz was more terrifying than anything she'd
endured in France, captures the blurred lines of a new
war that cared for neither gender nor class. '*The doctor was
not at all reassuring and every time I attacked a bomb he said, "Be
careful our wards at the hospital are filled with people with blown
off limbs who were putting out incendiaries!!" I may say he was a
rather casual and annoying onlooker.*' On the roof of burning
London Olivia discovered she was more than equal to any
man. While thousands of girls were still trapped at home,
she relished the exhilarating freedom war handed her.
That night they soon knew '*each other's life histories and were
very matey*'. Back down on London's midnight pavement,
the naval reservist decided to try his luck, asking his brave
accomplice out for a drink. Olivia was obliged to turn him
down when '*I suddenly realised that in my hurry to get out I'd only
flung on my overcoat over a stark naked body*'.

Privilege and personal grit guaranteed Olivia many
more close encounters. If the sheen of working for the
Free French was wearing off ('*I'm going to try and get a paid
job preferably not with the frogs, I'd rather something employed by
the English to do with the French*') London under siege was
electrifying. With more than six months of night attacks,
in hidden pockets of the city life had taken on vital new
intensity. Café de Paris, well covered in Piccadilly, was

supposedly the safest place in London. Olivia had arrived late from dinner at the Ritz and was sitting on the balcony surrounding the beautiful circular dance floor. Down below was a fusion of jazz enveloped in a warm fug of tobacco smoke and dim electric light . . . 'We were told if in doubt go to Café de Paris, but the bomb went straight down over the band. It hit a lot of people.' Britain's most famous Black performer, Ken 'Snakehips' Johnson, was among the thirty-four killed. In those first few suspended seconds after the explosion, Olivia involuntarily checked her limbs. 'You would not have known if your arms were blown off, not straight away.' Now almost stone deaf (her hearing never fully recovered), she remembers, 'There's euphoria for being alive. You don't think of anything else. I came out of the building and very nearly got run over by a bus.'

Like her experience in France, Olivia's Blitz was headline news. Small wonder in extreme old age she revels in a war that allowed her to buck the trend and be brave. In 1941 she was an exception to a female rule which had started to wear thin. In the first eight months of war, no measures were taken by the government to redistribute women in the workforce and although the growing need for female labour was identified in 1940, a national rethink had a lot of ground to cover. Particularly in historically male-dominated industrial and military roles, employers tenaciously held onto the idea of female inferiority.[4] Churchill was thrilled by the audacity of Britain's pilots, marvelling to his daughter Mary that 'it is very remarkable that the young should be so much braver than the old for they have so much more to lose'.[5] But youthful determination was not confined to men. Across the country, girls were discovering that sanctifying male heroism was no longer enough.

*

Daphne had returned from her grieving aunt and uncle to shop work in Feltwell, Norfolk. The detritus of war was everywhere. 'I remember moonlit walks with Reg best of all, standing by the gates after work, talking.' It should have been romantic, airman Reg and his young sweetheart but 'I was terrified, the bombers kept coming over cos of the aerodrome. It was awful, awful. I wanted to get away, the village lost several houses.' German aggression was matched by British bombers returning from raids on Berlin. 'I saw the blood once on the pilot's face, that's how low down they came.' Was it then she had the germ of an idea, that she, Daphne, might join the war effort and wear a uniform? 'I wanted to get away and join the forces. I wanted to go in at seventeen and a half but you could only go in at that age with parental permission and my mother wouldn't allow it. Absolutely not.'

If Hitler hoped to break British morale with the Blitz, his plan backfired. Instead, thousands of young girls began to question their role in a conflict that had become deeply personal. Meanwhile the War Office was waking up to the needs of an army whose manpower problems were acute; by early 1941 military operations stretched from the defence of British cities to the Mediterranean and beyond into the Middle East. A long war lay ahead; something had to give. Minister of Labour Ernest Bevin moved slowly towards the idea of female compulsion but he was wary of a public backlash and wanted to keep up the facade of voluntarism for as long as possible. The first major change was to introduce registration (the Registration for Employment Order) in March 1941. Under this scheme all women, in paid or unpaid work, received an official invitation to register their occupation at a local employment exchange. Girls between the ages of 18 and 24 who were neither working nor in essential occupations could be directed into industry. But crucially, although pressure could be applied, they could not be pushed into the forces.

Military obligation remained contentious. Girls in uniform was an emotive subject, particularly in the rough-cut serge and lisle khaki of the ATS, a service where support duties fell into five unremarkable categories: clerks, cooks, storewomen, drivers and orderlies. Status work was noticeable for its absence; according to ATS director Dame Helen initially only clerk 'was a trade in the army sense'.[6] The unpopularity of the Service was reflected in its sluggish recruitment figures, which saw the *Daily Telegraph* investigate the force in January 1941 amidst accusations it was both nannyish and intellectually limited.[7]

If the ATS was rarely a girl's first choice, parents were even less keen. Daphne's mother's resistance to the prospect of her daughter joining up and leaving home was a standard response from a generation who worried the nation's femininity and chastity were at stake. Women's role in wartime Britain saw heated debate in Parliament throughout 1941, with Labour MP Agnes Hardie arguing that female war work should be organised locally so that girls weren't 'dragged away from their own homes and districts' – an impossible ambition for the disparate forces and one that profoundly misunderstood the mindset of thousands of young women.[8] Penny, Vera and Daphne longed to 'get away from home' and 'do something' and it was girls like these that the ATS desperately needed to recruit.

7

Steel Helmets and Lipstick

Grace lives by the sea in Poole; she starts every sentence with 'my dear' and plies me with tea and biscuits. She also happens to have joined the ATS younger than any other girl in this book. 'I lied about my age so I could get in early, before I was seventeen and a half.' Unlike most other girls, she had no maternal guardian. 'You see, my mother died when I was eleven. It was terrible, really terrible. We came home from school and Dad said, "Your mum's taken ill." She was in Hornchurch Hospital, that was the first I knew of it.' For one week every evening after school Grace stayed with her aunt while her father finished his shift and visited his poorly wife. 'I remember he came to pick us up from Auntie and we were walking along, me holding one hand, Kit, my sister, the other and I asked, "Dad, who's with Mum now?"'

'"Nobody," he said. "Your mother's dead."'

Grace chokes on the memory, she wipes at her tears with a manicured hand.

I'm sorry, my dear, it always fills me up. Oh no, I've started you off. No, I'm not sure what she died of, maybe a waterborne disease, she's buried in Ilford cemetery. Me and my sister went to the funeral in navy blue velour coats, I remember because it was the first time we'd worn shop-bought clothes. Mum made all our clothes.

The pain is still raw and Grace's reaction to this gigantic loss messy and deeply moving. 'When she died I didn't get a cuddle no more. Step-mums don't cuddle.' How does a girl grow up without her mother? Grace shrugs. It was difficult, of that she is sure.

Between the wars Grace's father, Mr Clarke, worked for the Gas, Light and Coke Company; all over Ilford, Seven Kings and Chadwell Heath he went pushing his barrow, laying gas for the expanding population. But what was he meant to do with three girls on his own? Grace sighs. 'He always wanted a boy. He married again within a year and they had a son together, she didn't want us three girls.' Baby sister Ann was sent to an aunt, older sister Kit went straight into domestic service and within three years Grace had followed suit. 'I remember it was the summer holidays, I hadn't even had my fourteenth birthday and I was sent to work for a family with a toddler.' Grace carefully picks her way around painful childhood markers. 'I loved my dad, but he did what my stepmother wanted. She didn't want us so we had to go and he knew that I would have a clean bed, that I would be fed.' Domestic drudgery, the job that no girl wanted but one in four fell into, was Grace's lot. She dutifully donned a cap and apron and became the 'help' in someone else's house. 'I just did what I was told. I didn't want to be a skivvy, it was lonely. I didn't last long there.' Frustrated, Grace left her first job to work for a greengrocer and his family. A dark-haired, strong girl, she was on duty 'from the morning right through till the shop closed, taking errands, out on the bicycle, weighing produce, pricing goods, then it was time to get tea for their toddlers and of course there was my own meal to make.'

Grace almost looks surprised when asked for her opinion on the war. 'I lived in a vacuum, who was there to tell me anything? I was just focused on finding a better job. I wanted to go up in the world.' That meant working in a bigger house, with a large garden and a tennis court. Her next job was in Brentwood with a lovely couple who treated her properly. 'The Wilfords were business folk with a wonderful home. The lounge was enormous with a grand piano. I can see it now, the giant parquet floor I had to polish on my hands and knees. It looked ever so nice with a good sheen.' Grace closes her eyes. 'Best of all was their daughter Gabrielle, she worked in film. I loved clothes and she had rows and rows of beautiful dresses hanging on the landing, I would get her cast-offs.'

Dropped waists, full skirts, green satin, deep scarlet, chiffon, silk, the feminine silhouettes of the thirties finally belonged to Grace. 'Oh, I love nice things!' Once a week she stepped out of her pinafore into a dress and entered another world. 'Dancing was my favourite thing, and in Brentwood I would walk down every weekend to the town hall.' Grace smiles – the Blitz did not get in the way of her weekly night out. 'No, no bombs fell near me.' Brentwood dance theatre was her dreamland, where she relived treasured childhood memories: 'When I was dancing it all came flooding back. I was a little girl again and there was this stage in Ilford with a live band. My father always selected me or my sister to lead across the floor, and my mum, she would take the tickets at the cloakroom door.'

On Saturday nights in Brentwood Grace's torn-up past briefly blurred into a happier present.

'I met a soldier, he was stationed at Warley Barracks. Eddie Bill was his name, he was a blacksmith before the war in the Channel Islands. Yes, I suppose I was a catch, I certainly never sat out a dance.' The brush of Eddie's khaki uniform, his reassuring firm hold and musky smell as he led Grace through waltzes, foxtrots, quicksteps, how she lived for those snatched weekend moments. Back at work she served the Wilfords through their dining hatch and polished their wooden floor, all the while humming a tune, spinning the plates, turning softly on the ball of her foot and thinking of her boy, Eddie. 'War had thrown us together, I suppose. He was a private in the Ordnance Corps. It was the first time I had been properly hugged since my mum died. But then one day he told me he'd been transferred, he was going abroad.'

Grace was gutted. This was her first boyfriend, her replacement family, her main mucker and confidante. 'Oh no, dear, we didn't have sex, he was in his uniform, but it was still nice and tender.' When she counts the numbers on her fingers Grace realises she can't have been more than sixteen but Eddie had rocked her world and now the war was taking him away. 'Before he left, he made me a letter opener, a paper knife with my name stamped on it. I've no idea where he got the brass from. I had it as a keepsake, I kept it with me right through the war.' But it wasn't enough. What was this war that Eddie had gone off to? Where was Port Said? Why couldn't she go too?

He came to the door of where I worked to say goodbye, I can see him now with his kitbag and cap.

I missed him. I was isolated as a servant. I thought to myself, 'Now he's gone away, perhaps if I joined up I might be able to go where he is and be with him again.' It's a bit stupid when you think about it, but I really thought I would meet him again if I joined the army.

In this new patriots' war young women had different ideas about how to support their men. Back in London, Penny was fed up with the Blitz but would she have ever left her desk job at the ARP ('it was an essential service after all') had it not been for Ronald? 'Oh yes, we were going to get married. We talked about that, he said the next time he came home we'd get engaged.' The quintessential boy-next-door, 'tallish, fair, I like blond men', came from the neighbouring street, their fathers played in the same darts team, they had gone to the same school. Without the disrupter of war perhaps they would've already got married. 'But he was away in the navy aged eighteen and then one evening I was told by his brother that he was missing. Later they said he'd lost his life at sea.'

Penny's hope, her dream, her blond boy, was gone. Italy's entry into the war in June 1940 had opened up a new front in North Africa; Axis and Allied powers alike recognised the vital strategic importance of British colony Malta and in the air and at sea it was fought over with relentless ferocity. Ronald's vessel was hit by an Italian bomber near the island's northern harbour in the spring of 1941. Many years later Penny would go to Malta and pay respects to her schoolboy sweetheart, but back then, stuck in London surrounded by younger siblings, impotence was what she felt, a ghastly helplessness replicated in the bombed outline of the capital.

'I was very upset and my friend said, "Why don't we go to the pictures?" Before the film there was always a newsreel. That time it was Pathé news, and it showed you all about the ATS and what they were doing.' Penny stops and picks up her own personally crafted laminate featuring a range of ATS recruitment material. By mid-1941, along with thousands of other young women, she was being deliberately targeted by the Auxiliary Territorial Service. Grace can also recall numerous posters encouraging her to sign up. Neither girl took much persuasion. Penny went home, sat at the dinner table and announced to her parents, 'I want to join the army.' 'My mother said, "I am not a bit surprised, dear," and my father said, "Good show!"' They'd just survived the Blitz, surely nothing could be as bad as that?

Grace had no parents, and despite the posters, no real idea of what service in a female army might involve. 'I just thought that I would get to see Eddie again and I was lonely, I hoped I'd make some friends.'

*

The push factors motivating Penny and Grace were greater than any specific pull factor, but a promotional campaign helped direct their interest. Penny's coloured laminate peppered with ATS adverts showcases the combined efforts and contortions of the Ministries of War, Information and Labour to boost the reputation of the unpopular ATS. Crucially their belated recruitment campaign was preceded by a series of overdue structural changes within the service. In April 1941 the ATS was included in the Army Act. Finally the demeaning term 'camp followers' (all too often short-hand for prostitute) was dropped. For centuries women had risked their lives and lived on the edge to support men in numerous military ventures – only to be derided as 'hangers on'. At last camp followers were a thing of the past; in 1941 women were not called soldiers but at least as auxiliaries they had official military status.

The ATS's director Dame Helen was delighted – 'I was more fortunate than Moses: I had spent a month in my promised land' – but by July 1941 she had been dismissed.[1] According to a subsequent ATS director, Leslie Whateley, Dame Helen 'was so imbued with the military spirit that she was quite unable to see that women could not be treated like men'.[2] Therein lay the conundrum of female service by 1941. It needed mass appeal and had to attract a new breed of girl who was expected to submit to military duty while remaining sufficiently feminine to deflect critics. Dame Helen's replacement, the young and elegant Jean Knox, heralded a new direction and relations with the maverick FANY improved considerably. With a keen eye for branding (post-war she became the managing director of Sloane Square's department store, Peter Jones), Knox moved quickly to revamp the service's dowdy image and her first overhaul was the unpopular ATS uniform. Khaki would always trail the chic blue shades of rival Wrens and Waafs, but Knox did her best. Gone were Dame Helen's official-issue knickers and masculine jacket and in came a signature cap to replace 'that awful flat pancake affair'.[3]

Knox's revamp coincided with the arrival of a new kid on the block in the War Office. In 1941 talented military draughtsman Abram Games was tasked with designing a poster to banish the ATS's 'ugly and drab' image and bolster recruitment. The result was a stunning blonde profile; with ATS initials strapped across the picture in Union Jack red, white and blue, his poster stands out on Penny's laminate. She runs her finger down the image. 'Beautiful, isn't it?' The girl's lips are full and painted red, her hair is bleached and waved and the all-new cap sits at a jaunty angle. The result is almost provocative – and it certainly provoked new Director Knox. A demeaning 'lipstick advert' was her verdict, but the poster was already printed. Dubbed the 'Glamour Girl' and 'Blonde Bombshell' the image divided opinion.[4] Eighty years on and Grace is still unsure.

> I don't like the poster myself. She's not wearing a cap badge. You wouldn't go out without your cap badge. She could be anyone, nothing about her says ATS! She's too glamorous; the ATS had a reputation to look out for. No wonder people thought we were up to no good. Mind you, I like lipstick myself, I always 'ave. My current shade is *flame*, I like a deep red though the masks these days really mess it up.

Grace's ambiguous response sums up the problem. The ATS needed to appeal but it couldn't appear *too* appealing. Despite herself, Grace loved a twist of glamour, most girls did. Some workplaces encouraged the application of cosmetics on the basis they raised morale and *Woman's Own* agreed; standards had to be maintained.[5] But the Establishment railed against such gimmicks. Conservative MP Thelma Cazalet-Keir was horrified: 'It's not the kind of poster to encourage mothers to send their girls into the army.' But the image had caught the nation's attention. There were queues outside ATS recruiting offices and much rumpus in the press. 'While Hitler uses time with deadly skill, Parliament insists on wasting it . . . What is so very wrong with glamour? If Bevin wants another 140,000 recruits, how is he going to get them?' To no avail; ultimately Games's poster was deemed 'too daring for public consumption' and withdrawn.[6] Heaven forbid that girls (and boys) got the wrong idea.

Although temporarily sidelined, Games would design four more ATS posters before the war was over. His next head-and-shoulders image saw the 'blonde bombshell' remodelled; this time the girl is 'fresh and smiling . . . looking upwards with a gaze of enthusiasm', her military collar is raised and the headgear suggestive of serious, exciting work – she's wearing a steel helmet.[7] But it wasn't just the image of the ATS that had been overhauled; incorporated into the Army Act, by mid-1941 the trades available to women had multiplied exponentially. The stretched British war machine demanded that ATS girls were now recruited for work alongside numerous branches of the army including the Royal Corps of Signals, Intelligence Corps and the Royal Artillery, a move that was facilitated by the lifting of the ban on women undertaking operational duties. Grace claps her hands together. 'That's right, dear, I didn't know what I'd let myself in for. I never did see Eddie again but I sure was in the thick of it.'

8

Recruiting Gunner Girls

Careening around in a car, in a *'continual rush to get things done before the sirens go off'*, Olivia wore London's war lightly. Her work with de Gaulle was distracting and the world she inhabited afforded a rare sense of security amidst the chaos. A stint in the Mayfair Hotel was a case in point. *'Here one feels quite safe, the walls are so nice and thick and it's marvellous to feel that if the electricity gets bombed it's all their responsibility and one won't have to rush around buying oil stoves.'* Letters home reveal a startling absence of fear – *'I go out every night, it's such fun'* – and a refusal to see the downside. *'Really the damage is very slight and one has to go around looking for it.'* Her joie de vive was emboldened by an absolute faith in Britain's capacity to fight back. At night she slept with *'cotton wool stuffed firmly into the ears and windows tight shut to keep out the noise. The guns are terrific and our defences certainly seem to be having some effect.'* Olivia's belief in London's anti-aircraft defences adds grit to 'roar of the guns' Blitz mythology.[1] Belching and flashing into the night sky, AA Command certainly emboldened the capital's spirits, but beyond that, the guns' ability to bring down the enemy was found horribly wanting.

Churchill would write of AA Command that 'their main contribution came later',[2] by which time the service was predominantly 'manned' by women, including his own daughter Mary Churchill. Scottish Martha, whose first ATS seed had been planted at her dreaded 'coming out' season in 1939, is quite certain that the noise surrounding the headline decision to allow girls on gun-sites reinforced her own determination to join the service. With quiet authority she observes, 'It is remarkable when you look back at things that were controversial then, which now just seem like common sense.'

During the 1940–1 Blitz, relentless months of airborne attack had been little short of a disaster for the underfunded gunners and a lack of good men (siphoned off to frontline roles) made matters much worse. General Sir Frederick Pile, a man ahead of his time, had already proposed the unthinkable to the War Office when he suggested that ATS women should not just make up AA Command's numerical shortfall but outnumber men in all operational areas bar the gunpit; 'breath-taking and revolutionary' was the Under-Secretary of War's startled response.[3]

Not only had Pile thrown a bomb into the traditional parameters of wartime thinking, in which women were prohibited from occupying roles in operational areas, but he was also armed with the research to back it up. Before the war Caroline Haslett, an electrical engineer and world expert on the social and cultural relationship between girls and household gadgets, had been a regular Sunday fixture at Pile's male-assortment training unit on the Surrey Hills. At the end of her field research Haslett carefully concluded that women 'could do everything except the heavy work involved in loading, manoeuvring and firing the gun'. Without touching women's sacred 'non-combat' status, Pile had the 'proof' he needed that the gentler sex could solve his manpower problem.[4]

It was 25 April 1941 when regulations were finally passed permitting the employment of women on operational gun-sites. Girls had crossed a military Rubicon and Pile had skilfully negotiated a potential minefield with semantics. Crucially, women were not allowed to fire the guns, a ruling that allowed the War Office to pretend that no real gender threshold had been breached. Nonetheless, few men were enthusiastic about the idea; an artillery major spoke for many when he admitted: 'I didn't welcome the prospect of training them, thought they'd be a nuisance, thought they'd upset the battery and all that.'[5]

Martha smiles at the memory of her young self and the prospect of this exciting new role. 'From the start of the war there was a gun-site at Broomhall, my father's estate. We were near the Forth Bridge, which was the target of the very first Luftwaffe raid in Britain.' Long before the Blitz, Martha was familiar with the evolving form and work of anti-aircraft defence, her interest piqued by her father's Royal Artillery service in World War I. 'Certainly the prospect of air defence made the ATS more appealing. I suppose the other option was driving, it was considered the top job, but I was too small to drive in the army. You had to be 5 feet 2 inches. I missed it by an inch.'

The military landscape for women was rapidly changing, and the new state of play urgently required a cheerleader. Martha concedes, 'I didn't know Mary Churchill personally, although I was at school with her best friend, Judy Montagu, and in 1941 we all knew she was on the first mixed gun-site.' Although the Prime Minister's youngest daughter had always been 'in thrall' to the 'inherent glamour attached to the navy', and star-struck by her eldest sister Diana, a Wren who 'looked ravishing in her tricorn hat and black stockings', with AA Command's planned roll-out dependent on the ATS, in June 1941 it was not the pucker Wrens that needed a Churchillian facelift.

Mary and her friend Judy just happened to be staying at Chequers when 'one day we listened to a conversation between my father and General Sir Frederick Pile'. The latter informed Churchill 'that a project in which he had taken close personal involvement had just recently . . . come into operation – namely, the forming of the first heavy mixed (that is employing both men and women) anti-aircraft batteries'. The conversation worked like magic on open-eared Mary, who was stuck doing tweedy Women's Voluntary Service work in the Home Counties. The prospect of heroism and excitement on a pioneering mixed-sex gun-site sounded too good to be true – 'Judy and I were much excited . . . and intervened to say that we would both like to become "gunner girls"!'[6]

Pile had just landed his most famous recruit and Martha wasn't far behind. Out of school and aged nineteen, she too was sizing up her options. Duty was the lifeblood of the Bruce family; the local lord lieuten-ant, her father, had been instrumental in drumming up local girls for military service and finally it was Martha's turn. The ruling-class nexus would play a further part in deciding her fate when General Andrew Thorne, Scottish Command's new GOC, approached Lord Bruce and explained his youngest daughter, Pansy, wanted to join the ATS with a friend. It was the final nudge Martha needed. 'I thought it would be quite a good job, especially if I became a gunner. Pansy and I joined together and went to Newbattle Abbey training camp near Edinburgh.'

*

Before Martha (or indeed Mary) could get anywhere near a gun-site, overhauls in both the ATS and AA Command ensured all new recruits had to clear several hurdles, irrespective of their background or class. At the most rudimentary level girls were now subject to military discipline and for the first time prohibited from discharging themselves. In a nod to the public mood, Dame Helen's habit of promoting friends to officer rank had also been outlawed. On paper at least, the appointment of officers on the basis of birth and background had stopped and in the form of Mary Churchill, this all-new people's army had just landed the perfect auxiliary to show off its fresh approach. Before she was selected for service at Britain's first mixed gun-site in Richmond Park, Mary was put through her military paces.

Square-bashing, saluting, scrubbing, apparently nothing was beneath the Prime Minister's daughter. In what she later described as 'quite one of the BLOODIEST days of my life', her every move was captured on camera; like a blank canvas Mary's pale moon face registered discomfort as she sweated it out in front of the nation's press in uncompromisingly thick service dress. She couldn't have 'felt more mortified, embarrassed, or miserable' by the attention but the PR coup was too good to be true. Although several of her friends had turned their hand to a spot of nursing or driving, Mary admitted that 'relatively few . . . at this stage of the war were in the women's services', let alone the Cinderella ATS, when she 'took the plunge'. The wall-to-wall coverage, which Martha still remembers, saw an uptick in recruitment and even Mary acknowledged there were moments of levity. 'I was most diverted to see that amongst the press photographers dear Cecil Beaton had appeared on the scene – looking very elegant and completely out of place in this galaxy of determined khaki-clad women.'[7]

Minus a razzmatazz of media interest, Martha acquitted herself well during her own training at Dalkeith's imposing Newbattle Abbey. 'I enjoyed that very much because it didn't matter to me living in a barrack room with the ablutions and all that.' If high-blown ideas about battles being won on Eton's playing fields had less traction in World War II, Martha concedes that toughing it out at boarding school was good preparation for the army. The tinned food was revolting and second-hand physical training shoes particularly unappealing but she was used to spartan living and leadership came naturally to her. 'When it was our turn to clean the place I said to the other girls, "Let's make a good job of this." The washing facilities had never looked so beautiful.' Careful and kind, Martha was struck by the anguish of recruits who hadn't been away from home before and appalled by the ineptitude of the officers charged with their welfare.

> They were absolutely hopeless and younger than us it seemed. They didn't know what they were doing. One senior woman, I don't know who she was, but you'd have thought she was God practically. You weren't allowed to talk to her.

In 1941, with a vast recruitment process underway and an ambition to attract an additional 140,000 girls,

Martha had spotted a flaw in the ATS's grand plans. Good infrastructure and leadership were lacking in a service that was in the process of supplying AA Command with recruits Pile hoped 'would perform their duties more efficiently than some of the low-category men who were being allotted to us'.[8]

Exasperated with receiving the dregs of the army, in 1940 Pile had solicited the help of a Cambridge professor of psychology, who confirmed what the general already suspected; that his men were less able than the average army recruit. With Professor Bartlett's help, Pile promptly introduced aptitude testing, explaining to the War Office that 'a man who is to work on a predictor* requires a different type of mind from a man who is to handle ammunition at a gun'.[9] One year on and pioneering ATS recruits selected for anti-aircraft units were likewise expected to take a series of tests to assess their 'quickness and keenness of eye, sureness of hand and steadiness of nerve'.[10] Martha had left Downham School with a raft of top grades and aged ninety-nine, standing legs apart, hands on hips, fronting down a stranger mid-pandemic, there is no doubting her 'steadiness of nerve'. Surely she had been chosen for anti-aircraft training?

'No! When the list went up with the postings, I couldn't see my name anywhere. I wasn't on the gunners' list and I thought, "That's odd." And then I suddenly found my name and Pansy's in the corner, separate from everyone else, with hieroglyphics above them.' Martha's appointed

---

* A predictor was the first fully automated machine that could aim a gun at an aircraft based on observed speed and angle to the target.

military path was still no clearer to its recipient. She pauses and restates her case to become a gunner. 'In the interview I had asked to go into anti-aircraft defence because my father had been a gunner and I wanted to be properly involved in the war.' Sufficiently self-possessed to demand an explanation, she turned to the sergeant in charge. 'This must be a mistake. What does this mean? What are we training to be?'

'Oh,' came the bemused reply, 'you're training to be officers.'

Martha shot back, 'But we are not officers, we are just privates. Surely you cannot become an officer if you haven't been a private?'

Private Bruce was duly sent to see the 'god-like' senior commander. She inhales. 'I formed up my best man and entered the room.'

'What do you want?'

'Ma'am, I don't want to be trained as an officer, I want to be a radar operator on a gun-site.'

The senior commander looked at the small girl in front of her.

'Oh,' she said, 'you're just a baby. I'll transfer you.'

'And she did, she transferred me onto the list that was training to be gunners.'

Her friend Pansy Thorne, daughter of Scottish Command's GOC, was fast-tracked to become an officer, but not so Martha, who was determined to earn her stripes on the ground as a private. After all, this was a people's war and she wanted to be part of it.

*

Like Martha, Grace was also selected for work on a gun-site in late 1941. 'I wasn't quite seventeen and a half but I'd made up my mind.' Grace, who liked lipstick and dancing and her solider boyfriend, since transferred to Egypt, had 'never travelled as far as Leicester but it didn't bother me. I got on the train and it was a 1,500-weight lorry that picked us up and took us to Glen Parva barracks.' Austere and red brick, this high-Victorian military complex had spat out young men in World War I and now it was the girls' turn.

> There was a lot of discipline. You've got to have discipline. You all had to barrack your bed and fold your blankets. An NCO came in and you had to stand by your bed. Everything was timed, up at a certain time, abolitions at a certain time, breakfast at a certain time, we marched in and we marched out of the dining room.

Grace shrugs. 'I was used to discipline, my father was strict, I'd been in domestic service for years, I didn't mind. I wanted everything that the army could offer.' When she arrived Grace knew nothing of guardrooms, gun-sites, Mary Churchill or radars. Unlike Martha she wasn't in the military 'know'.

> After a few weeks of training, learning to salute that sort of thing, they said to a group of us, 'You're off to train with the Royal Artillery in Reading.' I s'pose I must've done OK in the tests. I don't say I was excellent but I was as good as anybody else. I didn't know what to expect, but being with all the girls, people my own age, was like a breath of fresh air. I loved it from the beginning.

Lady Martha came from a big house, Grace had worked in one as a servant (well, a mid-sized house in Brentwood), but in other ways the two girls weren't so different. Both had been away from home (Grace no longer had a home), both had worn a uniform ('more like a pinafore'), both understood discipline and structure ('I'd never missed a day's work, I never 'ave') and both wanted to belong. Eighty years later, in the lonely winter of 2020–1, both still hold fast to their former military identity, answering calls, finding photographs, allowing a writer into their personal space. 'I don't regret a day of it, dear. I remember signing on. I had to take a bus to Southend.' Alone, Grace dealt with the paperwork ('I didn't have any certificates, that's how I could lie about my age!') and passed the medical ('A1, I've always been strong as an ox') before returning to Brentwood, and getting on with her servant job. 'No, I didn't tell my boss. No, it would've been awkward. I waited till my papers came and then I said, "I'm going to war."'

Part Two

A LONG WAR

9

'YOU are wanted too!'

Daphne sighs. 'Reg didn't want me to go into the ATS. He worked with service girls, he said he knew what they were like.' And the ATS, rebranded Auxiliary Tarts Service in popular discourse, was stymied with the worst reputation of all the female armed services. Daphne shakes her head, 'It was most unfair, I've told you before that the Wrens had a higher pregnancy rate.' But retrospectively she has some sympathy for Reg's concern and concedes that she was 'an innocent flower'. Reg knew that; kissing and cuddling was all he'd been permitted before being posted away from Norfolk to Boscombe Down.* He missed his peaches-and-cream girl in Feltwell, all warm and welcoming, patiently waiting for his next leave. 'Maybe he felt I might meet somebody if I signed up, that he wouldn't have me to himself any more.' From her armchair, Daphne neatly articulates the conundrum that bedevilled military thinking: what were men fighting for if girls were forced to serve alongside them? The sanctity of home and its fecund promise of plenty and peace was a tantalising prospect for thousands of men living off thin rations in

---

* The Aeroplane and Armament Experimental Establishment was moved to Boscombe Down, Wiltshire, in 1939.

mean barracks. Labour's Agnes Hardie argued that 'war is not a woman's job . . . women share the bearing and rearing of children and should be exempt from war.'[1]

But by 1941 the bald realities of conflict on a giant scale called for a giant rethink. Additional girl power was desperately needed to plug the cracks in Britain's over-stretched war machine: defeated in Greece, occupied in Crete, pushed back in North Africa, haemorrhaging at sea, blitzed at home and desperately short of supplies. Given the ATS's poor start it's unsurprising that belated recruit-ment efforts failed to deliver the numbers of girls needed to bolster Britain's largest female service. For girls and parents alike, khaki simply didn't cut it and by December 1941 the British Government had made an unprecedented decision. Women must be compelled to serve.

Churchill's biographers are quick to talk up his jubi-lation when a Japanese attack on Pearl Harbour saw America enter the war on 7 December. Much less atten-tion is paid to his House of Commons address five days earlier.[2] In December 1941 the Prime Minister did a U-turn and argued that compulsion was needed to draw sufficient numbers of women into the armed forces, more specifically into the ATS. He'd long doubted the wisdom of forcing women to serve; his own daughters had all vol-unteered and he admitted feeling 'like an anxious parent inspecting a preparatory school' when he visited the female quarters at Britain's first mixed gun-site.[3] However, his apprehension regarding conscription was not about homesick young women but rather demoralised young men. Churchill believed that the 'vociferous opposition of men in the forces' to the idea of female conscription would cause unrest and the Defence Committee had agreed with him.[4] It was the indiscriminate reality of global conflict that forced their hand.

Indicative of the fraught implications of this volte face, in December 1941 when Churchill addressed the House, he reassured MPs: 'We do not propose at the present time to extend compulsion to join the Services to any married woman, not even childless married women.'[5] For the moment the National Service (No.2) Act (the word 'conscription' was studiously avoided) was confined to the call-up of single women, aged between twenty and thirty.

It's no coincidence that Reg, ten years Daphne's senior, asked her to marry him shortly after the introduction of conscription. There was the proposal and much discussion about the ring. 'It was beautiful, a daisy cluster, exactly what I asked for. He had it made in Boscombe Down.' But Reg's proposal came too late, Daphne's head had already been turned by someone else. 'Dorothy Lemmon and I were very close, we were school friends and her parents had already let her sign up, she'd joined the ATS.' Dorothy rang Daphne from distant Hull, where she was stationed on a gun-site. Buzzing with excitement, the two teenagers swapped notes; Daphne, still a year below conscription age, listened eagerly and contemplated her future. Her cousin William was dead, her fiancé had been posted away, her school friend was already serving – there was nothing left for her in Feltwell.

As had been the case in September 1939 with the passage of the first National Service Act for men, the prospect of compulsion encouraged a spate of volunteers and Daphne's mother's protestations paled in the face of her daughter's logic. 'I needed to volunteer early to make sure I got the job I wanted.' While the act's main target was the ATS, the political climate insisted conscripts were offered a choice between the armed services and munitions. Daphne had no intention of working in a factory and she was very clear about the job she wanted in the ATS. 'A telephonist, I wanted to be trained as a telephonist. I didn't want to work outside like Dorothy.' Headset, cables, receiver, notepad, uniform. Yes sir! 'If I could operate a switchboard, I would be able to get a good job at the GPO when I left.' The General Post Office, communication hub of the world, was Daphne's intended final destination. Nothing was to get in her way. 'I wrote to Reg just after I signed up and explained that we couldn't marry. I returned the ring. Mother was a stickler about things like that.'

What came next more than lived up to Daphne's expectations: 'Oh, it was lovely, lovely!' She's talking about her second training camp. 'After my initial three-week induction at Northampton, they decided I should go to the ack-ack training school at Melton Mowbray to be a teleplotter for a searchlight company. I'd explained to them I wanted to be a telephonist.' Daphne had read the mood correctly – entering the service as a volunteer gave women a degree of control over their military careers. 'I was learning how to log aircraft movements and communicate between sites.' There were tests every week; she still has her pencilled notes:

> *HOMING BEACON: This is a searchlight which*
>   *is used to guide planes home to their bases.*
> *Trace means plot but don't engage.*
> *Observe means each site reports its own area.*
> *Observe Free means all sites report All Clear.*

Within weeks this meticulous girl had been transformed into a soldier. Daphne enjoyed the routine, the discipline and wearing her uniform and was in full service dress when, out of the blue, Reg turned up at the gates.

'"Private Williams, an airman is at the guardhouse requesting to see you." That's what they told me. Captain Morris said he'd give me an hour off if I caught up with my lecture that afternoon.' Daphne dutifully went to meet Reg, neatly tucked into pressed khaki, her auburn hair waved under the new-look cap and her spectacles offset by the glint of the cap's badge. Poor Reg, he'd travelled across England to hear it for himself. There, amidst the rising sap of spring, catkins and catcalls, was his Daphne, irrevocably changed. 'We walked in a park in Melton Mowbray. I explained to him, "I love you, I still do, but I'm just starting out now, Reg. I'm training to be a tele-plotter."' Daphne pauses, perhaps understanding Reg's pain more clearly now than she did then. 'It was a long time ago, he was a dear man, but I had my life to get on with.' Goodbye, Reg.

*

Joan first appeared in the introduction of this book displaying her medals; she is one hundred years old and a soldier to her core. Ask her why military life demanded focus on bed-making, shiny buttons and appropriately positioned caps, she snaps her answer back: 'Discipline!' Be in no doubt, Cambridgeshire-born Joan Stittle understood what service meant and in late 1941 she had several reasons for wanting to join up (not least that 'the war was going so badly, I thought I better take a hand in it and see what I could do'). But in her diligently scribed notes Joan is clear about which service and why: 'having previously given much thought to such weighty matters, I decided I would look my best in the delicate blue of the Royal Air Force uniform.'

In the parliamentary debate that accompanied the introduction of female conscription MP Eleanor Rathbone expressed contempt for the focus on the ATS's new uniform – arguing that such feminine detail 'repels the best kind of girl'.[6] This Victorian feminist had apparently forgotten the more frivolous motivations of girlhood. Joan had made up her mind based on uniform and, fortuitously, in late 1941 she was no longer a teenager. The pending National Service Act had changed the dynamic at home for twenty-one-year-old Joan; her parents' reluctance to relinquish their daughter into the war was about to be overruled by a power greater than their own. Better surely to volunteer than suffer the indignity of being 'called up'?

A tiny stem of a woman wearing enormous sunglasses amidst the summer blaze of her beautiful Norwich garden, Joan and I first meet in July 2020. Fragile and unsure of her survival, time is short and she's frustrated by questions that probe into an early life before the war, when her father, a saddler and harness maker in Soham, had 400 shire horses on his books. England's famous fenlands were well served by Mr Stittle, of that Joan is sure.

> I loved the ripe smell of leather, it takes me right back, even today. Life was simple then, we travelled by pony and trap until I was eight, I'd never been further than Cambridge. No, I don't know why I was an only child, you'd have to ask my mother. They probably thought one was quite enough, my father had eleven siblings.

Her Victorian-born parents are long dead, but their daughter has kept a meticulous record of her wartime relationship with 'Ma and Pa'. Joan was a prolific letter-writer; perhaps as an only child she understood the pain inflicted by her wartime departure. Two of Mr Stittle's brothers had died in World War I and neither parent wanted their solitary 'ewe lamb' surrendered to the mercies of yet another conflict.

If, by the winter of 1941, parental objections were futile, the National Service Act anticipated fallout. Despite AA Command's overwhelming need for staff, no girl could be forced into an operational role, she had to volunteer. Gun-sites and airfields were optional, but service wasn't. This caveat smoothed Joan's domestic negotiations: her parents relented to the idea of active service provided their daughter 'could remain safely somewhere in England doing a sensible job'. In December 1941, while the parliamentary debate rumbled on, Joan seized the initiative and took a bus to Cambridge to clinch her place in the WAAF. 'Tomato soup and beans-on-toast in the local cafe for ninepence' delayed her arrival at the Wesleyan Church doubling as a recruitment office. Joan was locked out for lunch, but the air force's loss was the army's gain. In the adjacent room Joan met a 'stout, forbidding ATS recruitment officer'. Pale blue aspirations were exchanged for a khaki future.

However, the ATS demanded uniformity and that included robust physical and mental health; medicals were a compulsory first hurdle before Joan's admission into service and out of Soham. Just 5 feet 1 inch tall and weighing 81 pounds (the size of a small calf), medical officers found her slight frame bothersome (the defence of the realm on such inadequate shoulders?) but discovered no apparent fault as she stood naked among her aspiring soldiers. Marked A1, Joan returned home to recover her dignity and await summons to camp.

'Dignity!' Cornish Vera snorts; she's still recovering hers. With 'careful attention' paid to prospective service women's health, medical boards normally consisted of three qualified individuals, ideally including one woman,[7] but Vera only remembers the man. 'It was a young man, well, he looked young to me. I'd seen the other girls come out and I thought, "Crikey!"' This wasn't what Vera had bargained for when, aged nineteen, she decided to cut and run from her market garden job ('I could've stayed, it was war work too, you see') and signed up for the ATS in Plymouth. 'They pulled down me knickers! For scabies, yeah! They looked at everything, under your arms, down below. I nearly died, my face was like a beetroot.'

Vera's nether regions were her own very private concern, 'Yes, it was the first time anyone one had . . . !' In the 1940s modesty was jettisoned in the interests of national 'health and hygiene'. 'They looked at your hair, your nails, everything. I was 5 feet 5 inches with a 36-inch bust. Look at me now, it's all gone south!'

Fortified by fresh air, exercise and agricultural work, Vera was graded A1, but further 'inspections' were conducted on arrival at every new training centre and army barracks to 'eliminate infectious disease and to deal with the matter of head infestation'. Eighty years on and she's still muttering; her humiliation was not over. 'If you moved from another camp, you had to be FFI – Free

From Infection. Well, I went through all that again and I had nits in me hair! Everything had to be fumigated, my hair, my hat, my helmet. Everything, yeah.' Vera and her friend concluded that they'd contracted nits on the train between camps: 'We felt filthy for a bit, we daren't look at anybody.' Vera's emotional declamation is a reminder of the pitfalls of exceptionalism in a world of uniformity. Let it be known, the nits never dared return; Private Vera Edwards had serious work to do.

*

In the first week of 1942 nearly 2,500 women enrolled with the ATS; Daphne, Joan and Vera were among the girls who rushed into army life before the first conscripts arrived in March that year.

> *January 1942, Talavera Training Camp, Northampton,*
> *Dear Ma and Pa,*
> *. . . We were met by bus, about 50 of us, and brought to the camp. During the day another 200 more have come in. So far we have done nothing but queue up, wait, feed (lots of grub), wait, be medically examined for bugs, fleas, lice and lots more waiting etc.*

In her wry letters home, Joan acknowledges she has preserved the 'incidents and emotions of a different world and time'. They provide an invaluable antidote to the pitfalls of the human brain. The cerebral cortex selects and reselects the events through which we most frequently meander: sorting, refining, forgetting and re-remembering. The impact of this mental editing is as significant as it is hard to quantify but in Joan's letters any such distortion is avoided. When she started writing to her parents in January 1942, she had no idea what the outcome of war would be; her feted veteran status sat miles in future; meanwhile the present was an altogether more humdrum affair. As Joan quickly discovered, service life was far from glamorous.

> *Here is a list of requirements, which no doubt will be added to from time to time. Little pillow (and cover), bedsocks, toilet roll (most essential), one or two dusters, small teacloth, face cream, shoe socks, rat poison (for the people who snore).*

Joan can still recall the grinding of teeth and assortment of other nocturnal noises that accompanied communal living. Discomfort was the hallmark of those early days. The uniform didn't fit – *'new shoes play havoc with feet'* – and was inadequate against a particularly harsh January. *'I am wearing my own vest, the Army vest, pullover, cardigan, coat, skirt and I look very fat but I'm still COLD.'* And there was an obsession with gas.

> *This morning we had gas drill, through a tear-gas chamber with respirators on and then through it again without . . . needless to say my respirator was too big and I had to be re-issued with a child's size . . . we have gas lectures by the dozen, gas is dinned into us day and night.*

A hangover from World War I, like a poisonous pall, the threat of chemical warfare was ever present in World War II. Faced with possible invasion in 1940, Churchill asked his chief military assistant to investigate the possibility of 'drenching' the beaches with mustard gas. Two years later in early 1942, just as girls were billowing into training camps, gas was back on the agenda. The Russians expected gas would be used by the Germans in their next offensive and Churchill informed the War Cabinet that Britain should 'treat the use of gas against Russia as against us – we would retaliate against Germany'.[8]

Vera shudders. 'Oh, mustard gas. Oh yeah. We had to go into our hut with our mask on and they shut you up and then you had to whip it off quick show!' The ATS guidelines were explicit. '*The main object of gas training is to enable personnel to carry on with their work in the case of an attack*'[9] and recruits had to go through the gas chamber every three months. 'We were spluttering and choking. No wonder it killed some of the lads.' Vera's memory that men were killed with mustard gas confuses World War I with World War II, when gas was never used on the battlefields. With both sides fearful of retaliation, that horror was saved in its most fatal form (Zyklon-B) for the concentration camps. 'My goodness, we only had gas for a couple of minutes, we were all pushing each other out of this small door. I can't imagine what it must have been like.'

Basic training demanded basic good health and at Talavera Joan discovered invasive medical procedures were par for the course. She '*added to the world's misery by having two teeth out*' (the dentist was compulsory). '*One tooth refused to leave its mooring. Apart from a lopsided face I am better now*' and the demeaning impact of infestations was as bad as Vera remembered. '*A head inspection was due this morning. One of the girls in our hut didn't return from this operation so rumours are very busy.*' It was an unforgiving climate. '*One of the girls I travelled with has disappeared. There is a suggestion that she has scabies.*'

This zero tolerance policy had long military roots. World War I was the first major conflict in which more soldiers (on the Western Front) were killed by bullets than disease. Vaccinations and improved hygiene were trans-formative and by World War II compulsory. Every girl's service book is chock full of dreaded vaccination dates. Joan was no exception. '*An inoculation was timed for 5pm. We marched three-quarters of a mile over the camp-site to the hospital and stood out in the snow until 6.15.*' The following day she was '*reclining full length recuperating from last night's inoculation . . . I would rather have this than Typhoid – but I'd rather not have this. My arm has a huge muscle and I feel as if I've had flu for a fortnight.*' Within twenty-four hours several girls including Joan had a temperature and in her next letter she is '*frightfully proud of the fact that I'm the first one to have the vaccination "come up".*' With an arm as '*stiff as a poker*' she had to be dressed and undressed and was packed off to the local hospital for a check up. There '*the heartless nurse tells me it is a perfectly healthy vaccination*'.

Exactly seventy-nine years later, in January 2021, Joan sends me an email entitled 'Spring-ish.'

I have an appointment for a [Covid-19] vaccine on Wednesday afternoon at a surgery in Norwich. Old age has its compensations. Much love and good wishes, Joan.

10

'The girl behind the gunner'

Grace sits stoutly in her chair and smiles; nowadays this former servant girl is the president and oldest member of her Poole Royal Artillery Association. There's not much that fazes her, 'but I've got to say I am glad we're finally getting some recognition'. Signing up in October 1941, hopeful she might once more bump into boyfriend Eddie, Grace served in one of Britain's earliest mixed anti-aircraft batteries. After basic training at Leicester's Glen Parva barracks she was selected for Arborfield near Reading, where ATS girls were instructed alongside Royal Artillery men. She spent hours hunched over the ergonomics of different planes. Aircraft recognition was a vital skill and Grace can still recall Bakelite models of the British Spitfire and Hawker Hurricane, their proportions replicated in miniature, their tail fins and wingspan, versus Germany's deadly Messerschmitt and Focke-Wulf designs, long before she saw them flash in the beam of a searchlight. Designated a private in 495 Mixed Heavy Anti-Aircraft Battery (working alongside the largest 3.7 inch static guns), her next stop was Anglesey, with the couple of hundred men and women she'd work beside for the next four years. Grace was young and strong and fearless and she was no longer working alone. 'I loved the companionship, I loved it.'

Outside, weathering the gusting winds off the Welsh coastline, she adjusted herself to the realities of a technical war. 'It was a practice camp with live firing. You've got to pity the poor guy flying the biplane with a sock out behind.' With new expertise, Grace was filling a man's shoes. Narrated by a male gunner, an early Ministry of Information film illuminated the work of the ack-ack guns, painstakingly explaining that 'a shell takes half a minute to reach 30,000 feet. If the plane's speed is 200mph, in this time it will have gone two miles, so for accurate aiming we have to use special instruments.'[1] Special instruments that had niftily mechanised air defence (and the messy business of killing), neatly allowed women to step up in 1941 while preserving their sacred 'non-combatant' status. Grace was trained on the spotter and the height-finder. 'That's right, dear, you'd be standing for hours out in the open and before we had radar it was the spotter that suddenly shouts "PLANE!" and everybody looks and listens and as soon as you see it, you get your instrument onto it.'

With a cylindrical pipe and mirrored tubing and wheels that moved it up and down, left and right, the height-finder tracked the elevation and bearing of the plane. Grace is back following the aircraft in her mind's eye, face pressed against the viewer, watching out for the enemy, adjusting the bearings and the angle, calling out "on target" to the girl in front and 'this was just training, you know!' They hadn't even got as far as a gun-site. 'The big guns didn't move, it was the batteries that moved around in 1,500-ton lorries.' Private Grace and 495 Battery arrived on Crown

Hill outside Plymouth in 1942. 'When the sirens went you had to drop everything and run to the command post, you grabbed your steel helmet and you got going. No, not frightened. I don't remember being frightened.' Grace shakes her head, and repeats, 'I didn't really think about the danger, I were too busy.' A teenager without parental guidance, she didn't even realise that gun-site work was optional. 'I liked my job, but now you come to mention it, I was always in battledress, gaiters, boots with a tin hat on me head. So that tells you something.'

When addressing Parliament, Churchill had framed girls' new roles on gun-sites in the context of 'great quantities of anti-aircraft equipment' now 'coming out of the factories'. He argued that range finders, predictors and 'a host of elaborate appliances of a highly delicate and highly secret character' would do the fighting, not the girls.[2] The Prime Minister's verbal dexterity served him well; the press marvelled that 'modern warfare has not only created a new specialised job for the man behind the gun but has brought the girl behind the gunner', a 'mixed regiment being a unit consisting of both sexes'.[3] Britain recruited girls into anti-aircraft defence two years before Germany, aided and abetted by a prime minister who nipped and tucked the realities of operational service. After the 1940–1 Blitz, gun-sites were less dangerous than they had been, but they weren't risk free.

In April 1942 the inevitable happened. Nora Caveney, aged eighteen, 'was killed by a bomb splinter as she stood at a predictor on a south coast gun-site during a raid'. The press coverage of this first female anti-aircraft casualty enhanced the image of female soldiering. Nora, 'following an enemy aeroplane was "on target" when she collapsed' and, crucially, 'Private Gladys Keel . . . took Caveney's place at the predictor and continued to follow the raider and the guns were able to continue firing without a moment's delay'.[4] Royal Artillery PR made much of the uninterrupted action. The only indication of gender is that the death merited a report in *The Times*. Mid-war the defensive mission eclipsed the loss; now girls could die heroically too.[*] But eighty years on, Grace doesn't recall news of Nora Caveney and is sure 'we didn't think about the danger, not really. We learnt to operate and move as one.' There was security in numbers, the army made sure of that.

Vera is equally gung-ho.

Yeah, when the alarm went you'd run like mad. You'd have your dinky curlers in and they'd be tinkling against the helmet. If we'd been up all night, the cooks came with jugs of cocoa. Oh yes, it was always battle-dress in camp. Gaiters, trousers and boots, my mum went berserk when she heard I was wearing trousers!

Vera, like Grace, was assigned a MHAA battery (526). 'They just said, "You're operational and you're being trained for the predictor." "Crikey, what's that?" I said. "I shan't be able to do that!"' Vera laughs. 'But I did and I could.' She stops. 'What? I don't know if I was good at school. I left at fourteen and there was no focus on things like that.' It took a war to discover that Vera was bright.

---

[*] Estimates of the number of the ATS who died during WWII vary. The Commonwealth Graves Commission has the burial/commemoration details of 717 ATS members and that is the statistic frequently cited elsewhere.

'I was surprised when they said I was operational and they put me on this big machine with all these dials.'

Basic height-finding instruments had been around as early as 1917 but it was between the wars that the first prototype predictors were born. Clockwork-powered mechanical computers in the form of hefty black boxes, early variants 'bristled with levers and dials' which, when correctly operated, would determine the bearing, elevation and fuse-length for the guns based on the enemy's movement in the air.[5] Small wonder Vera was initially intimidated. There hadn't been much exposure to technology during a childhood in rural Cornwall.

In my first job as a domestic for Mrs Hawkins I always remember the telephone ringing. I was frightened to death.

'Go along, Vera,' she said, 'answer it!'

I remember I heard this voice, but I couldn't see it! I was terrified.

'Hellooooo, is Mrs Hawkins there?!'

Five years later and the predictor was an even more daunting prospect, with the 1939 Vickers model hailed as the latest groundbreaking invention that would save the nation. Vera peers at the Pathé footage on a smartphone. 'Well, I never! I was on the Vickers, it used to go up, I was on the telescope side and when we were doing drill in the morning you could look right through the barrel of the gun. We had to line up with them.' Anticipating the future position of enemy bombers was Vera's first wartime job. 'There'd be me on one side and Pat on the other and another girl, the No. 1, on the fuse.'

Pathé news boasts that wind speed and height-finder readings are fed into this high-tech machine and 'getting a line on the target' takes 'just a matter of seconds'. The girls' readings had to be spot on. As for the male gunners, 'they simply match the pointers on the dial . . . before you can say "knife" a well-directed gun is barking out a protest. Thanks to the predictor the visitor is in for a hot time!'[6] Vera's tickled, the footage has taken her back to a war where she was at the controls in an era before computer programmes and drones, when 'non-combatant' girls were guiding the guns. 'Ooh yeah, you'd see the shells go up! You could put a plane off its course just by firing.' Aged ninety-eight, she's animated, sitting up and alert in her seat, ready for action. 'I was posted to Liverpool first, it was terrible around the docks but I just thought of it as a job.' Imploding shells, puffs of smoke, the smell of cordite: Vera was riveted by her new life. 'Yes, you could hear the shrapnel coming down. Some of our girls did get hit. We were young and foolish, I s'pose, we never thought of it at the time . . . It never occurred to me I could get killed or anything.'

*

Daphne is holding a saucer in one hand and a cup in the other. Detail matters: there is a doily for the tray and milk must be poured first. A medical patch administers morphine: the dose has been cranked up, yet the pain persists. 'I'm ninety-seven, my body's given up.' Perhaps, but Daphne hasn't. She leans in. 'We were desk mates, good friends.' She's still talking about her school friend Dorothy Lemmon. 'I was very impressed that she managed to persuade her parents to let her go into the ATS as quickly as she did. She was only seventeen and a half, much younger than conscription age.' Frederick and Annie Lemmon's oldest daughter Dorothy was an athletic child, a runner, a jumper, an all-round achiever, perfect material for Britain's new-look female army. She badgered and bothered until her parents relented and three days after Christmas in 1941 Dorothy started her new life training at Talavera Camp, on the race course at Northampton, (four months before Daphne) and then on to Reading (just after Grace) to hone her skills as a 'gunner girl'.

Daphne was awestruck. 'It wasn't just that Dorothy got her way with her parents, but also she wanted to work on a gun-site and that is exactly what happened.' She breezed through Pile's aptitude tests and was moved onto Anglesey, where the great guns roared out to sea and Dorothy simulated action on a height-finder with her newly formed unit: 511 MHAA Battery. By the time Dorothy was in action defending the underbelly of Manchester against enemy fire, her friend Daphne was being put through her paces at Northampton. High summer and both girls had moved again, Private Dorothy on to Preston, a village just east of Hull, to shore up the city's docks against air attack and Private Daphne at her first posting with 65th Searchlight Company, back in Norfolk at Terrington St Clements.

'It was a terrible shock, terrible.' Daphne stops and puts down her cup and saucer. Dorothy is dead. She died seventy-nine years ago. It was a beautiful summer day, the Norfolk sky a giant blue basin against Earth's thin rim, when a telegram delivered its fatal blow back in Feltwell. 'We regret to inform you that your daughter, W/109181

Pte Dorothy Lemmon was killed in action in the early hours of this morning.' Decades later, her younger sister Verna would underscore what that action meant. 'When the air raid warning went, the girls alongside the men had to be on duty and were exposed to exactly the same dangers as the men, their only protection a few sandbags and a tin hat.'[7] Dorothy was caught by falling shrapnel and died instantly. Only just eighteen, in 1942 she wasn't old enough to vote but she was old enough to take a hit for king and country.

Daphne in nearby Terrington St Clements was granted a day pass and returned home for the funeral. She was struck by Dorothy's impressive military send-off. The whole village turned out to pay their respects amidst flowers and sunshine and men with reverse arms, ATS officers starched into khaki and a trumpet call so solitary and sad. 'I went to say goodbye, Dorothy was lying there in her front room, just one big bruise on her forehead and that was it.' Daphne, suddenly self-conscious in her uniform, shuffled out, head bowed. Parental grief is ghastly, she concedes. Later, there would be a marble gravestone in the local churchyard adorned with the ATS crest, Dorothy Lemmon's name and age and 'HER DUTY NOBLY DONE'.[*] Daphne nods. 'She's been made quite a lot of and her name is the last name to be read out on the Roll of Honour in Feltwell. She was a girl, you see, and it was different for girls.' Daphne's right, it was different for girls; as a non-combatant Dorothy couldn't be awarded a combat

---

[*] Dorothy Lemmon died on 1 August 1942. She was the daughter of Frederick and Annie and is buried in St Nicholas' Church, Feltwell, Norfolk.

medal. 'Oh no, her death didn't put me off serving, I was a teleplotter so I was inside on the switchboard.'

Daphne, having disposed of dear Reg and lost Dorothy, needed war to live up to expectations. 'I've already told you, I was in 65th Searchlight Company, Essex Regiment.' She sighs. In her head the image is picture perfect but the direction of this wartime scene into book form is proving somewhat harder to pin down. 'I have read a lot of what is written about the Second World War and none of it describes what I did.' What did Daphne do? 'I was on the plotting board and the switchboard (it was called a concentrator – make a note of that) and we were linked to all the searchlight sites in our battery. Right? It's simple.'

The planes came over, the searchlights went up, the guns went up and the planes came down. She nods. Daphne was back at base, coordinating the commands between sites, a small cog in a giant wheel of service that threw up the sabre-shafts of illumination Grace remembers so well. 'Oh yes, like minnows the planes were silver in the beams. When our fighters were up then we couldn't fire the guns no more.' Daphne goes through the rigmarole of a shift; that is how much it mattered, then and now.

'The Gun Operations Room (GOR make a note of that), when we were posted to Hull they used to ring up: "*HUMBER 1, HUMBER 1, stay on the line!*"' Daphne stayed on the line. A pause and more information: '"*HUMBER 1 to connect with the searchlight sites.*"' A raid was imminent. '"*HUMBER 1, take post, report when ready.*"'

Daphne leans in. 'If a site didn't answer, then the officer had to go to the site to make sure they were ready. That was it, you had to get the beam up, but not too soon, you didn't want to guide the enemy plane in.' She pauses.

It was a very, very interesting job, there were only two of us on the concentrator and one side dealt with the gun operations room, the other side the searchlight sites. We worked shifts and every evening at 6pm there'd be a rehearsal. The commanding officer would come up and everybody was ready for their job that night. It was intricate and lovely.

She stops; it's time for respite and coffee. 'No, not that tray, I have set out the coffee pot on the tray in the kitchen, the one I want you to use. Thank you. I have tried to explain to my carers that I can't help it, I have standards.'

*

Heavy and light gun batteries, searchlights, anti-aircraft rocket sites: the British landscape was peppered with protrusions, encampments, huts, mounds, lorries and guns. Vera and Grace belonged to heavy AA batteries, they were the girls behind the biggest guns, stationed mainly in clusters of four across more than a thousand camps. Vera began her service outside Liverpool, Grace recalls Plymouth, and like Daphne both can return to a snapshot moment, a frozen memory when 'the Jerry was in the air, the lights were up and the guns were roaring'. Grace was struck by the sheer size of the sky; a giant black blank canvas the enemy could penetrate at any time and across which she scanned at the helm of her height-finder. 'When the guns fired, you'd get a puff of smoke every time a shell exploded in the air, not just from our site but others further down the coast. We did our best but the sky is big.'

And so is Britain. Grace is puzzled and tussling still with a dark night when a German sortie (a Fringe Target attack, one of the many post-Blitz) capitalised on AA Command's split focus. Where to cluster guns bedevilled defensive thinking; should Pile prioritise the (random) Baedeker raids that mid-war aimed for Britain's beauty spots? Or reinforce the south coast to cover further troop embarkations to North Africa in 1943? Grace was stationed at Crown Hill, overlooking Plymouth, where there was a lack of Bofors guns to shore up the coast and American reinforcements were arriving and needed cover. The situation was made worse by Germany's deliberate mixing of attack strategies; high, low, inland, sea-borne. Fighting a war on two fronts, the Luftwaffe met the challenge of Britain's improved air defences with fierce cunning.[8]

'I remember the Messerschmitt most of all, with its wings, big, bearing down.' And Grace remembers being up all night with her optical quest, in khaki pants and greatcoat, taking down the bearings before they were yelled forward to the predictor. 'I didn't understand much about the war, but when I saw the Jerries, I just thought they shouldn't be over here and they shouldn't be bombing, we got to get rid of them, that's what I thought.' The stand-out raid was part of a six-day German sortie on Plymouth, Hastings, Deal, Brighton, Rye and Bexhill; AA Command claimed just two enemy fighters, and neither was downed by Grace's battery. She shakes her head: 'A lot of the time we were firing out to sea from remote gun-sites at the odd plane. Then, that night, we were in the right place but there were just too many of them. The flashing and the noise was dreadful.' A tin cup of warm cocoa at dawn was small succour for a girl whose identity was staked firmly in the work she did. 'We saw the bombs, you know, as they hit the town.'

'They called us Clarke, Bot and Crowe and the next day we were allowed down to Plymouth to have a look.' Drilling together, polishing, marching, exercising and fighting, the trio of girls who operated the height-finder developed a firm friendship. Grace had finally found companionship, and the prospect of unexpected free time was grasped with both hands. Grace Clarke, Lillian Crowe and Kathy Bot, still stunned from the night before, picked their way down the hill and into Plymouth. 'That's right, we had the morning off, we were allowed out.' The city's naval base at Devonport had been a magnet for the Luftwaffe during the Blitz and the Plymouth that Grace visited in 1943 still bore giant scars from those early bombing raids. In her young mind it was hard to discern the previous night's damage from the devastation that had ransacked the city two years earlier. 'It all looked very bad.' But vital and young and briefly free, there was also joy to be found in the sea air, wearing khaki, holding hands.

'In the centre was a street still clearing itself from the rubble and the shopkeepers were retrieving what they could.' Makeshift trestles and a table had sprung up amidst the fallen boards and bricks. Grace with her keen eye spotted a 'chappie, scrabbling and sorting out make-up, picking it up and popping it on the table.' A salvage job of sorts, the salesman with his wares freshly spilled out onto the street – and along came Grace. 'He even had bottles of perfume, I couldn't believe it. He had my perfume, Californian Poppy!' *As haunting as a Chopin nocturne . . . as dangerous as a tropical moon.* Californian Poppy was advertised with a disclaimer: '*Such a big demand, such a restricted supply – means that someone sometimes may be disappointed. Sorry!*' That day Grace bagged three bottles at sixpence a pop. 'He wanted rid of it. I love my Californian Poppy!'

Military and feminine, Grace was both at once.

11
'Top Ack!'

Grace is sure that there was no gun-laying equipment at her first two camps. 'No, the spotter was the first to know of an enemy plane. We didn't have radar at those early sites.' But when it was available, the emerging science of radar with its cabins and sci-fi dials and new-age screens proved a game-changer for anti-aircraft defence. The very first GL MK I radar* (able to pick up a target from seventeen miles away and feed in accurate information from eight) was born in 1939 and Martha had her eye firmly set on this hi-tech world when she defiantly rejected an officer training course in 1941. 'Instead I was sent to Devizes in Wiltshire, where all the operators of these new machines were trained in groups. Yes, we were exclusively trained by men on the technical side.' The Royal Artillery oversaw a course which rigorously put Martha through her paces, in a world where 'manning up' had taken on a whole new meaning.

Now in her hundredth year, these days Martha makes do with a telephone and an illuminated magnifying glass, but back then she was adjusting to a merry-go-round of constantly changing pioneering instruments and equipment.

---

* Gun-Laying Mark I Radar.

She remembers 'a plotting officer and a technical officer and a piece of equipment that searched the sky, and all this information was coming down onto a table with a little light underneath showing the progress of the enemy aircraft you're following'. Martha pauses; it's advanced stuff and establishing what happened at the Devizes training camp and what was later operational work is made harder by her prolonged presence at the former. 'I was told I was to stay behind, I was kept back to train squads of girls who kept arriving. Many had not had the necessary education, you had to have a technical aptitude.'

Martha commands respect, presumably she always did. Before she left Devizes this diminutive Scot was made lance bombardier, then bombardier. 'Look, I wouldn't normally say this but here's a picture of me that's really rather good.' The assured young soldier has a knowing smile and her gunner's white lanyard is bright and visible on the left, offset by the first stripe on her shoulder. Martha had earned her status and it pleased her, writing home: '*I'm becoming a little more used to being addressed as "bombardier". At first I kept looking round wondering who the people were talking to.*'

But she had not yet worked on an operational gun-site and the prospect of training often battle-hardened girls in a brand-new science of war was daunting. '*The first of the next intake has arrived, some of them look terribly superior and have been ack-ack in different branches before. They will probably be very difficult and full of their own ideas about everything.*' Despite the selection tests at early training camps, Martha often received a mixed bag. '*The last intake was ghastly and it's a tremendous relief to have some intelligent girls again. I have a particularly nice section at the moment, all tremendously keen and full of questions.*' Constantly trying to stay ahead of the game, she admitted to her mother: '*I'm always a bit scared as to what they're going to fire at me next, however I've stood up to it so far and I'm now perusing a book on wireless which I hope will stand me in good stead when they get more advanced.*'

A military greenhorn, Martha's own training ran concurrently with her teaching of others and the programme was rigorous. '*This afternoon we have another of those brain strain lectures. Yesterday's was awful. It looks just like a jigsaw on my page.*' Perhaps inevitably there was considerable competition with the opposite sex. '*Today's lecture was even worse than yesterday's and all the male TIs were there asking terrific questions and getting us all muddled up.*' But if Martha was put off her stride, she didn't show it.

> *Every morning now we parade at 8.15 and are inspected by none less than the Major himself. After that agonising process is over we do drill mixed! This is quite a new idea and works rather well, especially as we are far better than most of the men.*

Martha admitted to her mother: '*You know you always said to me it was much more interesting working with men instead of entirely with women, well there certainly is some truth in that statement.*' But a level playing field it was not. If gunners were traditionally promoted to lance bombardier and bombardier, Martha, who much enjoyed her new titles, was later told she could not use them. Officially ATS girls were privates not gunners, and corporals not bombardiers; a cruel reminder that they did not formally belong to the Royal Artillery. 'We were furious. Suddenly they came along and said this, it happened later when we were at a gun-site and it stopped us feeling like part of our battery. My father had been in the Royal Artillery, the titles meant something.'

Far-seeing Pile had favoured ack-ack girls' complete absorption into the Royal Artillery, but the ATS resisted this logical next step. Strictly defined roles insisted that they came under the authority of female officers and were subject to different (more lenient) rules. Women could be released from service for 'family' reasons and got a half holiday on a Sunday. Men couldn't and didn't. Women were also paid a third less than men for equivalent jobs. Further up the military food chain and the operational deployment of female officers was prohibited by ATS senior commanders. For them, an administrative remit remained the rule.[1] Dismissed as camp followers for so long, women, wary of losing hard-won ground, held back other women. Martha, when challenged about these disparities, is ever the practical soldier. 'You were in your own role, you wouldn't want to take over a role that wasn't yours. We weren't in a position to win a medal.' But men on the same gun-site were.

It was Pile who observed 'there was a good deal of muddled thinking which was prepared to allow women to do anything to kill the enemy except actually pull the trigger'.[2] But protest there was none. Just like their male counterparts, serving ATS girls were the bedrock of a deeply traditional society; the gentle sex knew their place. Martha explains, 'The guns were ridiculously big, and the shells were very heavy. You wouldn't want to take over that role. There was no need for it.' Sitting in her armchair, Vera hits a similar note: 'I think the guns were a manly thing to do, I can't see a woman going behind big guns like them.' Like Martha, it did not occur to her to challenge the status quo. 'It was just a job. I didn't question it. Not like nowadays when women do what they like, don't they?'

Grace sighs; she's been asked this before.

> Look, we never thought about it. I was on the height-finder and later in the plotting room underground, with earphones and a mouthpiece and we tracked the plane as it moved. We knew we were necessary and that the boys needed us. The girls could not have lifted the shells, we couldn't have run around with them. The girls wouldn't have done that.

Granted it may have required two girls to lift a shell, but elsewhere higher female replacement ratios had been promoted as reassuring proof that women were less physically able than men (at the end of 1941 AA Command expected to see the jobs of 15,000 men taken by 18,500 women and acknowledged that 'in heavier types of work a ratio of even 3:2 was found necessary'[3]). It wasn't the weight of the shells but rather the preservation of British girls' femininity, (and men's masculinity) that was at the heart of the non-combat rule. Vera's right; as long as women weren't involved, guns were 'the manly thing to do'.

*

Pile proudly declared 'British girls' were 'the first to take their place in a combatant role in any army in the world'.[4] He was wrong. British girls weren't combatants and Russian girls on the Eastern Front were mobilised in more lethal form. They remember their war very differently: 'I was a machine gunner, I killed so many . . . For a long time after the war I was afraid to have children. I gave birth to a child when I calmed down. Seven years later . . .' The Motherland's female soldiers took decades to recover. For these girls, manning the big guns that shot down fighter planes was often the easier option. Russian Vera was an anti-aircraft gunner. 'Fortunately I . . . I didn't see those people, the ones I killed . . . But . . . All the same . . . Now I realise that I killed them . . . I think about it . . . because . . . because I am old now. I pray for my soul.' The onslaught took its toll.

Valentina was an anti-aircraft artillery commander:

> At first I kept bleeding from the nose and ears, my stomach was completely upset . . . My throat was so dry I was nauseous. At night it wasn't too bad, but in daytime it was very frightening. It seemed the plane was flying straight at you, precisely at your gun. About to ram you . . . that wasn't for a young girl.[5]

Twenty million human lives in four years; war meant something very different on the Eastern Front. Three hundred thousand Russian girls fought in anti-aircraft units alone, where no job was out of bounds. Pilots of the German Luftflotte 4 and tank commanders in the 16th Panzer Division were shocked when they discovered the deadly fire ringing Stalingrad came from all-female batteries.[6] But this 'uncivilised' state was not replicated in western Europe, where women retained their non-combatant status.

Germany didn't allow women into AA batteries until 1943 and they never fired the guns, not even when the Russians came rolling into Berlin. In Britain, as late as December 1941, one of Churchill's justifications for directing women into the ATS was the possibility of 'inva-sion, which may never come but which will only be held off by our having large, well-trained, mobile forces and many other preparations in a constant high state of readiness'.[7] But his new ATS recruits weren't armed. Grace laughs. 'Every gun-site had a guardroom and two or three of us would be on guard duty in the day. We'd stop any arrivals. "Friend or foe?" we'd shout. The men always had a rifle, but us girls, we just had a stick, a truncheon that we'd kept in the guardroom.' Thankfully Grace met no foe.

Russian peasant-soldiers, male and female, bore the brunt of the German war machine from mid-1941; of this Stalin would constantly remind Churchill as he pushed the British Prime Minister to open a second front in the West. Meanwhile, back in Britain, the armed services, and AA Command in particular, grappled with a very differ-ent problem: how to keep batteries alert and committed when enemy raids were infrequent and unpredictable. In the words of one gun-site major: 'We were all so stale and edgy we'd have given our ears for sight of a Jerry plane.'[8]

Every woman in this book recalls endless exercise, drill, parades and fatigues. Compulsory daily rigour was the meat and drink of military life; service men and women had to be ready for action even when there wasn't any. Dame Helen understood that and argued girls required the 'right attitude of mind', a 'clear and comprehensible code' of conduct, and structured physical exercise and drill.[9] Finally under army law in 1941, the ATS worked hard to establish itself as a highly disciplined force; the absence of an immediate enemy could not be allowed to impact on performance, state of readiness or morale, but even the best equipped sometimes found the more humiliating trials hard to bear. Fatigue duty was dreaded with particular relish. Women were easy prey for this obligatory choring and Martha felt singled out at her Wiltshire training camp.

'We all had to do fatigues and that day I was the fatigue girl down on my hands and knees. It could involve anything: cleaning the ablutions, clearing leaves, but I was given the NAAFI.' The Navy Army and Air Force Institutes were the lifeblood of any battery, a neutral space where men and women could buy snacks and cigarettes and enjoy each other's company over simple refreshments. 'I was given the NAAFI after a sergeants' party; it was revolting, swilling in beer, a filthy room. And there were no cleaning products, nothing.' Martha has deliberately selected this abiding memory of tackling the NAAFI as an example of her ordinary war. Why was the filthiest of tasks given to her? Was it her aristocratic bearing? Her title? 'I think they thought this is Lady Martha, we will give her a nasty job; they tested your mettle.' They tried to humiliate her but the Royal Artillery had met their match in Martha, who cites the motto 'do it and complain afterwards'.

In due course she would get her own back, writing home: '*I was seized for drill by the female sergeant in charge. It was for the benefit of a male NCOs' course. They all took it in turns to drill the squad. One or two were good and the rest hopeless.*' Martha was pulled out of line. '*Just before we were due to be dismissed the RSM fixed me with a glassy stare and said, "Corporal come out and drill the squad."*' Martha did as she was told. '*I don't think the men were particularly pleased but the RSM complimented me, it couldn't have been too bad, perhaps they were jealous?*' A young woman barking at men shed a whole new light on army life and one neatly anticipated in 1941 when the Army

Act gave the ATS military status commensurate with the opposite sex. *Punch* summed up the novel state of affairs with a cartoon: Travelling on the London Underground a soldier offered his seat to a uniformed woman with the words 'Take my seat, Miss – MADAM – SERGEANT.'[10]

Fatigues and drill were accompanied by regular exercise. Every girl, no matter what trade, section or regiment, remembers physical training. Joan groans, 'I loathed PT.' And everyone hated the exposing 'dirty brown' uniform of shorts, aertex shirt and ill-fitting plimsolls. PT was dreaded by the rank and file and championed by the authorities. A 1942 parliamentary committee concluded: 'It has been impressed on us that the best menstrual – as indeed general – health prevails amongst girls and women doing strenuous and active work.'[11]

At her initial ATS medical Daphne recalls being asked: 'Do you suffer from heavy menstruation? Does it ever prevent you from working?' But despite the service's concern over days lost to monthly periods, Grace has no recollection of any pain relief being available ('my periods began when I was serving, they came as a terrible shock') and Daphne still remembers the excruciating embarrassment of collecting sanitary towels from the NAAFI. 'In case it was men issuing them we used to say, "Could I have a packet of silver teaspoons please?"' Euphemism abounded for the embarrassing inconvenience of periods, with physical training touted as the catch-all remedy that kept girls healthy, strong and occupied.

*

'The law changed and I had to sign up. I said I want to join the armed service with some sort of physical programme.

They told me the Wrens had no physical training, the WAAF a little but that the army had a very good structure. That's why I went into the ATS.' Beryl might be the last ATS anti-aircraft PT instructor alive, and aged ninety-nine, in a heatwave with swollen legs, life is hard work. She's worried about the modern world – 'I think there's more wrong today. It's harder for you lot' – and she takes comfort in a past when the enemy was defined, the hierarchy respected and her abilities recognised. 'I was a dance teacher, I'm still registered with the Royal School of Dance.' But in 1939 plans to teach in London were kyboshed by the outbreak of war. Instead she returned home to Norwich and taught local children to dance (her seminal dance book for infants can be found in the British Library[12]). With strong features and wavy black hair, Beryl was an only child and grew up craving companionship. She compensated for her loneliness with books and music and enjoyed the order that sprang from solitude. 'I used to try and teach my dolls dancing and conversation. Perhaps I am bossy, I do like things to be manageable and as they should be.' True to form, the army career of W/209659 Beryl F. Manthorp has been carefully preserved in a perspex folder, ditto her early life in a burgundy clip file.

Like Grace, Beryl endured basic training at Glen Parva Barracks in Leicester, followed by a non-commissioned officers' cadre (training) and a physical training course, (both necessary for PT supervisors) before arriving at the enormous Oswestry Barracks on the Welsh border. This was a first and formative pit stop in a peripatetic career that saw Beryl administer PT instruction from Aberdeen to Leigh-on-Sea. With Regiment 23 in Oswestry, she was assigned the radio location girls (Martha's equivalents) and testifies to their 'superiority'. But bright or otherwise, PT remained compulsory and was well accommodated in this military garrison with its four large identical gyms. 'I made sure we had a proper class, from warm-ups onwards. Bungee jumps, star jumps, sit-ups, press-ups.' If fitness was the primary raison d'etre behind these workouts, then bonding and camaraderie ran a close second. 'Rocking the dumbie. You stand absolutely still and fall face forwards and your opposite caught you and pushed you back up. Or running and then at a certain point jumping, leaping in good faith that your partner would lift you up.' Faith in each other, faith in the ATS, faith in Britain's war effort. Beryl smiles, 'That's right, building a community, army strong.'

News of this PT instructor – a performer, a creative, a dancer – got around. 'Lance Bombardier Jack Sprugeon cycled up to see me . . . he told me about the Music and Drama Society. I was soon co-opted into the dance section.' Ambitions abounded, the am-dram group was all ranks and, unlike Beryl's PT classes, included men. 'We had professional musicians, dancers, singers, and a conjuror . . . I did a pas de deux with Jack, and a solo, and I danced with a group of girls.' The locals were treated to performances at the Gobowen Orthopaedic Hospital.[13] Army life without enemy raiders need not be dull, although under Beryl's fierce tuition it was quite possibly a smidgeon scary.

Often miles from any town with their picture houses and cafes, AA batteries became proficient at laying on their own entertainment. Martha's letters testify to that. Six months on and still at the training camp in Devizes, great plans were afoot. '*The battery dance takes place on Thurs-*

day and some of us are trying to arrange a cabaret show to put on in the interval . . . luckily there is plenty of talent in the battery to choose from and I hope it's going to be pretty hot stuff.' The show was clearly a success because two months later Martha began meticulously planning another. Her mother, the Countess of Elgin, was given her orders:

> *First of all, before I forget, will you please send with all possible <u>speed</u> my two cotton dinner dresses. NOT to go on the razzle but for two people to wear for a cabaret show. You know the ones I mean, the white one with yellow spirals and the highly coloured striped affair with blue sash. If you haven't time yourself, please see that someone with sense does it because I don't want the wrong ones turning up.*

A 'coming out' season just before the war had its perks. Beryl in Oswestry concedes 'costumes were a problem', but not so for Martha, who confirms the dresses arrived in time for the aptly named 'Top Ack!' performance. 'I was also the porter in a sketch with that Glen Miller song, oh you know the one . . . "Chattanooga Choo Choo".' The memory catches Martha off guard, she bursts out laughing. 'It was about a train. Chattanooga!'

12

'Come into the army, Maud'

The second National Service Act was passed in December 1941, but it had not been an easy sell. One MP claimed that the ATS 'has a thoroughly bad reputation in the country at the present time. Conditions in the ATS camps are in many cases exceedingly bad. The physical condition of the girls themselves is exceedingly bad and the whole service has got a bad name.' Fears about the 'wrong kind' of women serving and living alongside men ran deep and he spoke for many when he argued 'the ATS is not the sort of service a nice girl goes into'. The *New Statesman* picked up on the mood and published a spoof poem – 'Come into the army, Maud' – in which the ATS was 'Queen weed in the garden of service girls'. Maud would need to 'de-rouge the nails and prune the curls' if she wanted to shape up and serve.[1]

'Ha, my real name is Florence, but everyone calls me Maud! Florence Maud Ward. I once worked for a doctor and he described me as "the woman with that delightful regional accent".' Born and raised in the Black Country, one-hundred-and-one-year-old Maud grew up in Stour-bridge: 'A lovely little town, always the same.' Nearby city Birmingham felt a whole world away, '"Birmingham people, they brummies! We don't know much about them" – that was the attitude.' Maud admits that when she joined the army in 1942 'we did it for ourselves, we didn't do it for their sakes. Because we said, "Let's get away and see what's happening in the great big world." We didn't worry about what they were saying.'

Perhaps not, but elsewhere the spectre of a disreputable service had whipped up a feeding frenzy of anxiety. Today Joan laughs at the whiff of scandal that clung to the ATS. 'Yes, I knew of it at the time. I just thought it was very funny. Apparently we were called officers' ground-sheets; it didn't mean much to me. We were terribly innocent in those days. At twenty-one, I didn't know any more about life than a twelve year old does today.' Grace is unimpressed; she is very proud of her military service. 'I didn't listen to the news before I went in. I didn't know about any scandal. Yes, I did hear about it later but I chose to ignore it.' Martha smiles. 'Now you come to mention it, I think we did have a more lowly reputation than the other services.' But she remains vague on the question of why.

In fact, the ATS was up against a toxic cocktail of social conservatism, sexism and snobbery. By far the biggest service for women and forced to rely on conscription, a large proportion of its girls were recruited from the lower socio-economic classes. There was a heft of snobbishness in a smear campaign that replaced the word Territorial with Tarts and simultaneously played on the macho culture of the army. Insisting a girl worked in a factory was one thing, putting her in a uniform and asking her to serve alongside men, quite another. The *New Statesman* goaded 'Maud' to 'come into the army now', but very few of the rarefied voices dominating the press and politics really knew what the average 'Maud' was thinking.

Between bites of toast – 'I have a morbid appetite these days' – (Florence) Maud Ward explains how her life began as a pretty young thing. 'Mother said I was like the sweet little girl in the Pears soap advert. Later I wanted to look like Rita Hayworth and people like that, but instead I always looked about twelve.' Born in 1919, Maud arrived as an afterthought to parents already over forty. 'We never went anywhere but there always seemed to be enough money; Father did the paperwork for a tobacconist factory in Wolverhampton. And Mother worked next door in a little delicatessen. She'd say, "I wasn't a waitress! I was on the cooked meat counter."' A couple with aspirations, (their oldest daughter had already trained as a teacher), when Maud turned fourteen, she wasn't allowed to slop out of school straight into a job.

Yet by 1935, with the worst of the depression over, Maud recalls a slew of options. 'Lots of my friends left school, there were plenty of jobs in Birmingham, the Typhoo Tips factory and the ones making suitcases, Cheney's luggage, so girls overnight got jobs and they became all high heels and make-up.' The train to Birmingham was full of off-the-peg fashion and lipstick; picture houses had allowed a girl to dream and mass production put an extra sixpence in their pocket and gave them something to spend it on. But Maud's mother had other ideas. 'She said I had to carry on to the British School of Commerce. The sign's still there over the door, in Easy Row in Birmingham. I learnt shorthand and typing.' Maud remained in education, and the factory girls would mock 'us lot on the train, they'd say, "Look at the school girls!" But I was pleased in a way. Their job was just repetitious piecework on a line.'

Long gone was the heyday of the male clerk with his quill pen and copperplate handwriting. A new breed of typist was at the vanguard of female emancipation between the wars, and Maud's training saw her ride the wave. 'I got a job at Stewarts and Lloyds. Even before the war they supplied the whole of England with steel tubing.' Already twenty in 1942, she wasn't obliged to leave her job as a clerk at the steel manufacturers; their work supplying the war effort was 'essential'. She remembers the Pluto project – a 'PipeLine Under The Ocean' – that would later deliver fuel to D-Day's invading forces and the 15,000 miles of tubing produced for beach defences. Maud was busy all right, but she was also bored.

> I always think of those little Cadbury's finger biscuits, you can still get them. I had an overall, a proper wraparound one, you put your sleeves in and there's a pocket at the front. Well, I kept these biscuits in it and broke little bits off and nibbled at them while this man was kerfuffling and spluttering, trying to work out the conversion rates for kilos. I just wasn't interested, and my friend said to me, 'Are we really going to stop here all war?'

'We used to talk behind the cabinets and have a little giggle and not worry too much about our shorthand,' is how Maud puts it. This youthful verve was drawn into sharp relief by the arrival of 'older married women'. After the introduction of female conscription the stakes kept being raised; by the summer of 1942 the upper age rose to 45 and then 50 by 1943. Headlines screamed 'Conscription for Grandmothers' and Maud found herself surrounded by stodgy middle-aged women who wanted to work locally. [2] Small wonder she decided to cut her losses and sign up. 'I went into the ATS because it was easier to get into the army. It was very hard to get into the Wrens, you needed to know somebody.' Maud wanted an escape from chuntering colleagues and the ATS provided the simplest route.

She didn't need Minister of Labour Bevin to decry the ATS's morality issue as 'nonsense'. [3] Maud knew about 'rude girls', she saw them every day on the way into Birmingham and there was the neighbour's lass who flashed her knickers when doing a crab and hanging from a tree. 'She was old enough to know better, but some girls were just like that. Oh yes, I'd heard about the reputation of the ATS, I just thought, "I know how to conduct myself, I'm not going to go to wild parties." I wasn't brought up to be open like that.' A centenarian these days, Maud still cuts pretty, with aqua eyes that demand attention and old-fashioned feminine features, and in 1942 she knew what men could be like.

> I had several offers. I remember one man who came from a long way away on a motorbike, from Newark in Nottinghamshire. He was short-looking and came unexpectedly once to visit me. I remember him standing in the bay window, we were looking out over the scrapyard through the little lead lattice frames. I remember him putting his arms around me from the back and I thought, 'I don't like this person coming at me like this, squeezing me from the behind.'

Maud wriggled free. 'I yelled to Mother, "I have to get to work!" and left her to get rid of him.' She stops and laughs. 'Something like that they wouldn't be allowed to do today. They'd say that you'd been attacked. I just thought "I don't want this"!' Maud knew that boys will be boys, but they also had their perks. 'Early on we were worried about them going away. I remember talking in the park just after war was declared, we thought we'd be left behind with the older men and the ones that were discharged because their feet were wrong or something like that.'

The prospect of service, like life, was a mixed bag. Above all Maud was excited about leaving the Black Country for the first time. 'We had to get this special train. It was laid on to take us to Fulford Barracks in York for our three weeks training. Yes, I suppose it was the furthest away I'd ever been from home.' But if Maud was sanguine about the prospect of army life, the government was much less so. Overnight, girls had broken free of their domestic shackles and the nation's moral barometer went into overdrive. In a war framed against a German enemy, politicians and the public opined that the real danger was young women's apparent inability to resist Allied soldiers (America's entry into the conflict in December 1941 fuelled that fear). Lurid tales and salacious rumour found fertile ground amidst a war-weary populace. MP Nancy Astor did not mince her words. 'There has never been anything more villainous than the campaign against the morals and the state of women in the ATS.'[4] With ambitions to recruit upwards of 3,500 girls a week the government acted swiftly and by early 1942 the Violet Markham Committee on Amenities and Welfare in the Three Women's Services had been established.

Grace is defiant. 'I don't know what they thought they were looking for, we were a proud and happy lot.' But Markham, a wily operator who'd served on a Labour

Commission in World War I, knew exactly what she was doing. Beneath a veneer of concern for conditions and facilities the Committee had a clear agenda which sought to address 'rumours derogatory to the Services . . . growing uneasiness was shown by parents as these stories gathered force and volume'. On a moral quest, the Committee made its way around the three female services, visiting 123 camps and stations across the British Isles.[5] Meanwhile the ATS's newest recruits focused on perfecting their identity as soldiers. Everybody had something to prove.

*

Maud went through the usual induction with its injections, ill-fitting uniform and teeth extraction ('they took two teeth out; I said, "I'll go to my own dentist at home," but they were having none of it!') before selection as a shorthand typist, when she was posted to Halifax. 'There was a colonel and he had a secretary from Gravesend but he wanted a stand-in because if she didn't hear from her husband she was inclined to take off.' Ironically (given the moral hoo-ha), single girls were considered more reliable. 'I remember going in and saluting, hoping I did it right and the colonel said, "We'll start now". He set to dictating notes about training on board a troopship. I wrote pages and pages and pages of shorthand. I thought, "I will never be able to read this back."'

All-important shorthand and typing guaranteed Maud a decent role within the service. She had a recognisable, transferable skill. Clerk was one of the five original trades open to the ATS and the army's humiliating clerk ratio of five women to four men was soon amended to 1:1. Irrespective of their background, most girls longed for a skill like typing, it saved them from more demeaning domestic roles. Even Olivia, who'd wowed her way across invaded France and by 1940 was driving and translating for de Gualle and his Free French, repeats several times: 'But I couldn't type. I never learnt that sort of thing. I suppose it was my class, I didn't need to learn.' She keenly remembers that utility was everything; her hands simulate typing. 'I was not as good for de Gaulle as I could have been because I could not type.' Before the war it was presumed upper-class girls did not need concrete skills, and the poorest girls couldn't afford to acquire them. The conflict changed women's perceptions of themselves. And so did military service. Maud wasn't just a secretary, she was also a soldier.

Protocol, badges and rank mattered hugely to girls operating in a man's world. In 1942 Penny had left bombed London and her broken heart behind and like Maud she was posted to Fulford Barracks in York, where she too became a clerk. Penny was in the army now, and in her head sometimes she still is. 'At the training camp, oh, the discipline. You always addressed an officer "Ma'am". Yeah. And you salute. Then you wait until they dismiss you and you salute again. And you don't question them, what they say is the law.' All ninety-nine years of Penny rises from the chair and she re-enacts a salute. 'It's the longest way up and the shortest way down.' Her fingertips touch her temple. 'Long up, short down.' Then there's marching, 'a special kind of marching' according to Penny. She points her shod foot onto the floor, 'Ball first, ball to heel. And the arms, they are swinging.' Five months shy of her hundredth birthday, Penny's marching in her living room, right the way across to the window. She looks back and grins. 'You know I only gave up ballroom dancing this year!'

Unlike Penny, Joan can no longer march across the carpet but she too experienced the minutiae of army existence. It impacted on every corner of a girl's life, and the more regimented that life, the less time there was for high jinks. She was still in Talavera training camp, Northampton. '*Ma and Pa . . . you ask what I do in the evenings, well, after tea I sit round the fire (if it will burn), write letters, clean buttons, badges and shoes and go to bed.*' The next day it was '*snowing again. We have been on a route march and came back looking like ghosts.*' And later that afternoon:

> *We've just been on parade again. Now we are free until 2.45 when we have got to have a shower; at 3.45 go and be fitted with new uniforms (we get two complete sets). In the meantime a compulsory lecture – so you can see how fully occupied we are.*

Joan was still a fledgling private. '*When we were in town yesterday we met an officer and as we hadn't had the faintest idea how to salute, we turned and stared solemnly into a churchyard while he went past.*'

The salute demanded eye contact, bestowed respect and acknowledged rank. Mid-letter writing in Devizes, Martha jumped to. '*My bike has come and everyone is thrilled not least the major, speak of the devil here he comes . . . I've just subsided having sprung to attention and given him a smashing salute.*' Her father, the 10th Earl of Elgin, held numerous military and honorary titles; Martha knew the form and much about service life felt familiar. She signed off: the major '*came rocketing across the field in his car rather as grandfather does*'.

Penny, Joan, Maud, Martha, most girls in this book excelled at the paraphernalia and routines that their new military existence involved. However, in 1942 it was not the quality of their salutes nor the sheen on their buttons that the general public (and the Markham Committee) were worried about.

13

'Rumours derogatory to the service'

Maud admits 'I am unusual, I think I'm quaint.' She is too. Confident, with a quirky sense of humour and good looks, she's always known how to stand her ground. 'Oh, there were plenty of *those* sorts of girls, yes, they would say, "Come and play table tennis," we knew what they meant. Goodness knows what they got up to. I didn't bother joining them.' Upon arrival at her Fulford training camp, Maud quickly discovered that the ATS was a broad church. 'They'd check behind your ears for scabies, you get that from sleeping in dirty blankets without sheets, cos there were quite a lot of poor girls, they just didn't own pyjamas or anything.' She pauses. 'The first two girls I remember were lying on the bed, cuddling each other, and would you believe it, they came from Birmingham! Yes, I think it was a sexual thing. The other girls said, "Take no notice, they are always cuddling on the bed."' Maud stops. Did she know what a lesbian was? 'Yes, I knew those two were, yes. Years ago people would say, "Be careful if so and so gives you a lift, she might put a hand on your knee." There was a sort of fear, because it was sort of illegal, wasn't it? Things have changed so much.'

It is ironic that while the Markham Committee was scouring the country trying to ascertain if there were any grounds for the 'rumours derogatory to the service' concerning girls and their conduct with men, the first thing that struck many ATS recruits was the inner workings, habits and preferences of their own sex. Maud thinks she knew what lesbians were and her vagueness over their legal status is understandable. While homosexual acts between men were illegal, gay women weren't prosecuted in the same way, but in the ATS lesbianism had 'a disciplinary aspect when it occurred'.[1] Penny is still amused by her own naivety. 'You had no privacy, you washed at the sink, so you'd be having a strip wash and you'd be standing and you'd see oooh, she's got big knockers!' Sharing a communal space, girls met other girls on their own terms often for the first time. Penny laughs, 'I tell you now, and this is the truth, I was in line for my NAAFI rations and this girl seemed to be getting very close to me, very touchy and when I got back to the hut the girl in the bunk below me said, "Oh, don't mind her, she's a lezzer!"'

Penny had no idea what a 'lezzer' was. '"Well, hen," this girl said (she was from Glasgow), "you don't know what a lezzer is? You're so ignorant!" She said, "They fancy other girls."' Penny shakes her head at the parallel universe she once occupied. 'Yes, that's what she said! Well, I had never met a lesbian before, we didn't talk about things like that.' Nor, when it finally drew its conclusions, did the Markham Committee. (According to ATS thinking, 'there was a danger of creating a problem by drawing attention to it'.[2]) However, in 1941 a memorandum entitled 'A Special Problem' set out the 'issues' surrounding homosexuality and attempted to differentiate between 'adolescent "crush", normal friendships between women, unhealthy friendships and true promiscuity'.[3]

Penny is back in Fulford Barracks, where being a woman had taken on a whole new meaning. 'Blow me, I thought "This is a bit funny." I couldn't think what they do.' Her story goes from the NAAFI queue to barrack bunk beds, 'and there was this girl below me, and another girl used to always come up. She'd still be standing there by the bed after lights out.' The midnight antics were drawn to a halt by a corporal who pulled Penny to one side the following day. 'What were they doing? Were they petting, or kissing?' Penny explained she didn't look down, that she had been trying to get to sleep. 'Well, the next thing I knew the girl got a posting!' Penny's story chimes with ATS guidelines, published retrospectively in 1945: 'As cases arose they were usually dealt with by posting and only a very few promiscuous lesbians had to be discharged from the Service.'[4]

If the ATS managed to keep the 'special problem' of lesbianism out of the press, they had less success with fears about the opposite sex. It was this area that the Markham Committee focused on. 'Virtue has no gossip value. It has been one of the tasks of your Committee to form some conclusion as to why the Women's Services have incurred so much criticism.' Under the caption 'SERVICE LIFE AND MORALS' the Committee explained they'd been unable to find a connection between the auxiliaries with their 'trim and soldierly bearing, their good discipline and high spirits' and the 'unfriendly comments often current'. Instead, they looked for 'psychological reasons' for the rumours.

> The British, though they fight when called upon to do so with unfaltering courage and determination, are not a military race. They cherish a deep-rooted

prejudice against uniforms; consequently a woman in a uniform may rouse a special sense of hostility, conscious and sub-conscious, among certain people . . . the woman becomes an easy target for gossip and careless talk.[5]

The Committee confronted the issue of society's response to uniformed women with platitudes and euphemism. The 'morality' question was branded a woman's problem and as an 'easy target' in much of the public debate girls were framed as unfortunate victims of gossip. Inappropriate male behaviour wasn't referenced and most men would presumably have been exempt on the basis of their 'deep-rooted prejudice against uniforms'.

*

'No, they were all wonderfully well behaved.' In our first meeting Daphne strongly resists the idea that (some) British men may have behaved inappropriately during the war. RAF man Reg, her former fiancé, never put a foot wrong, all the men in her unit were 'delightful' and later her husband too. 'I married as a virgin aged thirty-two.' Daphne keenly remembers that her war as a teleplotter in a searchlight regiment was fought alongside heroes; meanwhile today's more open permissive society reinforces her conviction that men were 'better behaved' back then. It is months later, when she has finally relaxed and dug deep and persistently into a past clogged with seventy-five years of commemorations and armistices that she concedes, 'During the war older men liked me.'

In 1943 Daphne's searchlight battery left Norfolk and headed for Rise Park, a stately home on the outskirts of

Hull. 'Well, when Mrs Harden on the local telephone exchange heard that I was going north, she said I must meet her sister and brother-in-law, so being a social girl I did just that.' Unless they were on leave, ATS girls had to wear their uniform at all times; Daphne, neatly tucked into her service dress, complete with beige tights, polished shoes and spectacles, arrived for dinner in nearby Withernsea. After a satisfactory meal, her male host offered to walk her to the bus stop. 'I can see him now with a trilby hat and raincoat, he must've been over forty; he wasn't in the war, I can't remember why not.' Daphne made polite small talk with this older gentleman. It was dark and when they arrived, the bus shelter was empty. 'That's when it happened, he tried to kiss me! He held me and leaned in and I thought, "God I don't want this!" I veered away. It was most embarrassing.'

Mortified, Daphne leapt on the bus; safely back at Rise Park she shared her story among friends. 'They laughed and said, "It's because he's been married for a long time and you were in uniform."' Daphne nods. 'Lots of people thought we were easy but lots of us came from good families.' Under her breath she admits, 'It wasn't the first time.' Closer to home in nearby Terrington St Clements, she went to visit a local family. 'Everywhere I went I had somebody in my village who knew somebody where I was posted. George and Dolly, they were called, and they lived on the road between Kings Lynn and Spalding with their little boy. I went a few times; George was an agricultural worker so not in the forces and one night he tried it on, he tried to kiss me when his wife wasn't there.' Daphne politely resisted George's advances: '"No, no! I'm not that type of girl."' Ninety-seven years old, she pushes away an imaginary man and looks up: 'He apologised so I visited them again.'

A repository for male desire outside military service, Daphne discovered that for certain men within the ranks, the ATS uniform also prompted meddling. A methodical hoarder she still possesses her physical training kit. Notorious for its brown aertex and tight slug-coloured shorts, the scarlet and white PT arrangement that's spread across Daphne's armchair is startling. 'We had to wear it when we went to Hull. There was this colonel, Chalky White, an awful man.' Daphne purses her lips. 'He did not like the ATS PT kit so he bought us all red tops and white shorts.' The colonel's curious cheerleading costume leers back at Daphne eighty years on; female uniform was exclusively the remit of the ATS and she is not entirely sure what motivated 'Chalky'. 'He didn't like the girls in the other kit. Yes, he was weird. A horrible older man.'

Daphne came across him one morning; she was enjoying a walk in a world of her own when she heard the colonel shouting in the distance. 'I thought he was shouting at his dog, but no, he was shouting at me. He accused me of failing to salute him, but I did salute him.' Defiant, she stood her ground. '"I did salute, sir, and you saluted back!" I don't forget these things, he wanted attention.' Chalky was eventually 'posted elsewhere. Some of the girls' parents rang and made such a fuss about him . . .' Daphne pats her red and white PT combo and smiles, 'But these came in useful later, when I went travelling after the war.'

Lest there's any doubt where the problem predominantly lay, Martha's 1942 letter to her mother spells it out.

We have two cadets attached to us for a fortnight, they are very nice lads and know the job backwards. They are here so that the battery command can decide whether or not they are suitable for a mixed unit. It's a pity they didn't start the system long ago, then perhaps some of the dirty old men would not be where they are today!!

Dirty old men. Concerned about the sexual dynamics of the mixed batteries, initially Pile had deliberately deployed older married men. Grace, serving in one of the first mixed batteries, remembers 'all the young men were replaced straight away. They were sent aboard after a few months and older men were brought in. They were probably only thirty or forty but to us they were old men, it was a bit like having your father around. They used to look after us girls.' At best their relationship with the much younger ATS was paternal and Pile quickly discovered these older men in their separate Nissan huts were a mixed blessing. They found the young women 'a bit tiresome'[6] and Martha's letters confirm the feeling was reciprocated. Camaraderie was easier to establish with junior officers who were 'hand-picked with meticulous care'. Increasingly the army only assigned newly conscripted men to mixed units, believing if they hadn't known any other army life, they 'would not find the atmosphere of a mixed battery so hysterically unorthodox'.[7]

The 'hysterical unorthodoxy' of their position was something girls had to get used to, in and out of camp. In Devizes, Martha and her fellow gunner girls enjoyed walking the Wiltshire countryside amidst *'masses of tiny villages with ridiculous names and lovely thatched roofs, truly olde Englishe'*. But the locals failed to live up to their quaint surrounds;

a '*herd*' of '*dense looking*' young men '*pursued*' the girls '*on one of our wanderings. They were most persistent but luckily from a good way off.*'

However, the focus of the Markham Committee, and public's attention more generally, was on the behaviour of service girls not 'persistent' men. The Committee's concluding thoughts underline the problem: 'War gives rise to many rumours. Vague and discreditable allegations about the conduct of women in the forces have caused considerable distress and anxiety not only to friends and relations at home but to men fighting overseas.'[8] The allegations were about 'the conduct of women' and in 1942 the Committee did not seek to reassure young girls, instead it looked to placate their parents and the traditional heroes of war: men.

14

Figureheads and Secret Work

'We had to cut the grass beside the instruments so she wouldn't get her feet dirty and we whitewashed all the walls. I remember going around with a paint brush.' Martha laughs but is adamant that the King's sister, Mary, the Princess Royal, was an exceptional controller commandant of the ATS. 'She asked all the right questions and was very on the ball.' It was later in the war and Martha had moved to a gun-site on the perimeter of London when the Princess Royal visited. It was a first meeting for the two women and Martha recalls a commandant who took trouble over her role; Mary was 'a handsome woman who looked good in a uniform' and 'put everyone at their ease'. One royal, the other aristocratic (although Mary was twenty years Martha's senior), the two had much in common, including privileged no-nonsense upbringings and an abiding respect for authority. Mary, the only daughter of George V, had been a teenager during World War I, when she embraced nursing with passion and by April 1918 her own mother, Queen Mary, was 'graciously pleased to assume the position and title of Commandant-in-Chief' of the Women's Royal Auxiliary Corps.[1]

With the tradition well established in World War I, the connection between female royals and military service was resumed at the beginning of World War II: consort Queen Elizabeth was immediately appointed Commandant-in-Chief of the WRNS, WAAF and the ATS. But this wartime Queen didn't become famous for her official military titles; she avoided wearing uniform, instead preferring to pick her way around bombed-out Britain in modest heels and two-piece ensembles, complete with a hallmark hat and sympathetic smile. Approachable and gutsy, Elizabeth was a figurehead who stood for normality and peace, leaving her more formal sister-in-law, Mary, to occupy the military space. Dame Helen noted that in 1939 the Princess Royal was quick to 'join the ATS and accepted the rank of controller in Yorkshire' at a time when women were still feeling 'self conscious' in uniform.[2]

The ATS grew and so did Mary's role; by 1940 she was chief controller and a year later controller commandant. At her passing out parade in 1941 new recruit Mary Churchill was sent for by the Princess Royal. '*I thought she was very kind and charming. She asked about Mummie and Papa and whether I was happy and whether the food was good – the beds comfy and the uniform nice to wear.*'[3] Martha nods; the Princess was a woman she both approved of and later worked for. 'After the war, when I was in the Territorial Army, I was asked if I'd be Mary's honorary lady-in-waiting from the military. I said yes because I had such respect for her.' Acting as the Princess Royal's personal link to the ATS's successor organisation, the WRAC,[*] Martha spent spare hours diligently replying to bishops and ladies on behalf of the Service's controller commandant, when once more she noted Mary's genuine interest and attention to detail.

---

[*]   The Women's Royal Army Corps replaced the ATS in 1949.

Lest there is any doubt about the Princess Royal's value, Martha spells it out. 'The whole function of the forces, the chain of command right down to the private, demands somebody to look up to and that is what the royals provided and Mary did it very well.'

Leadership, both symbolic and hands-on, was especially vital in the war years when the ATS expanded at an unprecedented rate. Out went old-school Director Dame Helen Gwynne Vaughan in 1941, to be replaced by 'glamorous', approachable Jean Knox, who served until mid-1943, a period when the ATS more than quadrupled in size to a service of 209,877 women.[4] According to the Markham Committee, this unprecedented expansion explained the growing pains in the Service's accommodation, uniform, equipment and selection processes. More worryingly, the Committee was unequivocal about the paucity of good leadership; there was an acute 'shortage of officers', a situation exacerbated by the insatiable personnel demands of AA Command. They recommended 'further recruitment from within the ranks of the Service' and 'more active propaganda . . . to give publicity to a policy of accelerated promotion for suitable candidates'.[5] A natural leader, Corporal Martha Bruce was once again targeted.

In August 1942 Martha had been '*allotted my team*' of radar (gun-laying) operatives, '*5 very nice girls. I hope we will do great things when we go into action on site.*' The prospect of finally 'going into the field' was thrilling. 'I thought, "Good show!" because we were going to get on with the war and help fire a gun.' But rapid expansion both within AA Command and the ATS had left chaos in its wake. At the girls' first two gun-sites there was no radar equipment, ditto the third, Mangotsfield near Bristol. A year earlier Martha had turned down an officer's training course, fearing special treatment, but by late 1942 things were different. She'd completed twelve months in the ranks, acquitted herself as well as any man and was deeply frustrated by an absence of gun-laying equipment. This time when they mentioned promotion to an officer, she said, *'I'd be quite pleased to change because I am not doing the job I was trained for!'*

The pre-officer cadet training unit was in Leicester, where Martha was 'taken back to basics'. She sighs. Once again the jobs were demeaning, but Martha was a soldier and did as she was told and had been taught. 'We barracked our beds, cleaned our kit, cleaned the ablutions and in came the sergeant: "My recruits would do it better than you are doing it! They would be down on their hands and knees scraping the floor with a razor blade! And look at that fire bucket, it is filthy!"' Martha peers out from her Orkney chair and smiles. 'I said to these other girls, "We'll fox that woman, we'll go down to the local shop and buy a new bucket and we will polish it until it sparkles and that will shut her up."' Martha outsmarted her senior. 'You should have seen her face!'

If there was a general anxiety about the quality of some of the officers being rushed through, Martha had little confidence in the course used to assess them. 'Next we were sent to clear nits out of the hair of a new intake and then we were presented with piles of rubbish.' The sergeant tipped the bins onto a tarpaulin and insisted the girls sort through the detritus. 'It was unbelievable, the training was non-existent. They didn't have the right people in charge.' The demeaning tasks enraged Martha and they were anathema to several girls on the course. 'A few of them had no idea how to barrack a bed.' Martha explains the process behind this unique military routine: a bed that shunts up into 'biscuits' a third of its length, upon which blankets are folded and sheets and greatcoats tucked up into the size of a gas mask. Then she stops and raises her brows. 'Some girls had come from a secret place and they had never barracked their bed, they thought it was nonsense. One of them failed the course. We didn't ask, we just accepted that they did secret jobs. Well, yes, now I realise they came from Bletchley Park.'

*

Betty laughs hard. 'Gosh, they were uncomfortable, those biscuits, they slid and slipped all over the shop. I wrapped mine in a blanket. Certainly before the military quarters were built at Bletchley Park I would've been unable to barrack my bed, lucky I wasn't on that training course!' In recent years Betty (aka Charlotte) Webb MBE has become the code-breaking Park's most celebrated veteran. To commemorate the 75th anniversary of VE Day in 2020, *National Geographic* featured 'The Last Voices of World War II' and Betty, looking fierce and forward, dressed in a sharp red suit, was their cover girl. Under the caption 'British Intelligence', readers were informed that 'Webb, 97, was 18 when she started at work at Bletchley Park, Britain's top secret code-breaking center'.

'German leaders believed messages encrypted by their Enigma machines were all but unbreakable. Bletchley personnel proved them wrong.'[6] Several of the Park's stellar cast have posthumously become big names, most famously the cryptanalyst Alan Turing, but beyond Bletchley's enduring reputation for eccentrics and boffins, three-quarters of its 8,000-strong staff were women, and a majority of those service girls. Betty's war involved long days spent sitting upright at her desk in a khaki tunic and skirt, soft brown hair neatly rolled two inches above the collar, blue eyes alert and watchful, picking her way through masses of 'groups of letters and figures on A4-sized sheets of paper'. On the first floor of the Park's red-brick mansion, Betty began her working life in a small room with an open fire and three middle-aged gentlemen. It was September 1941 and although intelligence operations had not been one of the trade options cited at her ATS Wrexham training camp, Ralph Tester's Military Section in Bletchley Park (otherwise known as Station X) was her new home. The Park had not yet begun recruiting service girls en masse (and when they did it would mainly be from the WRNS). Betty was an exception; perhaps she always has been.

Earlier in the year a stint on a domestic science course in Shropshire had proved exasperating. Four girls left prematurely and Betty was one of them. It was 'difficult to remain enthusiastic about cooking colourless food from simplified wartime recipes . . . Yes, I suppose at the back of it, it was about getting a good husband.' Betty had other things on her mind. She promptly swapped domesticity for an ATS training camp and her mother came to the station to see her off; 'If you don't like it, dear, you can always say you have to help me after my operation and come home.' Mrs Vine-Stevens had endured a pioneering mastectomy which never properly healed, but Betty was undeterred. With a military father, it's possible she already knew the army was her destiny; in any case she quickly found out. 'By the time I left the training camp I'd been awarded a stripe.'

Wrexham pulled in girls from across the region, including Liverpool and several Welsh towns. Betty remembers 'a rough lot, they needed a job and money. It was a real culture shock for me, I was from a middle class family where I had to behave very nicely at home and I thought they were horrid.' Betty didn't just think it. At breakfast, vast vats of scrambled eggs led to an unseemly stampede. 'Everyone just dived in as soon as it was put on the table, they were like animals at the trough!' Everyone that is, except Betty, who issued a call for order. 'Sit down! How dare you!' From one private to all the others, her action was brave if somewhat foolhardy, and she believes it paid off. 'I've often wondered whether my explosion at the breakfast table was the reason I was given that stripe rather smartly.'[7]

But top-secret Bletchley Park, with its hybrid academic, military and civilian staff, did not prioritise army stripes. Lance Corporal Betty's rapid promotion was a stamp of approval, but not sufficient on its own to guarantee her an early place at this extraordinary destination. 'No, I think it was because I had German on my CV. I am sure of it.' Despite her father's reservations, in 1937, aged fourteen Betty had gone to Saxony on an exchange visit. Her mother had been teaching music there when war broke out in 1914; a foreign national stuck in a hostile country with scarcely a word of German, Mrs Vine-Stevens made it her business to ensure her daughters grew up with the language skills she lacked. Beyond the acquisition of an accomplishment, the trip is a reminder that in the 1930s anxiety about fascism was offset by an enduring respect for the country of Gothe, Kant and the Weimar Republic.

Betty has fond memories of her devout host family, the Pauls, who lived in a flat on the Czechoslovakian border and abhorred the Hitler Youth meetings that their sunny young daughter was obliged to attend. There were dissenting whispers in the hallway and obligatory Fuhrer salutes in the classroom. Betty 'waved' her 'arm around to be diplomatic but I didn't say "Heil Hitler"'.[8] Instead she returned to Britain with serviceable German, a language that was in desperately short supply.

From Wrexham training camp, Betty was sent to an interview at Devonshire House in London's Piccadilly. Early on, the Park had begun earmarking the 'right type of recruit' and when the scale of the code-breaking mission became apparent, with Germany's endless radio communications leading to vast quantities of intercepted 'traffic', the military was tasked with finding German speakers. The onus would increasingly fall on the female forces (although the ATS girls never numbered more than a few hundred at the park).

Betty was interviewed in German by a major from the Intelligence Corps. 'He asked how I would communicate with someone in Scotland to which I responded, "I would do it by telephone, in writing, by telegram or by courier."'[9] In fact Betty's schoolgirl German wasn't sufficient to clinch a translating job in the Park, but her assured performance stood out. Still unclear about what her appointed trade would be, the next step was a train to Bletchley village in Buckinghamshire, where she was confronted with a vast document and forced to read it on the spot. Betty swore she would abide by the awesome demands of the Official Secrets Act. 'It is not something I will ever forget.'

A portent of the grave new world this eighteen year old had just stepped into was the gun which lay silently on the table.[10]

Ironically, for much of her time at the Park, Betty had little clue as to the wider purpose of what she was doing. Her first job in the mansion's south-west wing, above the ballroom, was not to understand but rather to register every message that passed her desk. 'All we were doing on the card index was putting things into date order and registering them under their call signs.' Beyond her department and rank, these intercepted traffic logs and indexes would be analysed for telltale patterns that might indicate enemy movement and intention, their coded contents would be deciphered, translated and evaluated and the final product filed for cross-reference purposes.[11] But none of that was Betty's business. She didn't even know what went on in the next-door room. And so it was that Churchill's 'geese that laid the golden eggs . . . never cackled'.[12] They swore they would not, and they knew not what to cackle about.

Beyond the long hours of secret shift work, Betty had plenty to distract her. Downstairs in the mansion's recreation room she enjoyed coffee and sugared buns with an assortment of 'different people . . . it was always social chit-chat. I think it helped you facilitate friendships because you couldn't talk "shop".' A spattering of crypt-analysts had been piloted in from America by 1942 and Betty had her first exposure to transatlantic culture. 'Side-walk, garters, pants, the accent can sound pretty awful!' Evenings were punctuated with long walks and sessions at a madrigal club: 'We had phones between some of the offices, and a chap rang up and said, "Are you interested in singing in a field tonight!"'[13] Betty laughs, still amused; it is easy to understand how Bletchley Park's extraordinary milieu distracted from her ATS status.

'Well, you see, to begin we didn't stay in army quarters, we were billeted with the locals.' Betty remembers her second Bletchley lodgings in nearby Loughton with fondness; the Foxleys were a modest, friendly family, there were meals with all three children and strip-down washes in front of the fire. It was a far cry from the standard drill, fatigues and discipline that most ATS recruits were subjected to. But as the Park grew, accommodating increasing numbers of staff became onerous and by 1943 army barracks were constructed for the Park's service personnel. Only when she moved into the camp was a (partial) military straight jacket imposed on Betty's life. 'It was an awful mix really because the military people wanted us to be military and we were just interested in working at Bletchley. By that stage I had an interesting job paraphrasing in the Japanese section.' She recalls Colonel Fillingham, a self-important man in charge of the army camp, who was 'hopping mad because he wanted to know what was going on inside the gates, he didn't understand and they wouldn't let him in or tell him anything'. The tight bounds of confidentiality saw a colonel excluded and operating on the perimeter of a secret world against which he retaliated by 'imposing all sorts of military detail on us. He made life difficult when we were on shifts.'

Betty, promoted to staff sergeant by the end of the war, was an exemplary soldier and did her best to accommodate these two conflicting realities, but even she had a tipping point. 'I've often wondered about girls in the army today, they can serve on the front line but how do they manage their periods? Oh yes, of course, the contraceptive pill, I hadn't thought about that, it wasn't available in my day.' Betty suffered terrible monthly bleeds, exacerbated by the Park's around-the-clock shift work; menorrhagia occasionally left her incapacitated, once so badly she was taken into the barracks on a stretcher. 'It was difficult. Good Lord, no! It wasn't something you could talk about.'

Like so many girls of her generation, Betty thought she was dying when she got her first period, 'and still it took me a couple of months to pluck up courage and tell mother what was happening'. Unable to talk about her menstrual pain, at Bletchley she made do with sanitary towels – 'most unpleasant things that chafed your legs' – and the odd aspirin. Life in the army camp exacerbated the problem. 'One time I was back at the barracks and had a terrible period and I went to bed and failed to turn up to a breakfast parade and I was put on a charge.' Military discipline executed by an unsympathetic colonel had no truck with Park life, let alone female biology.

Along with the vast majority of her fellow Bletchley comrades, Betty kept her vow of silence until Britain's code-breaking story was declassified in the 1970s. Since then she has written a book, given over 200 lectures and been awarded the French Legion of Honour for her wartime service and an MBE for services to the current Bletchley Park Heritage Centre. Regularly popping up on television programmes via Zoom in lockdown, she is Bletchley's most famous extant veteran, but it has taken eighty years for Betty to break her silence on the pitfalls of menstruation in the army.

15

A Reluctant Recruit

'She's an extraordinary woman, isn't she?' In old age, Glasgow-born Nanza has become a good friend of Bletchley Park's Betty Webb. Today they are contemporaries and near neighbours in Birmingham's large orbit, and discovered late in life that they share a common heritage. 'I read about Betty in the paper and all the work she did to support Bletchley Park. I got in contact with her and said, "Do you know my wartime job was related to what you did?"' In 1942 Nanza was selected as an ATS wireless interceptor (also known as Y-station listeners) and her work with Signals involved the interception of the German military's coded messages. Like Betty, she's entitled to claim her place among Bletchley Park's feted veterans, but she rarely bothers. Despite Britain's affection for its war heroes, aged ninety-eight, Nanza is surprisingly unmoved by all the fuss. 'The truth was I didn't want to sign up.' The only woman in this book who did not volunteer for military service, Nanza waited until she was conscripted.

She sighs down the telephone. 'I loved my job; I worked for an insurance company in Glasgow. It was pen work, sums, that sort of thing, I was calculating what we did every month. I was very disappointed when I was called up but there was nothing you could do about it.'

Other women remember a swell of patriotism propelling them into uniform, but not Nanza. 'My father had been in the First World War and I got it shoved down my throat, about how we didn't do as well as we should've done. He told me that I was a spoilt brat and that army life would do me the world of good.' She laughs. A bright woman of twenty with a stimulating job in a big city, the prospect of military service with a handful of near-schoolgirls did not appeal. But Nanza had been following the news. When the law changed 'we knew there was going to be a big call up and then a letter arrived saying to report to somewhere in Glasgow'.

At the beginning of 1942 the absorption of two million women into compulsory war work posed an 'enormous problem' for which a Women's Consultative Committee was appointed. The Committee's main target was girls aged twenty and twenty-one who didn't have dependents; crucially these women were identified as 'mobile'.[1] Nanza was one such girl and fell into the 'quarter or one-third' of women Churchill anticipated 'will be required to exchange their present employment for one more effective in the war effort'.[2]

Nanza's mother, Mrs Hughes, was 'absolutely horrified' by the idea of her only daughter going to war. 'She thought Father should do something about it. And when he stopped laughing I went into the army. It nearly broke Mum's heart but I had to go.' Mrs Hughes 'was a mother hen who wanted her children right by her'. Between the wars Nanza's father, a solicitor, commuted daily into Glasgow; meanwhile, back in Campsie Glen, Mrs Hughes perfected her role as a wife, mother and homemaker. It was a wrench when son Peter completed his apprenticeship on the Clyde and left for India (a marine engineer, he was in Hong Kong when it fell on Christmas Day 1941), and now her daughter was being sent away.

Nanza is a forthright woman who doesn't compromise her views to majority opinion, but rules were rules. 'My work was sad to lose me, they kept my position open and carried on paying my salary for a year.' Together with her friend Violet, she travelled to Scotland's east coast for rudimentary military training; it was the first time she'd been away from home and she missed it terribly. 'But Father thought it was wonderful that his daughter was going into uniform. Every time I was on leave I had to walk up and down to show him how it looked.'

It is between waves of coronavirus in the summer of 2020 that we arrange to meet in Nanza's back garden for a further chat. Two days later and the phone rings. 'Ach, Tessa, if I was in the ATS now I would swear! (Army life was all bloody this and bloody that!) Linda, my daughter, says I am not allowed to meet you because of the Covids, I am sorry.' Nanza is once more caught up in a national crisis and eighty years on filial concern has replaced her anxious mother.

'In that case we'll keep talking on the telephone.'

*

'Ach, we're a' Jock Tamson's bairns.' With Scotland's version of 'we're all God's children', Nanza pushes against the suggestion that she had a special role in the war but the ATS manual is clear: by 1941 'there were certain further tests . . . they were of course only given to recruits who seemed possibly suitable for the specific employments concerned'. Effortlessly, Nanza passed the 'S.P. Test 10.

Morse Aptitude. For Potential Wireless Operators' and was promptly earmarked for Special Operator Training, working alongside the Royal Corps of Signals.[3]* 'I did my training on the Isle of Man from June to December in 1942. Oh, it was beautiful, absolutely beautiful, I loved it.' Despite her initial reluctance, Nanza quickly discovered that service life had its perks.

Stationed in Douglas, Private Hughes's new home was a requisitioned hotel on the seafront of the island's breezy capital. 'It was very nice, there were hotels which offered a good meal at a reasonable price, and I had very good parents who never sent a letter without putting a pound note in it.' Nanza's cosseted upbringing served her well; girls were paid less than men and as part of the national saving scheme were encouraged to put aside nearly a third of their earnings; unlike many, Nanza had a disposable income. 'Father said, "Don't go smoking all those cigarettes!" That's right, I smoked Players. Most of the girls enjoyed a smoke. It was a bit of bravado, I suppose.'

The town's expansive bay encouraged bathing and paddling and when Irish ships delivered fresh food, clamouring uniformed men and women rushed down to the seafront to enjoy fried eggs and chips. The island was heaving with life: an RAF training camp, an officer's training unit and up on the hillside Nanza remembers lines of despondent Italians. 'They were on the other side of the island, we saw them when we went walking on the moors. We weren't allowed to speak to them.' Marshalling troops

---

* By the end of the war over 15,000 ATS women were employed on signals duties.

and holding detained 'enemy aliens' had become the life-blood of this one-time tourist island.

'Being a military man, Dad gave me a run down of what I should and shouldn't do. He always said, "Don't let anyone touch you, you are your own person and if some-one does touch you, get in touch with your commanding officer."' Tall and by her own admission 'forceful', Nanza had no call to report misdemeanours to officers who were 'too young to have any importance, maybe just a year older than us', and any homesick lapses were mitigated by hard work. Beyond the blue skies and fresh eggs, Nanza was there to learn the language of Morse, quickly and efficiently. More easily transmitted over greater distances than the human voice, Morse was used extensively as a means of communication by both sides in the war. Girls were expected to reach speeds of over twenty words (five-letter or figure blocks) a minute. For weeks Nanza sat with pencil, paper and bakelite headphones, listening to dits and dahs slowly at first, and then faster and faster. 'I'm told girls were much better at it than men, we were quicker and more accurate, keen to get things right, I suppose.' Those who couldn't keep up went back to the beginning, and match-fit recruits were sent out into the field.

'Well, it was a moor actually. We were sent to the York-shire Moors and stationed in Harrogate.' In large Austin trucks, girls headed across the top of England, were sorted into sets and put to work in purpose-built army blocks. At the coal face of Britain's gigantic interception project, hundreds of ATS recruits sat at desks and tuned into allo-cated frequencies, waiting for a sudden burst of Morse across the atmosphere. 'I always knew I was listening to a group of Germans, but beyond the Morse it was all in code, I had no idea what they were saying. In my head I imagined they were in Germany, communicating with each other.' The faceless enemy's intermittent appearances kept Nanza pinned to her seat for six-hour stints; every dot and dash was listed, every message logged, every sheet of paper rolled up and pushed into a tube. This undigested 'traffic' was couriered overnight by dispatch riders and at the other end of England Betty and her equivalents would receive it, making sure the raw material was logged, dated and sent on to be deciphered. The final product was called Ultra, and provided the Allies with extraordinary detail about enemy movements. This code-breaking war story has injected some glamour into Britain's wartime narrative but much of the work had an interminable quality. In the Park's post-war Labour Review under a section titled 'Medium or Low Grade Labour' is the observation: 'It was astonishing what young women could be trained to do.'[4]

Up on the moors there was little to go on: no human voice, no English language, very little German language – soldiers rarely let their guard down. One listener sat agog when suddenly she heard a German paratrooper cry for his mother – *'Mutter! Mutter!'* – amidst the bombed rubble of Italy's Montecassino Monastery in early 1944. Nanza's presumption that her group of Germans were in Germany was wrong; they were in occupied France. Girls were kept in the dark and secrecy was stressed. But if other ATS recruits on the moors recall stark warnings – 'Breaking your oath is committing treason! What you are doing is important. You speak nothing of what you are doing here!'[5] – Nanza, although aware her work was highly confidential, ('the training was all about secrecy'), has no recollection of an Official Secrets Act and shared certain stories with her father. 'I told him what I was doing; he had been an officer in the First World War and he was interested and proud. But I didn't tell my mother, ach no, she wouldn't have understood anything!'

Bletchley stalwart Betty (whose parents died before their daughter could tell them what she did in the war) is surprised to hear of her friend's indiscretion. Secrecy was the hallmark of the code-breaking operation, knowledge of its existence would have fatally undermined a game-changing mission. But Nanza, who at twenty-one was older and more experienced than many of her ATS unit, made up her own mind. Her father was trustworthy and intelligent. Was sharing her limited knowledge with him really such a breach? Did no one else break confidence among their closest friends and family? In a wartime narrative that's been impacted by decades of celebrated remembering, Nanza's detached take on her service years is a valuable corrective. She was very much her own woman.

> Oh yes, I got put on a charge for being unruly. We all did, about ten of us, we'd been arguing and making a noise in the barracks. Having been in insurance with such a good job, I'd a lot to say for myself. I got another good job after the war at Sun Alliance . . . it could be quite frustrating being a private.

*

A month before this book went to print, Nanza's daughter, Linda, emailed me. She explained that shortly after the war her mother married Tom, an RAF navigator who'd been shot down on his last trip over the Ruhr Valley in February 1945 and taken prisoner. Nanza remembers a man 'so thin I could have knocked him over'. Linda, their only child, was born in December 1946. Initially, Nanza found married life with a traumatised husband and a move to Birmingham, away from Scottish friends and family, challenging. Linda told me her mother decided the answer was finding a job:

> *[She] worked in the accounts department of a small insurance company, taken over in subsequent years by Sun Alliance. Working full time for women was quite unusual in the 1950s and I don't remember any school friends having working mothers.*
>
> *She stayed with the company until she retired in the late 1980s, having risen to the post of chief accountant, the first woman to hold this post in any Sun Alliance branch. She oversaw the computerisation of the accounts in the 60s and 70s, and work was her whole life. She was never a natural homemaker, but what I missed out on not coming home to freshly baked cakes was more than made up for by the role model she presented as a working mother.*

16

The Cookhouse – 'a woman's natural home'

'Well, I didn't want to be a cook. I would not even have considered it. I wanted to break away from being a domestic servant, I didn't want to do anything domestic.' Grace pauses. 'Of course, I mean, there had to be girls to help with the cooking on the gun-site but it wasn't something that I did. Only when you were on fatigues, and the people who didn't go on the church parade, they had to do a bit of "spud bashing" on a Sunday morning.' Grace didn't mind army food. 'Warm vegetables, a lot of toast and marmalade and bangers and mash. At teatime you might even have the odd kipper. That was a treat!' But she is clear, as are most of the women in this book: they did not join the army to cook. No, ma'am! This state of mind helps explain the ATS's 'main problem, which remained unchanged during the war . . . there were never enough cooks'.[1]

Bletchley Park's Betty sighs. 'Yes, poor dears, I mean I suppose being an orderly was worse, but I did not leave my domestic science course to become an army cook!' Barbara, who had always lived in Yorkshire, agrees. 'A cook? I didn't want to be a cook. I signed up early and was a volunteer so I had a bit of leeway regarding what I did.' Still at school in 1939, three years later Barbara was a young woman working in a makeshift munitions factory, 'but as soon as I was seventeen and a half, that was the age for signing up, I went straight away to register'. In fact, it was 2 January 1943, the day before Barbara's birthday, but the office was closed on a Sunday and she couldn't possibly wait another fortnight for her next day off. 'So I went to Kendal in a snowstorm; the recruiting office was in an old mill on an upper floor and the officer said, "Oh, we can stretch the formalities regarding your age."' So that was all right then. Barbara draws breath. 'No, I did not want to cook, I wanted to be a driver. There were tests so someone who wasn't, or didn't, perform quite as well would've become an orderly.' She stops, it's awkward but that is how it was. 'Some girls were brighter than others, some suited being cookhouse orderlies, I suppose.'

Barbara won a scholarship to her high school in the Yorkshire Dales and the thought of scrubbing and cleaning in an army kitchen didn't occur to her. Nor cooking, which for women still hadn't been elevated to a trade. At the beginning of the war male soldiers in the cookhouse received an extra 3d a day, but when an equivalent application was made for women to get an additional 2d a day there was uproar.[2] The pay obstacle was eventually resolved but the lack of trade status compounded perception problems. Barbara remembers, 'The food was pretty good, but I always found, and I could be wrong, but I found if we had a male sergeant in charge of the cookhouse the food was better than if we had a woman.' She pauses and gently adds, again, 'I could be wrong.'

'I can't scrub floors and peel potatoes . . . I want to do something exciting and difficult.' Leslie Howard's 1943 ATS recruitment film, *The Gentle Sex,* was an unlikely hit and in an opening scene, Joan Greenwood, just one of the stellar cast, lies on her army biscuit and laments: 'I wanted to get away on my own and be tough and independent. I have spent weeks dreaming about guns and batteries.' Most girls joined up to escape domestic drudgery and ATS efforts to increase recruitment with 'adventure through action' campaigns made matters worse. Greenwood's Betty in *The Gentle Sex* was reassured by a fellow recruit: 'If you are a good girl, they will give you a great big gunny wunny.'

This shortage of cooks was compounded by the importance of food in army life. Churchill was unequivocal. 'The British soldier is more likely to be right than the scientists. All he cares about is beef . . .'[3] But while an army of men marched on a belly full of beef, initially ATS girls were given a 'female diet', with less meat, bacon and bread, and more milk, eggs, fresh vegetables, fruit and salad.[4] Vera guffaws, 'A terrible salad it was too, more like shredded cabbage and carrot!' The practice was promptly stopped when AA Command discovered female gunners were constantly starving. Soon stodge predominated and four meals punctuated each day; Churchill was right, food mattered, and it remained a major preoccupation throughout the war. Martha, wielding her brand-new officer rank, had little truck with faddy gunners.

I took a mess meeting on Sunday and had an argument with the men who 'won't take salad'. Honestly they're not happy unless they have butcher's meat every day. They even make a fuss about eating cheese. They won't believe that civilians get so little because of course 'Mum' always gets in a nice bit of meat for the lad on leave.

But Martha had a fight on her hands. A male soldier's training diary noted the overwhelming greed in camp: 'You should see us at the table, the knives scooping more than our share of butter, the spoons heaped with marmalade . . . all our passion is directed towards food. Not women haunt our dreams but eggs and bacon . . .'[5]

When they came, meals were often found wanting; even Martha had occasion to grumble. '*The food has been getting worse and worse lately. Nothing but beans, uneatable porridge and a small piece of cold bacon for breakfast. Meat (so called), potatoes peeled and boiled and beans and some sort of depth charge pudding or else rice.*' Leaden explosives used to guard British trade convoys crossing the Atlantic were the synonym for inedible dessert. Over five thousand ships were sunk during the war; island Britain felt the pinch and institutional food, not a national strength at the best of times, was an unappealing prospect. No wonder most girls did not want to cook.

*

Diana laughs. She was not most girls. Given away shortly after her birth in Sheffield, brought up by Mrs Booth, a professional 'childminder' (who 'advertised in *Nursery World* or *The Lady*'), Diana was practical and unspoilt. There was no shortage of money, her biological parents made sure of that, and she's quite certain that she was Mrs Booth's favourite. 'It was a long time before I knew she wasn't my real mother; I used to call the Booths Mum and Dad.' Small, cute even, with sand-coloured curls and a friendly, unassuming manner Diana was the perfect charge. There were other children who came and went, some were sent off to boarding school, but Diana never left. 'I remember

Above. The ATS's first Director, Dame Helen Gwynne Vaughan, in her hallmark outsized cap, inspecting recruits, Exeter, December 1940.

Below. Heading towards the invading German army in late May 1940, Olivia's SSAF unit stopped in Bar-le-Duc, north-eastern France. She's sitting in front of the window, bottle of wine in hand.

Above. Anne talking to Tessa about her wartime service at home in Little Melton, Norwich, September 2020.

Left. A beaming Queen Elizabeth (later the Queen Mother) visits Mary Churchill's anti-aircraft battery in London, July 1943. The Prime Minister's daughter is standing on the right.

Right. Abram Games' first ATS recruitment poster: dubbed the 'Blonde Bombshell' it was deemed 'too daring for public consumption' and withdrawn from circulation.

Below. Prime Minister Winston Churchill with his trademark cigar and immaculate wife, Clementine, watching ATS girls operating a predictor on their daughter Mary's gun-site.

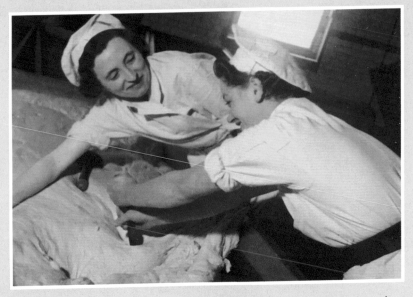

Above. ATS trainees kneading dough. The Service always struggled to recruit sufficient numbers in the cookhouse where Diana remembers the work as very physical.

Below. Martha, aged 99, talking Tessa through her impressive military career on the lawn at home in Limekilns, Fife, June 2021.

Above. FANY Joyce sitting atop her screwball horse Pinto at Thame Park, an SOE station in Oxfordshire, 1944.

Below. Anne, aged 18 in civilian dress joining the ATS, 1943; her mother standing to the right was the Service's first recruit – W/1 – in 1938. Always in need of good news stories, the ATS made much of the connection.

Above. Furthest right, Barbara is sitting on the bonnet of a Bedford truck at Motor Transport Training Company (MTTC), North Wales, where she was a driving instructor, 1945–6.

Below. Princess Elizabeth in her ATS overalls during a training session at MTTC, Camberley, March 1945.

Above. The Princess Royal, Mary, Controller Commandant of the ATS, meeting Britain's first West Indian recruits, 1943; Ena, who'd travelled from Jamaica, is the third girl from the left.

Below. Martha meeting her childhood acquaintance, HM Elizabeth II at the WRAC's centennial celebrations, Holyrood Palace, 2019.

Above. En route to an officer cadet training course in Palestine, March 1945, Anne's unit was delayed in Cairo. They made the most of their free time – Anne is the middle girl on a camel.

Below. Daphne, bottom left, on leave in 1946 feeding the pigeons in Trafalgar Square, London. Crouching next to her is Aunt Lucy, whose only child William died in France, June 1940.

when Peter Rogers arrived, he was a little boy and Mrs Booth suddenly said, "Oh, look over there!" And in that moment his mother disappeared. Peter was put in a room screaming and kicking. He was about four, he never saw his mother again.' Like a sensible older sister, when she wasn't at school or work Diana helped the Booths. 'I used to mix up the Christmas cakes, make marmalade, do the gardening, weed the pavements. And when the war came I brought rations too. Two ounces of tea, two of butter.' Off she went to the village store and weighed out the household's weekly provisions from sacks on the floor; back at home she was down on her hands and knees picking bits off the carpet and laying cones in the fire.

A military nurse in World War I, with a husband who always 'polished his medals for Armistice Day', it was Mrs Booth who steered Diana into the ATS when she turned eighteen. Conscription meant the move would soon be inevitable and Diana had to make her own way in the world.

> I didn't know I was going to join the army, Mrs Booth wrote a letter to the recruiting office in Brighton, she saw me onto the train. I don't think I wanted to go into the ATS. I said I wanted to be in the Wrens. She said, 'No! Go into the army, the King's shilling.' I did what I was told.

The following week, a freezing day in February 1943, Diana was travelling in a lorry heading to Guildford. There she went through the usual rigmarole: picking khaki clothes off a trestle table, holding out her arm for numerous injections and enduring a series of selection tests. 'I remember a blackboard with a list of the options. I couldn't do office work, I didn't know how to type, so

I said I would cook. I thought that sounded, well, it was something I could do.' And she still can: a large rhubarb and apple crumble steams on the table between us. Diana was a pragmatist; she knew she had to learn to stand on her own two feet and cooking was the sensible option. Posted to Warrington for a six-week cookery course, she was given a train ticket north and a packed lunch. 'A meat pie it was, with pastry that was too hard to eat.'

Diana had previously prepared food for local evacuee children and given Mrs Booth a helping hand in the kitchen but military cooking was on a different scale. There were 'recipes for 500 men and incessant lectures from a male army sergeant. How to cook 500 Chelsea buns, 500 doughnuts, 1,000 Yorkshire puddings.' Wrapped in white overalls, clogs scuffing on the concrete floor, a 'kerchief covering her rolled hair', Diana grappled with a giant metal chipping machine, a robotic hand that smashed batter, a vegetable larder as big as a house, a meat refrigerator with life-size haunches of Churchill's beef. The mechanisation of war included the cookhouse. There are official ATS photographs of strong girls crouched down, kneading into giant troughs of dough, handling baking trays the size of four full grown men; 5-foot Diana was dwarfed by factory-scale production. And outside there was field cooking. 'We did a lot of camp cooking, soldiers on a battlefield need fed.' A watchman stood over the fire; at dawn's break his shovel of hot cinders would start Diana's stove, a burst of warmth against the stone cold air. 'It was a big black cauldron, I had a job to lift it up to cook the porridge.'

Scale and mobility mattered. In early 1943 few knew when or where exactly, but surely a second front was pending, and the amassing and training of troops grew exponentially. By December 1943 detailed planning for Operation Overlord (the codename for the Battle of Normandy) had finally begun and staging-post Britain became ever more congested with military preparations. Cleaning firearms, preparing kitbags, polishing tanks, the ATS were stretched across the country serving men and their machines. The army and its ATS tentacles was a seething hive of activity and each and every khaki troop, male or female, needed fed.

Tins of meat and jam from America lined the walls of Diana's cookhouse. 'I was posted to Old Harlow near Epping Forest, I was cooking for the REME, the Royal Electrical and Mechanical Engineers.' Workshops littered the site in what was an impromptu military factory providing radios for fighter planes. Man's work in this case, and those men expected their elevenses; Diana 'got buckets of tea ready for them to take back to the workshops. I upset boiling water on my leg. I'm little and the buckets were heavy and awkward to carry.' Badly scalded, she was in bed for a week. 'The medical officer came by every day.' Miles from any guns, working in a cookhouse (according to Dame Helen, 'a woman's natural home'[6]), Diana was the only girl in this book injured during the war.

Her next wound was sustained in a battle with sliced bread. 'It was an old-fashioned cutting machine in a Nissan hut. I was up at 5 o'clock preparing a mountain of toast and I cut my thumb, there was blood everywhere.' Three stitches later and Diana was straight back to work: 'I just got on with it.' Situated in Essex, facing east, she'd snatch periods of respite and reflection in the parade ground, shading her eyes against the glare, watching 'all our bombers going over to Germany'. Churchill needed to assure Stalin that the Allies were actively helping ease the pressure on the Eastern Front and crushing German morale. Standing in her pinny that hot summer of 1943, Diana watched as new-model bombers with four engines flew eastwards to Hamburg, Germany's largest industrial city. She counted the planes on their way out and she counted them on the way back. 'Sometimes one was missing.' Diana's observations matched the latest hit by Ambrose and his Orchestra on the cookhouse wireless. '*One of our planes was missing, two hour overdue.*' What she didn't know (and could not imagine) was the firestorm the Allied bombers – '*comin in on a wing and prayer*' – left in their wake. Operation Gomarrah killed 37,000 German civilians and injured 180,000 more. Hamburg was destroyed.

Back in Essex, Diana wiped her hands on her apron and returned to work. Waste was a big issue in the cookhouse; all efforts were made to keep it to a bare minimum. There was 'wet swill' and 'dry swill'. Wet swill mainly consisted of scraps off plates. 'On no account' did it include bread or uncooked meat. The detailed cookhouse instructions were overseen by a commanding officer. Nor could bones be thrown away. They 'are boiled first for stock, then drained and dried on top of the oven'. ATS manuals note units received money for tins of crushed recycled bones; the glycerine alone was used in 'shells, grease, glue, fertiliser and dyes'. Likewise inedible fats were minced and rendered down on a slow heat. Diana drained off the 'first-class fat', then added water and rendered again, a 'second-class dripping' was saved and last of all, 'cracklings' – the excess fat used in rissoles. What remained was packaged in 'non-returnable cartons' and sent by rail to 'the same contractors as the bones' and 'used for the manufacture of munitions'.[7]

More instructions insisted that the 'dry swill' bucket only included 'legitimate parings of vegetables and fruit which are unfit for the stock-pot'. Diana nods, the swill buckets were a science all of their own and had to be scrubbed out daily with boiling water after the contents were handed over to the local farmer. 'He came to get all the waste for his pigs; in exchange he brought us bunches of flowers.' Diana recalls the pungent aroma of sweet peas, their colourful heads adorning the cookhouse window. Wartime Britain was a barter society and the military was no exception; small gifts and sweet meats became valuable social currency both in the mess and among servicemen and women.

*

For Martha, access to a Scottish estate and an elevated social network came with perks. She wrote home, '*I haven't thanked you for the partridges, which were delicious and enjoyed by the whole mess.*' Mrs Walker, the family cook, was also thanked for '*delicious shortbread and gingerbread*' and Martha's mother was beseeched to buy more chocolate as none could be found in the NAAFI. A bag of cherries cheered Martha up in Oswestry and the prospect of strawberries and cream made her mouth water. Grow-your-own had taken on a whole new meaning. Martha's battery travelled overnight from Chatham to Manchester with '*a flock of geese, 2 dozen hens and rabbits and a dog. The truck (not the passengers) smelt like I don't know what when it was opened.*'

Diana doesn't recall plucking or gutting; the prizes individual units procured depended on their connections and, perhaps inevitably, Mary Churchill's MHAA Battery 469 was one of the most fortunate. It benefited from her parents' largesse, including a large 'Christmas cracker and delicious goodies' for the barrack room. '*The girls were simply delighted & we had a lovely party on Christmas evening & the officers came & we pulled the cracker and ate the cake.*' When royalty visited Mary's battery, the rank and file enjoyed the same menu – 'pie and summer pudding' – as the Queen, 'who thankfully did not spill gravy down her august neck'.[8]

Mary, like her father, loved good food. Churchill was convinced that the way to lose the war 'is to try to force the British people into a diet of milk, oatmeal, potatoes, etc., washed down on gala occasions with a little lime juice'.[9] Food and the conversations it inspired provided a familiar and comforting connection with home for new recruits, often away from their parents for the first time. Joan reassured her ma and pa back in Soham:

> *We always come from meals busting full. Sunday tea was salmon, beetroot, watercress and, what tickled me, bread and butter and golden syrup. A bit messy. Last night we had herrings on toast, b. and b. with jam and doughnuts. When I was fitted with my tunic I had the belt on the third hole, now I can only use the first. A remarkable discovery, we've just found out that supper is at 6.30pm. We didn't know there WAS any supper. We had beefsteak pie.*

Food mattered; Diana had an important job and by mid-1943 highly qualified female cooks were finally promoted to 'tradeswoman'. An OCTU manual of the same year insisted on the 'training and upgrading of cooks' and stressed that 'cooking is both a profession and an art'.[10]

see that unlike other ATS girls we took our leather
strap over the top of our cap. That was a privilege
passed on to us and it was greatly defended. It dis-
tinguished us from the rest. We were very proud to
be drivers.

Barbara had been biding her time. Sixteen in 1942,
she left school and 'answered the telephone for Armstrong
Siddeley, they'd gone over to aircraft production and had
been bombed out of Coventry'. But this improvised factory was only ever a halfway station until Barbara was
old enough to sign up. Her mother had been in military
service in the Great War; a member of the WAAC, she'd
prepared the troops' bully beef and catered in the officers'
mess. Barbara shakes her head. That would never do for
her. No, driving was her goal. 'My parents didn't have
a car, ordinary people didn't have cars; driving to me
seemed something useful, exciting and different.' A family
car wasn't forthcoming until 1943, when her father was
promoted to police sergeant and moved across Yorkshire
from Dent to Settle. But by that time Barbara had already
left home.

'My papers came through very quickly; I reported to
Lancaster Castle. We were issued our kit before we went to
Bowerham Barracks for our basic training and then went
back to the castle for our passing-out parade. Oh yes, I've
always had a good memory.' Aged ninety-five, Barbara
also has extraordinary hearing.

> Yes, I do. At the end of the selection tests, I was called
> over with another girl; they said, 'We're obliged to
> bring to your notice something you may not be aware
> of.' Apparently I'd passed the ATS hearing test with

flying colours and they asked if I would consider a specific job, but they couldn't tell me what it was, just that I would spend long hours listening.

Briefly Barbara is silent. She takes her present-day veteran duties very seriously; not only is she the last woman standing in her local Royal Artillery Association but, smothered in medals, Barbara is now the British Legion's go-to poster girl on Armistice Day; I found her in the *Yorkshire Post*. However, few wartime accolades can compete with the gloss that accompanies Bletchley Park's achievements or the romantic danger associated with Special Operations Executive (SOE) spies. 'I now realise I could have been a Bletchley girl, I was given the choice; it was something to do with agents and listening. They asked me if I knew Morse code.' She sighs and wrestles with the decision she made as a seventeen year old. 'It was the lack of detail, they couldn't tell me anything and it seemed a bit flimsy so I told them I wasn't interested. The other girl signed up, I didn't.' If back then Barbara was hooked on her driving dream, eighty years later it's hard not to wonder what might have been. Career choices for 1940s women were few and far between.

'Anyway, it was the right decision for me. I was sent to Motor Transport Training Company in Camberley, where the Queen trained, only she wasn't the Queen then and she didn't join up for two more years. Did I tell you I've met the Queen?' Barbara is back on track; if her wartime choices require vindication, HM Elizabeth II provides it.

I've always felt I had a lot in common with the Queen. When I was a little girl I had a Ladybird book all about Princess Elizabeth, it had sepia pictures. Elizabeth and I were born nine months apart, got engaged the same year, got married the same year, had a son the same year, had a daughter the same year.

But perhaps most importantly, Barbara and Elizabeth both trained to be drivers in the ATS. Currently the world's only living head of state to have served in World War II, Britain's future queen also completed a mechanics and driving course in Surrey, but Barbara got there first.

'We had all sorts of mechanical tests to see if we were any good with a screwdriver and a spanner. I was lucky because growing up I lived next door to a boy called Ken, and he had Meccano!' Barbara's early years were spent crouched over Ken's Meccano set creating cranes, engines and automobiles. It turned out that she was a dab hand at mechanics and earned status as Ken's special friend. But like all friendships, it had its limits. 'He wasn't so interested in playing with my dolls.' Barbara believes she had a good balance; dolls and Meccano were supplemented with climbing trees and riding bikes. This was a girl who knew her own mind: pictures reveal a determined face and strong frame. Barbara was not put off by the long journey south, nor by the girls at the Surrey camp, many of whom were FANYs from the 'upper bracket'.

'I had to convince my parents though. I sat them down and explained that just as they had both served in the First World War, I wanted to join up as soon as I could in the Second.' Barbara's parents were reluctant to say goodbye to their only child; war work in a local factory felt like a safer bet. By 1943 this familiar tussle between parents and teenage daughters was being played out across the country and impacted most families, even (especially) the House of Windsor. Princess Elizabeth was eighteen and the war was almost over by the time she was finally permitted to join the ATS.

*

It was December 1936 when beloved Uncle David gave up his divine inheritance as King Edward VIII in favour of a life with American divorcee Wallis Simpson, and overnight ten-year-old Elizabeth, who enjoyed ponies, playing games and a spot of gardening, became heir to the most prestigious throne in the world.[1] The abdication had left a dent in the Windsor brand and the new King and his family were tasked with repairing the damage. It was the war that gifted unsure Bertie and his smiling, comely wife, Elizabeth, the perfect opportunity. The dutiful King fronted up to his country that had been 'forced into a conflict' and for the sake of 'the world's order and peace, it is unthinkable that we should refuse to meet the challenge'. Meanwhile his consort acquired a revolver and rumour has it she practised her shot against the bombed-out rats at Buckingham Palace. The royal couple quickly became synonymous with the nation's fortitude and bravery, facing down danger and refusing to leave London. Unlike other little rich girls, their daughters, Elizabeth and Margaret, weren't sent to Canada and in October 1940 Elizabeth delivered her first wireless address: 'Thousands of you in this country have had to leave your homes and be separated from your father and mother. My sister, Margaret Rose, and I feel so much for you.' Meanwhile their mother stoutly insisted: 'The children will not leave unless I do. I shall not leave unless their father does, and the King will not leave the country under any circumstances whatsoever.'[2]

Instead, Princess Elizabeth spent an isolated war at gloomy Windsor Castle in the company of the Grenadier Guards. 'They wouldn't have kept anybody out but they kept us in,' lamented little sister Margaret.[3] The confinement chafed and like many of her peers – Betty bored in a domestic science college, Barbara biding time in a munitions factory, Maud giggling behind the filing cabinets in Stewarts and Lloyds – Elizabeth longed for a bigger role in the war. There was the occasional benefit concert at the castle and frequent photo opportunities with her sister – inspecting bomber planes or at home with their dogs – aimed at boosting national morale, but these trifles felt inadequate in the face of a war narrative that increasingly looked to include women. When Elizabeth turned sixteen in 1942 she was permitted to sign on at the local labour exchange but was offered no work. She complained, 'I ought to do as other girls of my age do,' but like so many men of his generation, George VI had a very low opinion of the women's services. When his daughters' nanny Crawfie suggested she might leave and join the WRNS he was indignant. 'You would only be cooking some old admiral's breakfast.'[4] Crawfie stayed put, and so did Elizabeth.

But despite George's reluctance to relinquish his daughter, Elizabeth slipped inevitably into adulthood. Aged seventeen, she became the Honorary Colonel of the Grenadier Guards, a role that delighted her, and, although small, she wore a military uniform well. In 1943 the conscription age for women was lowered again, this time to nineteen, and by the following year, when Elizabeth turned eighteen, the War Cabinet supported the idea of her joining the forces. The princess would be an excellent propaganda weapon. Only George VI remained unsure, and it was the end of 1944 before his daughter, who persistently 'bothered the King', managed to persuade him otherwise. The choice of the ATS was presumably decided on the basis of the Colonel of the Grenadier Guards title Elizabeth already held. That her Aunt Mary, the Princess Royal, was controller commandant of the Service provided additional reassurance with the option of driving no doubt attractive to a princess who was yet to learn.

Barbara laughs. 'It turns out she wasn't so different from the rest of us.' Perhaps not, but unlike Barbara, who only had to turn up to a recruiting office in Kendal, Elizabeth's entry into the ATS involved a convoluted exchange of letters between the ATS's chief controller and the Queen's lady-in-waiting, Lady Katherine Seymour, as well as several meetings at the palace, including one with Camberley's commandant and the King and Queen in the presence of their eldest daughter.[5] Security, exceptional arrangements and the question of the princess's rank all had to be taken into account.

Seven decades later, at a Buckingham Palace Garden party, Penny, who swapped the ARP in London to be a clerk in the ATS, was frank and funny when she met the Queen's daughter, Princess Anne. 'I said, "Your mum, she joined the war later than us and she never slept in barracks like the rest of us!" How we laughed together when I realised I'd called the Queen "your mum"!' Penny is gleeful and her understanding of the princess's special set-up accurate. She didn't sleep in barracks but was collected daily from Windsor Castle by Junior Commander Wellesley, 'far and away the finest driving instructor', who used the journey to and from Camberley 'to instruct HRH Princess Elizabeth in driving'.[6] Like Penny, Barbara is proud that she served with Elizabeth when she was a princess but after a quick appraisal of the latter's proposed syllabus and training programme observes that her own motor transport course was 'more intensive'. In an early discussion between the Queen and the ATS deputy director: 'Her Majesty felt that the 10 weeks recruits course would be rather a waste of time, with which I wholly agreed, as HRH has a brain already trained to learn.'[7]

Unlike Barbara, the princess didn't arrive at Camberley as a private but held the honorary rank of subaltern in the ATS and was fast-tracked onto a cadre course for noncommissioned officers. By the beginning of April 1945 'extremely urgent' communications were being exchanged between the Palace and the ATS to ensure Elizabeth had sufficient clothing coupons to cover her uniform as a newly commissioned officer.[8] There was anxiety over the public reception to her special status with questions and answers prepared in advance of press interest. The stock response to queries about why the princess was not going through the ranks was 'because of the time factor'. As for the motivation behind the course, apparently that came from Elizabeth herself and was undertaken 'in order that Her Royal Highness may get an insight into what the women in the Services are actually doing in this war'.[9] And to an extent that's what she got. Barbara confirms Princess Elizabeth's truncated timetable at Camberley had much in common with her own Motor Transport Mechanical and Maintenance training course undertaken two years earlier.

*

Barbara learnt to drive army-style. 'It was everything to do with handling vehicles. I always remember the sergeant at the first lesson telling us, "You drive with your hands and your feet and the seat of your pants."' With four learners, including Barbara, to one instructor, new recruits took turns to go out. 'It was exhilarating and unnerving, and wonderful when you knew you'd made it through.' The accident reports from Camberley confirm that not everyone passed with flying colours. One girl confessed 'to avoid collision, I ran into the other lorry', another 'knocked over a man. He admitted it was his fault as he had been knocked over before.'[10]

While Barbara established the basics amidst a mixed bag of girls at Camberley, initially Elizabeth learnt to drive alone in the confines of Windsor Castle; Junior Commander Wellesley reported in daily at 9.45 am and stayed all morning. The first lessons were on blocks so the princess could master the controls before progressing onto changing down from top to third gear and reverse manoeuvring in the ground's nursery field. A bout of mumps saw Elizabeth's training delayed by five days; 'the driving hours thus missed' were 'made up by an extra half an hour's driving practice on the way from Windsor' when she began the second leg of her course at Camberley in March 1945.[11]

The *Telegraph* exclaimed that Princess Elizabeth 'becomes an excellent Truck-Driver' and the centre's commandant later confirmed that behind the wheel of her Austin utility she had 'a wonderful time!' getting stuck in traffic jams, dodging American soldiers and driving through London alone.[12] According to Barbara, 'You became part of the vehicle. If you were enthusiastic enough, you could feel it through your body. It was mainly trucks that we learnt in, Bedford trucks and Austins and Austin K2 ambulances.' There is an extraordinary energy and precision to Barbara's descriptions as she rattles off World War II vehicle models.

> I remember the Bedford three-ton truck; now that was not the weight of the vehicle but the weight it carried. The Bedford 1500 weight carried eight soldiers with full kit and then there were smaller utility trucks, Austins and Morrises, they carried 800 weight – four soldiers and full kit. The biggest trucks carried twenty troops. Oh yes, I could drive a big truck.

Barbara pauses; briefly she's back there among her comrades, marching into the day, onwards high up into the truck, tanking along the road and then back down below, under the bonnet.

Examining Elizabeth's proposed mechanics programme, now held in the National Army Museum, Barbara picks out the lessons she most vividly recalls.

> Practical mechanics! I could take a Bedford engine apart now and put it back together again. We had to learn the working of an internal combustion engine plus all the mechanical side. The propeller shaft – that's the bit that takes the power from the engine to the rear wheels of the vehicle . . .

Along with eleven other cadets, Princess Elizabeth also discovered how to use a spanner and take an engine apart, declaring, 'I'm a mechanic at last. I've scraped the skin off my knuckles' and later confessing 'everything I learnt was brand new to me'. Newspapers took great delight in reporting that the princess's practical training 'included changing wheels, cleaning plugs, and greasing and maintaining cars'.[13] She quickly became front-page news, gingerly tinkering beneath the bonnet of an army vehicle, while her visiting mother smiled expansively behind Elizabeth's shoulder. During the same visit, the King, flushed with pride, infuriated his daughter by 'nipping off the high tension lead to the distributor' when she was midway through a fault-finding vehicle check.[14] And a close look at the press photographs reveal that, just like Barbara's, the princess's cap strap runs across the top of her head. Yes, Elizabeth was heir to the throne but in spring 1945 she was also a subaltern and driver in the ATS. 'I've never worked so hard in my life,' she would later conclude, and admitted to post-war politician Barbara Castle that 'it had been the only time when she had been able to test herself against people of the same age'.[15]

However, Elizabeth's experience was never intended to be rank and file. Above all, her participation was symbolic; a royal endorsement of women's unprecedented wartime role in the armed services. Yes, she shared in what Barbara describes as the thrill of driving a big truck, and the pride all recruits took in their new knowledge and uniformed status, but the princess's timetable was pared down before she'd even arrived at Camberley; drill and physical and gas training were exempt and apparently the other cadets felt a bit excluded when Elizabeth was whisked away between lectures and slept in a castle at night.[16] Although most of the press coverage was positive, early on the *Daily Mail* had a gripe about the princess failing to get her hands dirty.[17] It was an inaccurate charge and an unfair one. Talking to Barbara some eighty years on, there's a sense that perhaps it was Elizabeth who was short-changed, not the other recruits. Because Britain's gutsy princess never stayed in barracks she missed out on much of the camaraderie of army life.

'In Camberley we were in huts in the grounds, at least twelve of us in each and we'd chat away in the evenings.' Only child Barbara was riveted by communal living and a favourite story is the Glaswegian woman three beds down. At forty-four years old, from the Gorbals, Marianne MacDonald had 'an accent you could cut with a knife – as rough as they come', and was 'quite open about being a prostitute, in fact I think she still was. She was a blousy sort, not the escort type.' Barbara, at just seventeen, was terrified of Marianne but discovered 'a heart of gold'. 'She'd call me young 'un and warn me about all sorts of things I'd never heard of!' Barbara laughs and pauses briefly before concluding, 'I expect the girls the princess trained with were hand-picked.'

Elizabeth was Britain's future monarch. It was perhaps no coincidence that war ended just one month after she passed out with officer status in April 1945. From the King's point of view, the timing was impeccable; his daughter was the first female member of the royal family to serve full-time in the military, but not for long. When asked by the commandant at Camberley if she would become a regular ATS officer, the princess's reply was unequivocal: 'I'd give everything I possess to be an ordinary person like one of my own friends and to be an ATS officer. But I cannot do that. I have to always be at everyone's beck and call. Therefore I should be of no use.'[18] HRH Princess Elizabeth was subsequently made a junior commander that July and has ever since remained a dedicated supporter of Britain's armed services, particularly of the men and women who served alongside her in World War II. But if the princess's passing-out parade in spring 1945 effectively marked the end of her wartime service, the opposite was true for Barbara. In her case, a stiff ten-week training course in Camberley was just the beginning of an extraordinary three-year adventure.

18

Gun-site Life

'My first posting was to a place called Norton-on-Tees up in County Durham, just over the river. It was a light anti-aircraft unit, I was a driver for the battery head-quarters and one of the 57,000 girls who served with the Royal Artillery alongside the men.' In 1943 the number of women on anti-aircraft sites across Britain peaked, and Barbara was one of them. She sighs. 'For years we were the forgotten army, it was much later that they made us life members of the Royal Artillery Association.' This belated badge of honour is important to Barbara, and her ability to recall the minute building blocks of regimental life are indicative of her inner soldier.

> We were stationed right in the middle of heavy indus-try – Britannia Steel Works, Dorman Long Steel, ICI works – they were like small cities in themselves. Each battery was just one gun and one gun crew of seven. They used 40mm Swedish Bofor guns, rapid fire, 120 rounds a minute; mind you, they overheated before they got to that. You couldn't have heavy guns near a city cos of the shrapnel, so there were separate guns dotted about . . .

Barbara shoots out the information, effortlessly segue-ing between tasks and times, detailing what she describes as her 'routine job making sure the gun crews were supplied with everything they needed': picking up provisions, loading goods and munitions, ferrying gunners. She was the human link that joined the dots of gun-site life. 'That's when you really learn to drive, when you're out on your first trip with no instructor. I was driving an officer and very keen that I should get everything right.' Barbara's most important relationship was with her vehicle. Daily, fifteen minutes were assigned to maintenance, when every driver would examine an allotted part of their truck. The system – established on a fourteen-day rota, backed up by a task book, which Barbara still has, and overseen by a mechanic – was foolproof. 'If you were a driver in the British army, you checked the same section on the same day, each day checking a different section. By day fourteen the whole vehicle had been given a once-over.' On the fifteenth day, Barbara, clad in overalls, proudly presented her vehicle for reinspection by an artificer, before the rigmarole began all over again. For its simplicity and efficiency, the process still delights her. 'It was a brilliant idea. It meant that no fault could be more than two weeks old. What could really go wrong? Every vehicle was so highly maintained.'

Grace nods. 'Well, yes, I suppose the vehicles had to be in good nick. They couldn't afford to break down. I mean, a lot of the gun-sites were in remote locations and there were lots of us travelling in these trucks. I was in there with me kitbag; we'd always sing, you couldn't help but sing in a 1500 weight.' Uniformed, khaki-clad girls, each facing the other, four, eight, ten in a row, moving between camps, heading down to town for a day off or an occasional big night out. 'You are my sunshine, you make me happy when the skies are grey.' Grace starts humming. She's alone in 2021 and the skies are still grey, but there's cheer in her voice. The jaunty lilt of an American vibe, imported into wartime Britain by myriad big-time artists, was harmonised by ATS gunner girls. 'We had a great descant going on. I do remember once the American soldiers sent a lorry to get us girls to their dance. I went on that occasion.' But despite their glamorous reputation, Grace refused to have her head turned by the thousands of 'Yanks' that poured into Britain in 1943.

> They'd pick up a young girl in uniform and automatically assume you were easy. Yes, we got oranges and bars of chocolate and we danced all night, but I kept me knees together. It didn't mean I couldn't have a dance but don't forget I had a young man back at camp.

Grace is almost surprised to hear that Barbara drove for AA Command, 'because, you see, it was only men who drove trucks in our battery. That's right, dear, that's how I met my Bob, he was our driver on site and the mechanic.' Somewhere between Cheltenham and Gloucester on a gun-site she can no longer name Grace fell in love. 'They broke the mould when they made my Bob.' She swallows. This was the same dark-haired, leonine-featured girl who had joined the army believing she'd be reunited overseas with Private Eddie, her one-time sweetheart posted to Port Said, when suddenly in the green glades of Gloucestershire she found another. 'Well, it wasn't quite like that. Eddie and I wrote to each other, but we didn't always get our mail. And then you might get three or four letters all together. And the same must've happened to him.'

Sitting on her bed, coming to terms with the sudden, late arrival of an overseas letter, the envelope stuffed into her greatcoat, Grace absorbed Eddie's words as he spilt his soul across the page. '*I haven't heard from you for so long, I assume by now you must have found another boyfriend . . . I really hope if I ever meet you and your new boyfriend, I would tell him what a lucky guy he is.*' Grace pauses. 'I thought, "That's nice."' But no, she didn't write back. Eddie in the filthy heat of the Middle East had generously relinquished his love and set Grace free.

'I'm not sure when I first met Bob. I think it was in the NAAFI.' Grace was having a smoke, and Bob, mid-weight and mid-height, a regular bloke, was propped up at a nearby table. 'It was the only place we had to go off duty, and you could chat to anybody in there.' So Grace chatted to Bob in his REME overalls. 'We never dated off-site, just in the NAAFI. We were attracted to each other. What's that, dear? Well, no, it wasn't very private. Oh, I knew he liked me, you can always tell by looking in someone's eyes, if there's a dance in them.' Bob's eyes shone and their knees touched beneath the table.

And a little cuddle, yes, you see outside the NAAFI on a gun-site there was a small crossroads between the command posts and the offices and accommodation, the girls were on one side and the boys on the other. So yes, perhaps a little cuddle outside. It might seem strange to young girls today but that's how we fell in love back then.

*

Young men in war were a precious and often fleeting commodity. Barbara met her man Stan on leave in late 1944.

It's a funny thing, both our fathers were in the police force, that's how we met, our parents knew each other. I was invited to this party and I arrived in battledress and stood out like a sore thumb. Stan was there, he was in the air force and he had a blonde girlfriend in a red chiffon dress. We spent the rest of the leave as a four with her and his friend Chips.

When their time was up, Stan asked for Barbara's address and they exchanged letters; Barbara received missives signed off from Lofty (Stan) and Chips. 'Then the letters started arriving without the name Chips at the bottom, it turns out it was just Stan writing to me all along.' The blonde girl in red had also disappeared, meanwhile RAF man Stan maintained his correspondence with Barbara, waiting patiently until war's end. 'It's not so different really from the way the Queen found her husband and, like I say, we both got married within a year of each other.'

Barbara's right, as usual. Princess Elizabeth had her first meaningful meeting with eighteen-year-old naval cadet Philip in 1939 when the King and Queen went to visit Dartmouth Naval College just before the outbreak of war. It was the beginning of a relationship that developed slowly through an innocent correspondence, one which, like Barbara's, was heightened by the respective danger the two men faced at sea and in the air. In both cases the parents were heavily involved. 'You know, Stan never asked me to marry him, he wrote and asked my father instead; he told me that Father was delighted to give his permission!' By all accounts George VI took a bit more persuading.[1]

*

It's fortunate that Barbara met Stan on leave, because working in gun-site transport the pickings were slim. Initially, she was one of four female drivers servicing remote light anti-aircraft units, sites which were small and mobile and therefore deemed unfit for women. Apparently they violated 'the acceptable standard of female accommodation' and it was feared they 'offered insufficient security from prowling, sex-starved men'.[2] Barbara didn't have much face time with the individuals concerned. 'We'd just drop off their provisions and so forth and go on to the next site. They seemed quite old to us, I think they went back to their wives when they were on leave.'

Housed at the headquarters, in a pre-war drill hall, Barbara worked hard:

> Just as hard as the male drivers but they were paid 3s 6d a day, and we were paid 2 shillings. And men got an extra sixpence for driving ammunition, and a red flag front and back. We didn't but we also drove ammunition. Did I complain? No! There was no one to complain to. That was the way things were. It was a man's world.

Nor was Barbara's job confined to mechanics and driving. 'They decided, the powers that be, that we girls also needed to train as a group of searchlight operators.'

Light AA Command units couldn't be mixed sex for fear of hanky-panky, and similar rules were initially applied to searchlight units. The prospect of a handful

of women 'in some bleak and desolate spot, five miles or
more from the nearest town' operating a searchlight filled
the authorities with dread. Unarmed and (one presumed)
virgo intacto, 'how would they deal with possible intrud-
ers, with saboteurs?' General Pile lamented that 'there
was all sorts of horrid doubts confronting us'.[3] Barbara
laughs. 'Well, they'd clearly stopped worrying about them
by 1943.' But even though 'women proved just as hearty
as men', outstanding worries persisted and in the end the
experiment was limited to just one all-female searchlight
regiment, the 93rd.[4] However, the ambition remained,
which explains why driver Barbara's battery was roped
into a searchlight operation on the roof of their northern
drill hall. 'We weren't keen but we went along with it.'

Barbara was in charge of an adapted truck fitted with
a generator. 'At a given command I had to throw a switch
and a lever was plugged into a set of fittings which connected the searchlight to the electric supply.' The little
team practised all day. Gradually the skies closed in and
darkness fell; after hours of waiting Barbara was on the
cusp of action. 'I was standing there, I was very pleased
with my bit. I threw the switch! But . . .' and she starts
laughing, 'it all came unstuck.' The carbon rods that
concentrated the phenomenal wattage had been wrongly
assembled; instead of an iconic white beam, a lurid sea
of light spilt out across the night sky. Middlesborough
and the surrounding area were bathed in extraordinary
fluorescent light. It was a bomber's delight and girls were
at the helm.

Barbara stood agog, staring upwards at the luminous
glare. 'Put that bloody light out!' (Not the order she had
been trained to expect.) Barbara jumped to and pulled the

lever back. Middlesborough vanished into black and the following day the searchlight mysteriously disappeared. The incident was never mentioned again.

The story still tickles Barbara. At seventeen years old, everything felt vivid and important and would prove unforgettable. As was the case for so many girls, Britain's war bumped into Barbara's emerging adulthood and has yielded purpose and stories ever since. 'I only gave up driving recently, an old Rover. I had a hip operation. But I really miss it. I used to drive around Yorkshire giving lectures about the Second World War.' Both Barbara and Princess Elizabeth trained as ATS drivers in Camberley, and ever since delicious garrulous Barbara has compensated for the Queen's silence about her service.

'After that first posting I was moved on to Redcar and 129 Regiment, 455 Heavy Anti-Aircraft Battery.' It was wintertime and Barbara was back in Yorkshire. This was a wet and cold version of Yorkshire and Redcar a rundown out-of-season seaside resort. 'It was a bit rough, everywhere was a bit like Covid times in a way, everything was drab and grey and boarded up.' Barbara recalls mined beaches covered in barbed wire, pillboxes and tank traps, great slabs of concrete protruded from the sand; the vista was a rude reminder that she wasn't there on holiday. 'Mind you, there was a bit of hanging about; the battery I'd been posted to had just come from Dover and needed a rest.' But the ATS, keen to keep their girls occupied, prioritised physical training. A small slice of beach right opposite the camp had been deliberately cleared of mines so girls could perform their obligatory exercises. 'It was horrible! In flimsy little shorts and a cotton shirt we had to go down and do this PT and one of the young officers in full battledress, a scarf and gloves, came with us.' The officer loathed the girls, and the girls loathed the officer and her dog. 'She shouldn't have had a dog, it was against rules.' (Barbara was and still is a stickler for rules.) 'We weren't allowed pets, and it was a horrible dog, it used to sit beside her and watch us.'

Press-ups, sit-ups, star jumps, squats, all in front of a dog and its owner until one morning the dog took off along the beach. 'It broke away into the minefield, trailing its lead.' The officer screamed, "COME HERE, COME HERE, COME HERE!" The dog kept running, dodging in and out between the columns and the concrete. The girls stopped and stared; it was only a matter of time. Sure enough, 'There was a big bang and a whoosh of sand!' In an explosion designed to kill a human being, the mine made mincemeat of the dog. 'The collar came down, and little bits of fur and blood. That was all that was left of 'COME HERE'. We shouldn't have laughed . . .' Barbara is still laughing. 'The officer was absolutely stunned.' Her beloved dog was collateral damage, killed in an inhospitable place, otherwise known as the home front.

19

Becoming a FANY

Olivia smiles and shrugs and searches a tired brain for an answer that no longer exists. She can't remember when she stopped working for de Gaulle, and indicative of human nature's tendency to hold onto disappointment more resolutely than success she is sure that her services were relinquished before she was ready to go. But exactly when and why she left are less easy to pin down. It is possible de Gaulle's strained relations with his British hosts coupled with the arrival of increasing assistance from occupied France hastened the end of Olivia's tenure with the Free French, although correspondence with her mother suggests she was still working for the General's organisation in January 1943. Olivia's final letter is sent from the Comité National Français (a title de Gaulle used from September 1941) and contains another possible, more likely reason for her imminent departure. In it Olivia refers to a pending ski trip in Scotland the following month with a certain Major Peter Jordan, the British soldier she'd marry that summer.

In her personal archive there's a photograph of their wedding day at Claridges Hotel; petite, with a dash of dark lipstick and clutching white roses sugared with stephanotis, Olivia looks euphoric. Despite frequently running herself down (in her dotage still believing she was the ugly duckling among four sisters), in 1943 Olivia's gamine and lively appeal won her a prize that in war was more coveted than even the Croix de Guerre: marriage to a man of decent standing. Her French uniform had finally been replaced with a white silk dress, nipped in at her dainty waist and offset with an intricately embroidered lace veil. Among her papers Olivia has kept several congratulatory telegrams and they include one from General de Gaulle; he sent the couple his most sincere wishes of happiness (*'mes voeux de bonheur les plus sincères'*). It is highly likely it was her marriage to an English major that called time on Olivia's French adventure. She was a woman after all.

Life as Mrs Peter Jordan did not completely curtail Olivia's wartime efforts; her nephew is certain she worked in some capacity in GKN, an aerospace and automotive factory on London's South Bank. But that's not what she remembers. No, her two great achievements were those early hair-raising escapades driving an ambulance across France and later collaboration with and driving for de Gaulle in London. By mid-1943 Olivia's service in French uniform was a thing of the past but her actions were not forgotten. Amidst her papers in the tricolour's blue, white and red is a 1993 invitation to the unveiling of the Statue of General de Gaulle in the same Carlton Gardens where she once worked for the great man.

Olivia has carried those seminal years with her for the rest of her life. Not many British girls were in the eye of the storm as early as 1940. Driving an ambulance carried a whiff of glamour, as did a war on the Continent, where few female service personnel were permitted until 1944. Olivia managed both. She nods her head and reminds me once more that she was 'the equivalent of a FANY but in the French army'.

*

Joyce stopped playing tennis last year. 'It's because of this dreadful virus, but I think I probably had to anyway; I'm ninety-seven next birthday.' A fan of Kate Middleton's style, sitting at a safe distance under a sunshade in her Petworth garden, she looks exquisite in a mottled-grey smock with matching hair cropped short. We are still sifting through her large collection of FANY memorabilia. 'The main thing you had to be sure of was security. You had to have two references and two weeks training in Banbury. I know we came under the umbrella of the ATS but we always kept our separate identity.' That identity included the FANY's elite reputation and the freedoms and privileges that came with it. The First Aid Nursing Yeomanry's acronym had long made people laugh but they took themselves very seriously.

Barbara has vivid recollections of the FANYs at Camberley driving centre. 'One or two were aristocratic, certainly most of them were well bred. I had not come across women like that before.' She remembers a strident brigade of older female instructors, several of whom had been FANY drivers in World War I. 'We didn't see much of them. The officer class were separate anyway.' Martha echoes a similar sentiment: 'In the ATS, the FANYs were looked on as the posh people who we didn't like particularly. They drove the generals around and actually I think they probably worked really hard.' In fact, the FANYs were much more than mere drivers to the military top brass in World War II, but that was the image they were best known for, and true to form they provided the army with 1,500 driver-mechanics as early as 1938.

Joyce readily admits, 'I had this feeling with my friend Primrose that we ought to join up. We chose the FANYs because we hoped we could be drivers, and because we thought we'd be driving men around, just like in *Foyle's War*.' Teenage Joyce was in the privileged position of having access to her father's Rover and knew better than most the thrilling liberation that came with four wheels. 'I was quite popular because I could use Daddy's car. He had a little business as a supplier of vegetables and mushrooms and I suppose we must have got extra petrol. The produce was boxed up and sent to Covent Garden.'

Like Olivia, Joyce occupied a southern version of upper-class England; she'd been a day girl at a boarding school in Surrey. 'Manor House in Limpsfield, the Churchill girls went there. Mary was just a couple of years older than me, I knew her quite well.' Joyce recalls 'Clemmie', Churchill's wife, arriving at school functions 'always looking lovely, dressed in a mink coat and not much else!' and she still has Mary's bold signature in her autograph book. But by 1943 school was a thing of the past and Mary had since become a pin-up for her pioneering role in anti-aircraft defence. Despite her mother's disinclination ('Father was injured in the First World War, he had a breakdown afterwards although these things were never really talked about'), Joyce wanted her own role in the war. 'So Primrose and I made our way to London to sign up as FANYs.'

Joyce is one of two English girls in this book who joined the FANY in 1943; Lancashire-born Jean is the other. A robust, healthy child, Jean enjoyed an affluent rural upbringing in Newland Hall, a large sandstone manor house inhabited by three generations of Owtrams. Her parents identified as local 'squirarchy – one below aristocracy' and the men of the household boasted an impressive lineage of military service; a tradition which saw Jean's father, Colonel Carey Owtram of 137th Regiment, set sail on SS *Dominion Monarch* as part of a twenty-strong convoy heading out to the Far East in September 1941. Jean had waved goodbye to him after a bracing family holiday of hunting, shooting and fishing in Scotland and reluctantly returned to Wroxall Abbey, a provincial girls' boarding school in Warwickshire.

Letters home record her abundant good faith: '*My own most darling Mummy . . . I expect I'm a fatalist or something, but I'm quite certain that he'll be all right, because he's so very precious and God doesn't let anything too awful happen.*'[1] Jean's religious fervour came to nought. By the beginning of 1942 Colonel Owtram's regiment was in retreat, backing down the Malay Peninsula to Singapore, which fell to the Japanese on 15 February. This apparently impregnable stronghold yielded some 80,000 Allied prisoners to the enemy in a catastrophic blow to the prestige of the British Empire, and Jean's father was among them. His 'missing' status did little for Jean's intolerance of boarding school with its petty rules and regulations. Now in her mid-nineties, she laughs. 'Yes, you see, my older sister, Pat, she had been a prefect but not me. I would duck down to the basement and smoke cigarettes and play the piano very loudly.' There was a war on, her father was missing and Jean was desperate for a slice of the action.

*

Jean is quite certain that 'I was accepted into the FANY on my eighteenth birthday – that was the youngest possible age. My sister, Pat, was in the Wrens but by 1943 the Wrens were only looking for cooks and bottle washers. I didn't fancy that so I went for the FANYs.' It was her godmother, 'Aunt Marjorie', who tipped Jean off about FANY girls who were having 'a very good time in London'. This was not an organisation which actively recruited, relying instead on its reputation, and although the FANY had been incorporated into the ATS in 1940, the remit for its 6,000 girls was closely guarded and often highly confidential.

Similarly, Joyce believes she had 'heard of the FANYs through a school friend', which conforms to the idea of a closed social network. At this stage in the application process it was less about girls' abilities (Jean and Joyce profess to have had little interest in academia and no secretarial skills, preferring sport, in Joyce's case high-level tennis) and more about a class-based faith in their good name and conduct. As Jean delicately explains: 'There was still a sense that the FANY chose their recruits from a certain kind of family under the old-fashioned notion that girls who had been sent away to boarding school would be of the "right stuff".'[2]

If ATS recruits all recall the rigours of the medical test prior to entry into the service, FANYs had to clear a different hurdle. Joyce was asked to provide at least two references. 'My doctor gave me one, he knew my parents well, and my bank manager the other. Yes, I did have an account; when I was fifteen my father gave me a cheque book and a small allowance.' Reputations mattered, and Joyce's family was well known in Oxted, the local Surrey village. 'I was summoned for an interview at 31A Wilton Place.' Tucked neatly into London's Belgravia in a rent-free vicarage for the duration of the war, the FANY headquarters oversaw the recruitment of new girls and it was here Joyce was confronted by 'two terrifying women'.

The first was Marian Gamwell, one of two indomitable sisters who ran the Corps. Veterans of World War I, pilots, motorcyclists, farmers and fighters, the Gamwells' ability to hold their own had been tested against the mettle of Dame Helen, the ATS's doughty first director. She met her match in Marian, who fought tooth and nail for the Corps to remain autonomous. The first showdown came with the organisation's motor companies, which eventually relocated to Camberley in a move that heralded a FANY–ATS fusion. These were the FANYs Barbara worked with, who (reluctantly) gifted the tradition of the cap strap over the crown of the head to their ATS comrades. In the later 1940 ATS marriage deal with the remaining so-called Free FANYs, the Corps kept their own uniform, their own headquarters and their own leadership.[3]

Despite Dame Helen's best efforts the FANY retained its individualism, and to young recruits like Joyce the service's stylish élan was especially appealing. At the interview, Gamwell was flanked by 'a beautiful woman', FANY secretary Phyllis Bingham. 'She was very elegant, not over the top but very attractive and I'm not sure you'd say intelligent but she was definitely charismatic.' Bingham wasn't the only FANY who cut a dash; the whole Corps took uniform very seriously. Joyce was measured by a London tailor. 'I suspect he came from Savile Row. It was wonderful really, because it all fitted so well. The jacket and skirt were made from a worsted barathea, that's the smooth cloth used for men's dinner jackets. It was absolutely super.' This handmade wool-weave uniform was completed with a Sam Browne leather belt, cut by the local saddler, and a FANY insignia on each lapel. In Joyce's studio photograph, the girl staring back with her thatch of dark hair, prominent brows and pursed lips is handsome and looks older than eighteen. 'We did grow up quickly. As well as the interview there was a training course, and it was all terribly secret.'

Having held onto its deliberately small, selective recruitment process, the FANY was in prime position to undertake what Marian considered its 'most important work'.[4] Glamorous Bingham was much more than a mere FANY secretary, she was also the close personal friend of acting Brigadier Colin Gubbins, the prime mover behind the Special Operations Executive (SOE), a secret organisation formed to conduct espionage, sabotage and reconnaissance in enemy-occupied countries. With the blessing of Churchill, Gubbins' approach to warfare was uncompromising: agents were instructed to blow up trains, bridges and factories and help foster local insurgents and guerrilla warfare. Most of the leading players were men, often with Commando training, but the organisation didn't conform to gender norms. In much the same way that Bletchley Park initially relied on a nexus of familiar friends and relations to staff its very secret mission, this 'Ministry of Ungentlemanly Warfare' pulled in help from those it could trust. For Gubbins, Bingham was one such woman, and the Corps she belonged to, with its classy reputation and refusal to be forced into an ATS strait-jacket, the perfect vehicle through which to recruit staff and new agents. Sitting in front of her intimidating interviewers, above all else Joyce was being evaluated for trustworthiness. Could she keep a secret? Was she reliable?

In August 2020 she puckers her brow; it is very hot despite the sunshade and this was all a long time ago, but there are some things you don't forget. 'We were collected by army trucks and taken to Banbury. It was all rather new to me because I hadn't been a boarder at school, and some of the FANYs were really rather frightening.' Joyce and Primrose had made it past the Corps' gatekeepers, and were packed off on a two-week training course.

We stayed in a big house, Overthorpe Hall; the FANYs always had lovely accommodation. No, there wasn't much route marching, just lots of lectures. A chap came down from the War Office, he was an officer and it was drummed into you that you must not talk. My mother and father never knew I worked for the SOE. They thought I was at a wireless training school for overseas forces. That was the cover story. Oh no, goodness no! I wasn't dropped into France. My French wasn't nearly good enough for that!

Joyce laughs and then lowers her voice; it's hard to hear above the cacophony of English birdsong. 'But the people we were working with, we knew what they were doing was dangerous and that we most probably wouldn't see them again. They were amazingly brave because they knew exactly what they were in for.'

20

Deadly Parlour Games

At the end of their two-week induction Joyce and her friend Primrose were allotted their wartime roles. Wannabe drivers, the girls were despondent when informed that they'd be 'transmitter hut attendants'. 'Good God!' thought Joyce. 'Is that cleaning a loo? An attendant! It didn't sound very glamorous.' Their FANY supervisor quickly supplemented the description with the words '"at a wireless training school". That sounded OK,' admits Joyce, 'so we didn't go on about the driving.' Instead the girls were ferried to a second stately home in Oxfordshire. During the war Thame Park mansion had become Station 52, a special training venue for SOE agents and a transmission centre, receiving clandestine messages from France. For the next year this was Joyce's new home.

In Britain's World War II hall of fame perhaps no name shines brighter than that of Violette Szabo; posthumously awarded both the British George Cross and the French Croix de Guerre, she is one of the most famous SOE agents. A bilingual working-class Londoner, shortly after her French husband was killed during the Second Battle of El Alamein Violette was recruited into the SOE, the organisation that would pilot over fifty female agents into France. Violette was one of thirty-nine who also belonged to the FANY, which with its *je ne sais quoi* provided the perfect cover (including a pension and uniform) for a pool of women whose work was a matter of life and death. Sixteen of the girls died, thirteen in concentration camps, including Violette. She was captured and interrogated during her second mission in occupied France and was shot aged twenty-three in execution alley, Ravensbruck, north Germany.[1]

Standard British service girls with their non-combatant status couldn't be armed, but no such rule inhibited FANYs operating in SOE; Violette had a sten gun and was reputedly a good shot, but it did not save her life. Another renowned SOE FANY was Polish-born Krystyna Sharbek, codename Christine Granville, who survived missions in Poland and France only to be stabbed to death by a jealous ex-lover in 1952.[2] However, it's wrong to see the FANYs' role exclusively through the lens of a handful of extraordinary individuals who risked their lives beyond enemy lines. Most of these women did not identify with the FANY (Krystyna wore her uniform just once), and they were a small minority compared with the 2,000 FANYs, including Joyce and Jean, working in Britain and abroad with ciphers and signals and in special training schools, providing vital support for SOE's overseas agents and insurgents.

'At Thame Park I didn't work in the house. In the grounds there was a thing like a garage, inside which were machines – receivers – that looked like microwaves with twiddling knobs. That's where we were.' Joyce was at the coalface of a highly sophisticated traffic network which SOE had aggressively developed to enable agents and resistance movements to communicate back to base in Britain. With her friend Primrose she spent hours and hours in a small hut with a giant aerial.

> It was picking up communications from France – it had to be big! The signals office would ring you up from the main house with a frequency, and it was a bit like tuning a radio with these needles that would dip up and down. Eventually at a certain time you'd hear dudududuuuu. That was the Morse coming through the airwaves and you'd know it was ok.

Joyce in her hut with a concrete floor was a link in a chain between France and the Park's signals office. Nothing more, nothing less. There she sat, sometimes with knitting, sometimes without, an attendant: the connection between two countries waiting to take an order to tune in or tune out. The communication chain depended on someone somewhere in France, an agent with a wireless set, making contact. The provision of supplies, reporting of enemy activities or the extraction of personnel – on numerous levels it was essential to know what was going on.

> I'd hear the Morse but it wasn't my job to write it down. I wasn't Morse literate, I didn't decode, that happened back at the house. The worst thing was if it was a live transmission and suddenly without warning it stopped, then you knew they'd been found out and probably killed. A lot of the agents died.

While Joyce sat in the transmission hut, Thame Park's SOE trainee agents were put through their paces: wireless operations, escape and evasion, uniform recognition, communications and cryptography, firing practice.

Well, they had their own programme. They spent some time in the woods. But we didn't ask, we knew not to ask. Yes, I have heard of Violette Szabo and Krystyna Skarbek but they weren't at Thame Park. They became famous after the war. One didn't know their real names, they were given false identities, which must've been the most difficult thing.

Joyce remembers a 'good mix of interesting people', mainly men: Canadian, Norwegian, French and at least one Pole. She pushes a pile of photographs across the table, several feature a screwball horse; in one Joyce sits astride this handsome mare and in another on the same steed there's a uniformed man, ram-rod straight with a wide proud face staring beyond the horizon of the picture. 'He was a Norwegian agent, we called him Bjorn; I believe he was quite aristocratic. I remember him saying, "If you have something unusual," which I did, I had a horse and a dog, "you always get remembered."'

Joyce didn't travel light. Pinto the horse couldn't stay at home (his field was on the flight path to Biggin Hill), but thankfully the FANYs were allowed pets, and a local farmer provided hay. 'If you were in the services, people were always ready to help. My dog, Tiger, slept in the cupboard; he was a cairn and when I was on duty the other FANYs took him to the pub because he was the best way to meet people.' Joyce stares back from the grainy photographs; the striking teenager possesses an assuredness in stark contrast to the precarious future of the men and women who surrounded her. 'There were about thirty agents and a whole lot of army and us FANYs. Thame

Park was quite a large station. We had a recreation hut and there'd be dances.'

A faded yellow Thame Park entertainment programme boasts 'Joyce Chamberlain, Soprano' with two 'selected items and an accompanist'. 'I'd done a lot of music at school, piano, violin, that sort of thing, which helped. I think I sang "Cherry Ripe" that evening.' She smiles; her coral lips still hold the same shape; Joyce remains irresistible. Back then, as Norwegian Bjorn noted, she was certainly memorable. Joyce laughs. 'No, we didn't do physical training, the FANYs' exercise was parties!' Privileged and pretty, Joyce wore the war lightly, and briefly thrown in among a firebrand of freedom fighters, it's hard to escape the conclusion she was a vital and pleasing distraction for a disparate group desperately trying to live in the moment.

*

Training for SOE recruits was gruelling and relentless (there were refresher courses and 'finishing schools'), and each agent had their own strengths and weaknesses. Violette Szabo spoke French like a native but passed out of her first training school at Winterfold House with a 'moderately favourable report'; this patchy performance didn't inhibit her selection overseas, nor a practice parachute jump when she badly twisted her ankle, an injury which fatally slowed her getaway in France.[3] After many weeks 'spent on the roofs of various Cairo buildings with her SOE suitcase transmitter bleeping and whispering' agent Krystyna Sharbeck still 'could not get the hang of her wireless' and although 'very bright', she struggled with coding; apparently this was the kind of repetitive work that didn't suit her temperamental personality.[4] Later Gubbins wrote that the best signallers and coders were 'girls straight from higher education who had not lost the classroom'.[5] Cue eighteen-year-old FANY Jean. Alongside the likes of Joyce who established connections with agents in the field, legions of FANYs were trained to communicate with and decode the agents' messages and Jean was one of these girls. By 1943 she had left Wroxall Abbey, her provincial boarding school, and been subjected to an interview at FANY headquarters in Wilton Place.

'It seemed to go well, but I was somewhat confused at the end when they asked me if I liked crosswords. I thought they'd run out of things to talk about and that perhaps I'd failed the interview!' In fact the crossword question was deliberate and, fortuitously, Jean had spent many childhood hours puzzling away with her grand-father. ('Reading, music and crosswords – that was our home entertainment!') She was a prime candidate for the FANY's expanding role in code and cipher. Promptly dispatched to Overthorpe Park for basic training, Jean then returned to Wilton Place, where, 'when I wasn't marching around Hyde Park, I was taught how to use various coding methods'.[6]

As well as Morse, in her own autobiography Jean describes two additional techniques, the first of which she learnt at training camp. 'Playfair' had been around for nearly a century and involved the encryption of pairs of letters, which increased the coding options in a standard alphabet from 26 to 600 while the decoder required noth-ing more than a pen and paper. Once she'd mastered the basics, Jean was informed of her first posting. 'I was to be working with SOE' and was required to sign the Official Secrets Act. 'I felt more important than I had ever felt before as I proudly signed my name.'[7]

A year earlier, in 1942, Leo Marks, genius cryptographer and maverick wordsmith, had been recruited into SOE as their head of coding. He recalled his first meeting with a room full of FANYs.

> The average age of these girls was twenty . . . and most of them had been selected as coders on an arbitrary basis because they happened to be available when coders were wanted. After the briefest of training they were dispatched to one of the most secret establishments in England and left to get on with it. They were never allowed to meet the agents whose traffic they handled and who were only code names to them. The Gestapo had no more reality for these girls than when they'd joined the FANY.

Marks understood that messages sent in haste from the field, with the enemy's 'direction-finding cars' hunting agents 'like sniffer dogs', often contained errors, errors which made them difficult to decipher. It wasn't good enough for FANYs to master basic coding; they needed to be able to unravel messages that contained mistakes. Resending a message was out of the question, it took too long and risked discovery and death.

In order to instil a professional gear change among the FANY, Marks realised they needed to understand what was at stake. He told them a story about a Yugoslav partisan, eighteen years old, who had been caught with a wireless transmitter, had refused to betray the organiser whose messages he was sending and was eventually taken to the mortuary 'no longer recognisable as a human being'. Appalled by this brutal story, two days later Marks received a message from those same FANYs on a teleprinter: 'WE HAVE BROKEN OUR FIRST INDECIPHERABLE.'[8]

One year later, after a sea change in working practices, it was into this FANY rank that Jean entered. Equipped with a cover story ('if asked, I was to say I worked in "personnel relations and training"'), and getting off the bus a stop early as instructed, Jean took her seat in a spartan office in SOE's Baker Street headquarters (discreetly initialled ISRB – Inter Service Research Bureau) and applied pencil to paper. Messages arrived randomly via teleprinter ('it's possible some came from Thame Park. I don't know. You didn't ask. We didn't ask') and she methodically worked her way through the pile.

When Jean first joined SOE, all overseas agents were known by their codenames and they frequently communicated using prearranged poems or 'anything they could easily remember' as a formula to encrypt their messages. According to Marks, this 'concept of clandestine coding had been adopted by SOE because of a theory . . . that if an agent was caught and searched it was better security if his code was in his head'. Initially, Shakespeare, Keats, Poe, Tennyson and the Bible were SOE's bestsellers, and far too easily recognisable. As Marks put it: 'Even works less familiar to the Germans than the National Anthem – the Lord's Prayer perhaps – would cause them no problem.'[9] So, at his instigation, several coders also became part-time poets because 'if our future poem-codes were original compositions written by members of SOE, no reference books would be of the slightest help tracing them'.[10]

However the poem-code system had a number of weaknesses (it was eventually replaced), which included the need for each message to be at least two hundred letters long. The result was vital communications interlaced with nonsense words. Jean recalls 'some arriving as fragments of poetry or jumbled letters'. Transmissions relaying the need for munitions, numbers wounded, location of troops, were stuffed with deliberate booby traps. 'A friend got a message all down, the agent had filled in as many words as possible so it was difficult to decode and the last words were "I wish I were a woolly lamb with fur upon . . ."' The friend promptly replied, '"Upon what?"' Jeans smiles; levity was important. But the longer the message, the more likely it was that mistakes would creep in. Here she admits, 'I found out I was rather good at it, at deciphering the indecipherables. If someone had made a mess of their message, if they were under pressure, I would think what might this mean? What's this about? What could be behind this?' Leaving school aged sixteen, convinced she was really only good at sports, it turned out Jean was a wizard at the 'deadliest of parlour games'.

The past is somewhere vague now, but she keenly remembers a rapid promotion to shift leader. Soon Jean headed up a small team of girls and 'if they weren't getting it right, it was passed to me and I would think, "What could they have done? Could they have shifted this column over here?"' She waves her arm gently and smiles. 'But we were just girls.' She never worked under Leo Marks and was not part of his poet's corner but as a distinctive, dark-haired man, Jean knew who he was, they all did. 'It was almost Christmas and we were feeling terribly excited one evening when he blew into our room.' The FANYs jumped to and wished their senior a resounding 'Merry Christmas' but the greeting was not reciprocated. 'It is not a merry Christmas, Europe is burning. People are dying out there.'[11] Marks launched into diatribe about the horror of war. Jean stood agog. Of course, yes, her father was in a Japanese prisoner-of-war-camp! Tears pricked her eyes. 'War does that, it gives you terrible mood swings.' The girls returned to their desks, sombre, depressed even.

Later they would discover Marks's ominous outburst had been triggered by the death of Ruth Hambro, his girlfriend ('the woman I wanted beside me for the rest of my life') in a plane crash, an episode he later shared in his autobiography. 'I went up to the roof of Norgeby House, which was the closest I could get to her . . . there was a quick way down from it but she wouldn't have approved.' Instead Marks stood staring at the sky from No. 83 Baker Street and 'transmitted a message to her which I had failed to deliver when I had the chance'.

> The life that I have
> Is all that I have
> And the life that I have
> Is yours . . .

Perhaps the most famous code-poem of all time, within three months Marks had given his touching four-verse composition to Violette Szabo just before she left on her fatal final mission to France. But that Christmas Eve it remained between him and his beloved Ruth. According to Marks, he then 'went downstairs and wished the girls a Happy Christmas'.[12] That is not how Jean recalls his brief, dramatic appearance in their office, but she was receiving the message not delivering it.

21

Multi-racial War

From the beginning of the war the south-east of England was disproportionately impacted by Britain's expanding war machine. Joyce recalls that by 1940 in the surrounds of Oxted, her Surrey home, 'there were Canadian soldiers, two regiments, with their tanks rolling into our fields. We had never seen that sort of thing. We felt involved and excited. They gave us chocolates and we were very keen on making them feel welcome in the house.' Joyce has a playful laugh. 'Yes! Lots of men, it was terribly exciting, they were all wonderful. Oh yes, there was lots of flirting! And there were also New Zealanders training to be Spitfire pilots at Biggin Hill; we got to know them rather well.' Needless to say Joyce's mother didn't share quite the same frisson of excitement but, ever the hostess, sandwiches and tea were forthcoming.

This predominantly male uniformed presence across Britain would steadily grow. By 1943 Beryl Manthorp was a regimental PT specialist and had been promoted to sergeant. It was a peripatetic job that saw her cross vast swathes of Britain and by 1944 she was heading down into England once more as gun-sites proliferated along the southern coast in anticipation of the Allied invasion into France. Beryl's wartime notes annotate detailed information concerning her movements, accommodation, transport and fleeting friendships. Occasional commentaries on wider issues stand out. Stationed in the centre of an American tank regiment in Dorset, one morning she was waved into the adjutant's office. 'As he put the phone down he turned to me: "You know the tanks are moving; I've just been told a company of Black troops are coming to clear up. However shall I tell everyone?" I told him we all knew that was the way the Americans worked. "Oh," he replied, "I didn't know."'[1]

Long before the details of Operation Overlord (later remembered as the D-Day landings) were pinned down to mid-1944, Britain was the recipient of Operation Bolero, the arrival of American forces on British soil. Angus Calder in *The People's War* argues that of all the Allied, Dominion and Colonial troops in Britain by late spring 1944, the Americans made a big impact because of their 'affluence and directness'.[2] There is no doubting the latter, but as Beryl's retort implies, the stark cultural segregation between Black and white soldiers in the American army was also a talking point among British service personnel. Unlike America, Britain had a very small Black population (predominantly highly educated, from the colonies and residing in metropolitan centres[3]) and its imperial Black and Asian troops invariably occupied separate colonial regiments and often, though not exclusively, defended local territories. But if in World War II the race buck stopped with America, white Britain was on high alert and Black American troops were distanced through a deliberate 'othering' process.

Beryl details the preparations of her white MHAA battery prior to the arrival of their new neighbours. 'A visiting officer gave us a very good talk on the characteristics of Black people and how to live with them in close proximity, all nations have their own physical and mental identities.' On the telephone she supplements this description. 'We were always told if they come along, "Say hello, don't ignore them, but don't get involved."' Hands-off Britain hedged its bets with clear protocol written by a white ruling class educated on the inferiority of the Black man.[4] Beryl described what happened next.

> The tanks went and in came the clear-up regiment. The next day two of us went into Bournemouth. As we approached the stile two very large Black figures appeared from the other side. 'Hullo, you now going out?' in broad USA accents. We climbed over the style saying, 'Yes, we are just hurrying for the bus.' That was our first encounter with our new neighbours. None of us went out alone and we never had any problems; they spoke to us, we replied and they gave us lifts in their jeeps. The US army allowed the Black troops one late night out a week. That night all white troops were CB [confined to barracks].[5]

Beryl steps back into her twenty-two-year-old self, recalling the official warnings that were issued. She admits, 'I don't think I would've wanted to have been on my own' in a jeep with a Black American soldier, but she thinks she might've got into a vehicle with a white officer. It was different then, of this Beryl is certain.

Eighty years ago, ATS girls were trained to acknowledge a gulf between themselves as white British women and Black American soldiers. But in the summer of 2020 as Black Lives Matter protests swirl across the country, Beryl is once more peering down at the uniformed image of her younger self. The girl looking back has an open face and thick, wavy dark hair tucked up, regulation-style. 'My mother was born in Trinidad; my grandfather was serving over there in the British army when he met my grandmother. I don't know if there were any Black relatives in her family but my mother was quite dark-skinned and I'm certainly not fair.' Beryl, aged ninety-nine, with her walnut-lined face and very few extant biological relatives, is questing to find out more. 'My grandmother and my mother's two sisters all died of malaria, so my grandfather came back to Essex, where his sister brought up my mother. The link with Trinidad was lost.'

Beryl's British-Trinidadian mother was born into a late-Victorian world deliberately defined by race. Back then, academic books propounded on the principal divisions of man with the 'mental characters' of those in the 'Black' categories falling into the lowest groups, coupled with derisory tags: 'sensuous, unintellectual, fitful'.[6] The climate was rigid and unforgiving; 'mulattos', the pejorative term for persons of mixed race, were at a distinct disadvantage. Growing up in Essex, Beryl's mother identified as a white woman; likewise in the war her daughter, white and British-born, was encouraged to see herself as different from the Black American soldiers she served beside.

But eighty years later and still in Britain, Beryl no longer focuses on difference, instead she wonders at what might once have united her with her Black comrades.

*

ATS propaganda film *The Gentle Sex* closes with narrator Leslie Howard confessing: 'Well, there they are, the women. Our sweethearts, sisters, mothers, daughters. Let's give in at last and admit we are really proud of you.' But pride wasn't enough, more girls were needed. In 1943 extensive preparations for a second front competed with Allied military campaigns in North Africa, Italy and Burma; the British army and its support service, the ATS, were stretched like never before. Martha, a subaltern in AA Command with a team of girls under her, clicks her tongue: 'They started scraping the bowl, the standard of the average recruit went down and down.' Posters, films and newsreels soliciting girls to sign up jostled for attention and beneath the patriotic words lay obligation; women aged nineteen and above had to join the war effort.

Vicar's daughter Anne, having finally left school aged eighteen, 'applied to join the ATS in the spring of 1943 and the elderly woman officer in charge was delighted to enlist me, as voluntary recruitment was slow'. The same officer was even more delighted when she discovered that just five years earlier Anne's mother, Marjory, had been W/1, the first woman to serve in the brand-new ATS. The story was a PR coup in a long war where new recruits were hard to find. The local newspapers all featured the same photograph of young Anne, still in civilian clothes, signing a large document under the matronly gaze of her mother. The image underlines just how much had changed. When Marjory joined up as part of an early wave of uniformed women, female service was little more than a hobby for well-intended local ladies; five years later it had become the bricks and mortar of public life.

With an upbringing defined by the family's Anglican mission in Burma, ideas of duty and service were stamped deep into Anne's psyche; an eager Girl Guide, she had long awaited her turn to 'fight'. It was a crashing blow therefore when she failed her ATS medical. 'The shock and disappointment were enormous.' Every other woman in this book passed with an A1 health check, Anne was the exception. She could see perfectly well, but only with one eye. Hampered with a disabling patch at school, willing her lazy eye to work harder, Anne had bumped around campus, missing chair seats, failing tests, sitting out matches. The stress of trying and failing was so humiliating it had made her ill, but surely by 1943 that was a thing of the past? The patch had been removed and the good eye more than compensated for the bad. No. Rules were rules – unless of course you had the wherewithal to contest them. Anne's parents supported her in the quest to overturn the decision. 'I demanded my right to a second opinion, and saw another ophthalmologist, who (somewhat reluctantly) was prepared to sign me on, allotting me the very lowest possible medical category in existence.'[7]

Anne was finally in the ATS. Others weren't so lucky.

*

Despite the shortfall in numbers and the desperate efforts to enlist more girls, it is striking that the War Office resisted pressure to recruit women from the British West Indies, holding out against the wishes of the Colonial Office for over two years. There was no official colour bar in the ATS, and overseas the service employed local women; in the Middle East, 3,684 women came from countries in the region and it was ATS girls who trained the Women's Auxiliary Corps of India. In a similar vein, the War Office hoped that a focus on local deployment would stem ambitions to bring women of colour across the Atlantic. In December 1941 (the same month conscription was announced in Britain), they released a statement.

> The army considers it would be wrong to encourage coloured women to come from the West Indies . . . as they would be unused to the climatic conditions and modes of life in England . . . any demand by West Indian women to be enrolled in a uniformed service would be better met by local organisations.[8]

The Mother Country wasn't ready to welcome its daughters.

Aged one hundred and three and currently staying with her daughter in Barbados, Ena is full of laughter. It is hard to distinguish her words in a pre-recorded Zoom, but the sentiment is clear.[9] There was to be no stopping this woman. The pokey conservative mindset of the War Office, too slow to support the recruitment of girls at the onset of war and then prevaricating over the enlistment of West Indian women, had met its match. Born in Jamaica and losing both parents young, Ena was used to looking out for herself. There are striking similarities between her fortitude and Anne's; both were children of Empire and both are passionate lifelong Guiders. Today the oldest known living ATS veteran, Ena's life philosophy, which she attributes to the Guides, is similar to Anne's: 'You have to give back to society.' While Anne is still the vice president of her local Guide Association, Ena was honoured as a Member of the Order of the British Empire (MBE) for her work with the Guides. But for all that unites these two women, in the eyes of the War Office there was a defining feature that separated them: race.

Born in 1917, Ena grew up on an island where white colonial men occupied the top jobs in a system that openly discriminated. Early on, Ena mastered the art of pushing back; given the role of temporary clerk in Spanish Town's courthouse when they had only advertised for male applicants, by the time war broke out she occupied a permanent position at Kingston's Criminal Court Office.[10] Her focus was never on barriers but rather opportunities, and pre-war Jamaica proved a useful training ground in a decade that witnessed a wave of nationalism, exacerbated by dire economics and inequality. Ena belonged to a generation of Jamaicans determined to deliver change, and what better way to prove your worth than to fight as a woman in imperial Britain's war.

The Colonial Office was desperate to enlist eager West Indian girls like Ena, believing a larger role in the conflict would stem the restive stirrings of independence across the region. 'The coming together of so many for a common cause' is the way Ena's daughter describes World War II in an email. But was it? The War Office looked unlikely to capitulate over the question of recruiting Black women into Britain, claiming as late as spring 1943 they could not 'agree to accept any coloured women for service in this country'. Their hand was eventually forced when ATS Controller Jean Knox decided she needed girls from the Caribbean to work in Washington alongside Britain's newest and most important ally, America. In the States, segregation insisted those women were white and that, the Colonial Office claimed, left no option but to recruit Black West

Indian women into Britain. Presented with a fait accompli, the War Office relented; thirty Caribbean women were permitted to join the ATS in Britain as a 'symbolic act'.[11]

Sparkling, with pearls combed into shining grey hair that falls across a floral smock, her delicate silhouette offset against a sun-orange wall, Ena nods and chats. 'Yes, yes,' she was one of those very first girls, having spotted a small advert in the classified section of a Jamaican newspaper.[12] The bar was set high; in this so-called people's war, most West Indian women had to pay their own fare, a means test that prohibited the poorest from crossing the Atlantic. Arriving at No.7 ATS Training Centre Guildford in December 1943, Ena did not find the weather cold (she had a serge uniform to keep her warm), and in those early days there was plenty of company, including the press and the Princess Royal. Against a book-lined wall, Ena stands out, with her confident grin and proffered gloved hand. ATS Commandant Mary, the Princess Royal, reaches to accept it, her distinct, slightly puffy Windsor profile almost smiling back.[13] This was a first: the Empire had come home in female form, and the photograph of a Black girl with her West Indian colleagues snapped a deliberate feel-good moment.

Ena vividly remembers a very warm reception in Britain, nodding her head, recalling the names of cherished friends both Scottish and English. Repeating the word 'welcome', she reminds her daughter of the Collymore family, who shared their name and had seen Ena's picture in the paper. 'They got in contact with the War Office and that first Christmas, when the camp was closed, this lady invited me to stay and also invited my friends as well. Real kindness.'[14] The description conjures up a picture-book scene, Ena and her girlfriends from a far-away land tackling rationed turkey and sprouts within four very British walls. Ena's overriding memory is of a Merrie England and such was her eager disposition (then and now), it is hard to imagine how she could have elicited any other response.

Ena was among the first of a 'privileged' few West Indian women recruited into Britain, a country that needed all the help it could get. Arriving from the colonies, the girls had novelty value and the War Office made sure it stayed that way. The number of Black ATS recruits was kept to a bare minimum; meanwhile their extensive exposure in the media pointed to a double-handed game: the impression given was one of inclusion, when government policy predominantly focused on exclusion. In total, no more than a hundred Caribbean women arrived in Britain to serve in the ATS in the run-up to D-Day, although several hundred more were deployed locally. Ena's recollection that she met no racism but rather overwhelming friendliness suggests that by ruthlessly limiting the numbers of girls coming from the West Indies the British Government lost out. Ena's story is testimony to the unifying force of war and the power of individual kindness.

22

'One can look but one must not touch!'

In accounts of preparations for the D-Day landings the overwhelming impression is of a man's war, but invariably it was girls who were helping ready kitbags and munitions, servicing supply chains, writing up training programmes and copying out the logistical movements of troops.[1] The devil was in the detail. Penny nods; a private who wore her uniform with pride, in 1944 she was working as a clerk in Fulford Barracks, York.

> I was in the company office to begin with, writing up general duties pertaining to the army, then I was moved to Unit Command, where they were all senior officers. Commander Kennett and Senior Commander Morrison is what the ladies were called. The men were called brigadiers and it was very hush-hush. I knew my place, I did typing and teleprinting, and although I wasn't connected, I had an idea of what was going on.

Penny lowers her voice. 'Because at that time there were units all over England preparing for the second front.' In the months before the D-Day landings, Operation Overlord necessitated the writing up of highly confidential detailed plans that coordinated troop flows and big training exercises and, tapping away on her typewriter in Northern Command headquarters, Penny was an invaluable member of this logistical behemoth. Private Daysh '*has an alert brain and can be relied upon to use initiative and common sense*'. She is '*competent and trustworthy in every respect*'. Penny's service book testifies to both her ability and personality, which was judged '*pleasant*'. This private was '*very popular with the officers and the other ranks alike*'.

And just as the Overlord build-up changed her working life, so too did it change Penny's social life. 'Oh yes, there were a lot of men. It was raining men for a time.' She laughs. 'And the Yanks came over here and invited us to their dances.' Penny was a great dancer.

> I was a bit giddy, I was young and the Yanks were good movers, they were jivers, so they were, but not everyone liked them. They had more money and better uniforms than our boys. The Yanks – over here, overpaid, over-sexed! And they used to have nylons and chatted up the girls and the girls then used to go with the Yanks. And a lot of them got into trouble.

Penny pauses; for a few minutes she nibbles at her sausage roll and peruses memories of close dancing and close shaves. 'I did fall in love again, you know, after Ronald was killed.' (Her teenage sweetheart who died in an Italian bombing raid off Malta.) 'My new fella, Tom, wasn't American, no, he was a Londoner like me. I met him at a dance, he was a sergeant in the Rifle Brigade. They were training near us in Yorkshire. Oh yes, he was movie-star good-looking; I thought Ronald was good, but Tom was even better.'

Penny loved York with its imposing minster and peal-
ing bells, the Roman walls and wonderful weird street
names. 'Whip-ma-whop-ma-gate!' Blitzed London felt a
long way off and handsome Tom and this ancient city
quickly became her new world, but it couldn't last long. 'I
knew about pending troop movements 'cos of my work.
Tom would be sent away.' Dating took on new and vital
urgency, but privacy was hard to find. Penny laughs.

> At Fulford the men were in the barracks and the girls
> were in the Nissan huts away from the men, there was
> nowhere to go for a pet. But just beside our Nissan
> huts they'd park the army ambulances so when we'd
> been out on a date, we'd get in one and have a kiss
> and a cuddle!

Penny giggles, her hand clasped to her mouth. Petite
and definitely pretty, there she was leaning over the gear-
stick, having a fondle with a man who might not be around
much longer, when there was a rap on the foggy window.
She shakes her head. 'A corporal was doing the rounds,
they were a bit aware of their stripes, some of them.'

The following day Penny was punished. 'The sergeant
said I'd been a fool, and that I shouldn't have been there
and that she had no choice but to put me on a charge.'
All these years later it feels unduly severe, to punish a girl
for having a consensual smooch in a safe, dry space, but
Penny's story is indicative of the ongoing national obsession with female chastity. Pitting one generation against
another, this hot topic acquired a whole new dimension
with the arrival of over one million American soldiers.

The hope that the Markham Committee's findings
would kybosh parental anxiety was short-lived. The

numbers of soldiers gathering in Britain peaked in the early months of 1944 (American troops alone numbered over 1.5 million), and so too did worries about venereal disease and unwanted pregnancy. The former had sky-rocketed since the beginning of the war; a 70% increase in syphilis cases showed no signs of slowing and just before the arrival of the Americans, official warnings about VD went public. A swathe of explicit adverts appeared in women's magazines. Syphilis was 'dangerous, a killing disease', the first sign was a 'small ulcer near the sex organs'. Gonorrhoea gave its victims 'a discharge from the sex organs . . . chronic ill health and the inability to have children'. Fast treatment was essential and the publications were in no doubt as to the best course of action: 'Clean living is the real safeguard.'[2]

Penny nods, 'One can look, but one must not touch.' Girls knew the rules, and for those that didn't, they were drummed home pretty damn quickly. Teleplotter Daphne in 65th Searchlight Company was a good girl; she had neatly disposed of her RAF fiancé before things got heavy and her own sexual health was not a subject to which she gave much thought. 'I once got cystitis, does that count? The officer said I had slept on a damp bed. I was sent to the Camp Reception Station until I was better.' But in the ATS she recalls an increasing emphasis on 'personal hygiene'. 'At the training camp in North-ampton we had our first lectures about venereal disease; having never been into the world, I didn't know much about it.'

By 1943 those early lectures were no longer considered sufficient. 'I operated my regiment's switchboard and one day I was told to get everybody to listen at a certain time to a special broadcast. Well, we all thought this message was to do with the war. We were desperately hoping the second push would start.' Daphne, naturally efficient, set about transmitting the message to all the individual searchlight stations. 'But there was one site I couldn't reach, the signal was down. I was very worried they wouldn't know what was going on.' Relief came in the form of an army vehicle. 'I saw it and rushed out. "Quick quick!" I said to the chap driving. "Are you going to that site? You must tell them to tune into this very important communication! Don't forget."'

That lunchtime, Daphne settled down with her colleagues to listen to the much-heralded lecture. Mortified, she closed her eyes. 'I couldn't believe my ears. It was a programme about venereal disease and I had made such a fuss.' Eighty years on her cheeks still flush pink at the memory of that 'special broadcast'.

*

Anne is forthright on the telephone. 'I think you asked me too many questions about sex. We didn't think about it that much. It wasn't a big part of our lives.' I am chastened and search my notes to identify what might have triggered this controversial line of questioning. Anne took her wartime service very seriously; to this day she vividly remembers her ATS number, W/258922, and is a leading veteran in her church's Remembrance Day parade. I don't want to cause offence.

And there it is: in Anne's detailed memoir, a seemingly innocuous sentence: during her first posting, aged just eighteen, she 'had to take my share of patrolling the local pubs (on the lookout for drunken behaviour) and of doing guard duties at night'.[3] On further questioning it transpired that Anne, unable to capitalise on her excellent selection test results due to poor eyesight, was given a rapid promotion and stayed on at Wrexham, North Wales, to train as a junior non-commissioned officer. Her first posting as lance corporal at an ATS training centre involved the disciplining and education of women often older than she was. The experience was an eye-opener and Anne admits 'one of the worst things I ever had to do' was don a red armband and police her contemporaries. 'If we were on duty, we had to go around the pubs at night, and if we saw girls cuddling with army men or RAF men, we had to separate them and the girl got charged.' The story is reminiscent of Penny's escapade in Fulford Barracks, and Anne's discomfort a reminder of a process that pitted contemporaries one against the other. 'It was awful, I always tried to get out of these police duties. No, you hardly ever had to physically separate them because they were frightened of us, even the promiscuous ones. Nobody wanted to be put on a charge.'

Despite dreaded policing duties, Anne enjoyed her time at the training centre. 'One of the things I am most grateful for was that I met a huge number of people whom I wouldn't probably have met otherwise.' Anne trained recruits of 'all shapes and sizes'. The majority were conscripts, aged nineteen,

> who'd been called up from London's East End, nearly of all them having nits in their hair and boys on their minds. For days on end I did little else but delousing, and in the process was engaged in lengthy conversations with my 'patients', receiving graphic lessons on

sexual matters – some of them quite startling (even shocking) to a well-bred vicar's daughter![4]

Anne marvelled at a sexualised language and landscape she previously had no knowledge of ('I'd barely kissed a boy'), and in turn the new recruits were surprised by her lifestyle and naivety. Retrospectively, Anne is staggered that 'we got along tremendously well. We had been completely differently brought up and our values were pretty different too, yet the friendship was there.' Today it is still possible to see the glimmer of a girl whose natural assurance allowed her to lead before her time.

'Do you know Paragraph 11? Well, the army regulations had this famous Paragraph 11, which was to deal with women getting pregnant. They were sent home immediately. Absolutely immediately.' Anne is certain about that, but less sure about the contraception available to those girls who were sexually active. 'No, they didn't use much contraception. It didn't really exist. The chap very often was asked to withdraw. Yes, it was an incredible risk. I was very aware of that terror, the terror of getting pregnant.'

*

Grace did everything with Lillian Crowe and Kathy Bot, the two other girls on her height-finder. 'Well, almost everything, until Kathy got 'erself pregnant. I don't know how it happened. I mean it couldn't have happened in the battery, there was nowhere to go. Yes, perhaps it did happen when she was on leave.' Grace still sounds surprised by the news of Kathy's unfortunate condition. 'She was a pretty girl, tall and slim, she told us she was leaving. That she'd been sacked. Well, I presume after she missed a period the medical officer checked her over and proceedings began to get her out. You couldn't have someone pregnant in the battery. Oh no.' Kathy left and Grace never heard from her again. Clarke and Crowe had lost their Bot. Grace is matter of fact. 'Those were the rules.' And they mattered: female military personnel were judged on their 'illegitimate pregnancy rate', with the Markham Committee tersely insisting that pregnancy out of wedlock was 'certainly less common in the Services than out of them'.[5]

Fear helped control behaviour. Grace still recalls the lectures on venereal disease, 'but it didn't matter much to me because I wasn't having sex'. Her Bob had to wait, there was far too much at stake; unlike Kathy, former servant Grace didn't have a home to go to. Pregnancy, the enemy from within, potentially had more sinister repercussions than anything a German plane could deliver. Heroic death was surely preferable to a life of ignominy and poverty?

FANY Joyce nods: yes, there was a 'party girl at Thame Park who got pregnant. She was a bit bonkers, she liked to be outrageous. I think because she had very well-heeled parents; her father was an admiral and she wanted to kick back, a bit like Churchill's older daughters.' Joyce remembers the girl's unlikely boyfriend ('I did feel sorry for him. He was a nice little man, a sergeant. He'd come and service the transmitters'). And she pauses. 'This girl, I think she went somewhere locally near Thame Park, it was near Oxford. She had a private abortion and then she came back to work.' Illegal and often unsafe, abortions were all private in wartime Britain. 'I'm not sure how she fitted it in around her leave.'

Joyce shakes her head. 'We were terribly innocent. It sounds awful but it was presumed because the FANYs were educated privately they would behave better.' She goes over the story again, the wild pregnant FANY with her sergeant boyfriend. 'I think she did actually marry him in the end, although I don't think it lasted. They clearly had a deep affection for each other but pregnancy out of marriage would've been unacceptable.'

23

Boys, Girls and D-Day Landings

Penny loved Tom. 'I just knew it. He was shrewd and good-looking and ambitious.' The two Londoners were careful not to make the same mistake twice. 'Oh no, we weren't caught canoodling in an ambulance again, but we did meet up whenever we could. He was posted just outside York and I'd send messages to him via a dispatch driver. We'd go to the movies, or perhaps for a drink, and I loved to dance.' They'd met on the dance floor: Tom's regiment, the Rifle Brigade, had their own band and sent for twelve girls to make up numbers one Friday night. 'I'm not being big-headed when I say I was a good dancer.' Tom was awestruck. 'He came up and said, "I can't dance well but I've been watching you and excuse me, but I want to get to know you. Would you dance with me?"' Penny smiles; she can still remember the conversation she had with her mother when next on leave.

'Are you enjoying life in the army, dear?'

'Oh yes!' replied Penny. 'I love it!'

'And have you met anyone nice?'

Penny answered cautiously; her first love, Ronald, had been a local lad and a friend of the family. 'Well, yes, I have as it happens.'

Penny's mother put an arm around her daughter's shoulder. 'That's good, dear, it means that Ronald and you weren't meant to be.'

'I realise that now, Mum. Tom and I have got a lot in common.'

But like Ronald three years earlier, Tom was about to be sent away. 'He said to me one evening, "This might be our last meeting. Just so you know, if you don't hear from me, don't worry, I'll write when I can."' Penny nodded. Obligatory discretion prohibited the sharing of knowledge but the truth was she knew better than Tom where he was going. 'I was typing notes up in the day about the troop movements.' Her voice drops to a whisper. 'I knew his battalion was going to Kent, somewhere near Dover I think it was. There was a big movement from north to south but where they were to be stationed and all that had to be confidential so the Germans didn't get wind of the second front.' Penny held on hard to her secret information; handling it helped manage the fear. She's still not sure if it was worse being the girl left behind or the boy going off to fight.

*

In May 1944 girls up and down the country were jolted into a new reality. Men, nearly two million of them, were on the move. Larking around together, the anticipation before a dance, a firm hold and the pump of adrenaline – for months soldiers and their regiments stationed across Britain had broken the monotony of service life and now they were leaving.

Maud's and Charlie's story is striking for its simplicity. Maud was another ATS recruit who'd signed up to get out of a dull job and see a bit of the world beyond Birmingham. 'Then I was posted back to Birmingham within two months. I worked at Hollymoor, the military hospital.' A large Edwardian psychiatric hospital for serving soldiers, Maud signed in new patients. 'Their main diagnosis was anxiety – chronic anxiety, nowadays it would be called stress.' She tries out a new form of words, Post Traumatic Stress Disorder, and smiles. 'The severe cases went south to a mental hospital near Southampton, they'd be wearing royal blue and sitting in the back of the truck with the nurse and were given a dose of Pentothal, it kept them drowsy for the journey.'

Maud remembers the hospital for its group sessions and even some laughter; there were plenty of japes and sick men playing 'silly buggers' in groups. By 1942 Hollymoor had become the home of the so-called first Northfield experiments, where two pioneering psychoanalysts focused on patients' improved morale through 'good group spirit'. Briefly, exercise, conversation and handcraft activities were prioritised, with the men gathering in a daily parade. Maud doesn't remember the handcrafts, 'but they put their hands around me once or twice, and would try and steal my cap, silly things like that!' A young girl 'just doing my job', she skirted around their pain. 'I wrote up their psychiatric assessments. Those that were out in Burma had seen beheadings and terrible violence, but a lot of the time I think they were just bored. War can be very boring, you know.'

Boring unless Charlie Ward was around. A seasoned soldier, he'd arrived back in England in 1943 from a long deployment in the West Indies, and Maud and her friends were amused by this new arrival, seven years their senior, in charge of Hollymoor's medical depot. 'He was full of tall stories, he tried to tell us he'd just been to Hitler's Germany to put someone's glass eye in. We weren't having any of it.' But Charlie's 'swagger' provided much-needed levity. 'There was a tailor who worked in the shop next door, he'd complain about the clatter and the language when we were having our lunch. Effing and blinding, that sort of thing. You had to be careful you didn't get put on a charge, mind you.' After work there'd be drinks at Edward's, four girls all in a row, including Maud, and Charlie, who quickly dubbed the ATS clerks 'Charlie's chicks'. He was good fun and looked good too, with tanned skin and a twinkle.

Then suddenly one day everything changed. 'I remember my friend saying, "Look, Charlie's going, he's leaving. He's joined the Commandos! Maud, don't you want to say goodbye?"' Propelled forward by a feeling in her gut, Maud admits, 'I wanted to run after him; I couldn't do my work or anything that day.' It was true, Charlie was really leaving.

> I often think, 'What if I had a louder voice?' I have dreams in which I am the opposite of what I really am. I stood outside and watched him go, they were all singing farewell. It was early summer and the wallflowers were out; if I smell wallflowers now, I go straight back to that time. I felt down, really terrible after he left.

Charlie was heading south into the unknown, a crack troop in the Commandos, and Maud hadn't managed a proper goodbye. She hadn't said what she wanted to say.

His absence left a gaping hole. The sick men weren't so funny without Charlie there. What these soldiers had been through was real, and now it was Charlie's turn; first the training in Wrexham, twenty-five miles a day with a pack on his back, and then the landings in France. Maud looks up; age has not dimmed her startling blue eyes. 'After he left, oh yes, I listened to the news; we weren't told everything but I listened.'

The fifth of June 1944 came and went; bad weather conspired against the Normandy landings that day; the coast, including the five carefully selected invasion beaches and drop zones, had to be clear. The following night delivered a perfect glassy calm. The sea was flat, the sky inky black and Churchill rose three times from his bed to visit the map room. He could not sleep, confiding to his wife: 'Do you realise by the time you wake up in the morning twenty thousand men may have been killed?' The Prime Minister was anxious, and so was Maud. Later that same day Churchill addressed the Commons. 'During the night the first series of landings upon the European Continent has taken place.'[1]

On 6 June 1944, 156,115 men scrambled ashore, sufficient numbers to secure a French toe-hold from which the Allies could begin to push back the German occupiers, and by 9.05 am that included No. 3 Commando and Maud's Charlie. Among the second wave to come ashore, the unit was tasked with linking up the 6th Airborne Division on the eastern flank of Sword Beach. Maud knows this now, but she didn't then. She didn't even know if Charlie was alive. 'I saw the newsreel with them getting out of the landing craft. I couldn't focus on work, I thought I hope to goodness he can stay up. He was only 5 foot 7. I was so worried but I knew if he can get out he will, because he's got that in him.'

Penny nods. She is still whispering. 'I heard the news, that the landings had happened, but my Tom didn't go on 6 June, he went at the end of that week.' She nods again, fervently trying to get her words across without actually saying anything. Penny's training burnt deep tracks. You did not talk. What she wants to say is that Tom went in the second push, she knew this because of the Highly Confidential memos she was writing. Yes. More nodding. 'But no, I didn't know if he was still alive. Letters took two to three weeks.'

24

Operation Diver

'We were sent down to Suffolk for the start of the invasion, to provide air cover. It was on the cards, everybody knew something was happening. For three days you couldn't move on the roads, they were absolutely jam-packed.' Behind the wheel of a Bedford bowser (mini tanker), Barbara struggled to contain her impatience; the three-mile journey between her battery's two gun-sites was a protracted affair. 'It took ages to get across the road, one convoy passed through and another one was straight behind it.' In the spring of 1944, the nation's giant shuffle of troops and artillery included AA Command; Operation Overlord needed air cover for all its embarkation posts and hundreds of new gun-sites were established across England's southern flank. Never before had anti-aircraft defence relocated so many guns,[1] and the girls went with them.

Barbara wasn't far enough south to see the convoys set off from Normandy but she quickly heard the news. 'The first of the wounded were back on British soil by noon that same day, back in a British hospital in Southampton.' She hangs over the sentence, owning the sentiment; it's almost as if she was personally involved in their retrieval. Perhaps in some small way she was; surely that was the whole point of the uniform, the national messaging, the cleverly fostered patriotism? German horror saw Britain pull together as one in the same direction, irrespective of gender, age, sometimes even race.

After basic training in Guildford, Ena, who'd been a typist in a Jamaican courtroom, was given the trade of clerk. With troop numbers and munitions escalating rapidly in the months before D-Day there was no shortage of paperwork, but this ambitious twenty-six year old had not crossed the Atlantic to sit in front of a typewriter. No, sir! Talking over Zoom more than eighty years later, it's clear Ena was an adventurous girl. 'I wanted more responsibility and more action.' Of the few arrivals from the West Indies, most recruits were happy to stay put, but not Ena. She made her feelings known and was duly sent for further ATS evaluations. 'I was tested and they said I could go into any unit.' She smiles. 'Anti-aircraft, that is what I selected. I became a radar operator.'

It's AA Command's PT specialist Beryl who recalls that gun-laying girls, those selected for work with radar, 'had to be of a high standard of intelligence and education'. Pioneering technology demanded pioneering minds. Martha, until her promotion to subaltern, had been one such girl, and now Ena was amidst their ranks. By 1943 the ATS had changed significantly from its earlier class-bound days. Well-established systems identified talent and girls were often surprised by promotion. Vera, a one-time domestic servant and farmhand, was given a stripe in 1943 and made No. 1 on the predictor. 'The officer fetched me in and I said, "No, I don't want to do it." I didn't think I was ready. You had to tell people what to do and give commands. I didn't think I could do it, I ummed and ahhhed, but you know, in the end I done it.'

Meanwhile Ena joined the elite gun-layers in their curious black cabins with giant aerials and screens. The science of radar had progressed beyond recognition and by 1944 the arrival of American super-tech started to make a real difference. It's possible that Ena was operating a SCR 584 radar, which when married to a BTL Predictor offered fully automated tracking and aiming. Once the target had been locked on, technology could do the rest.[2]

*

Martha's battery was relocated to Poole, near Bournemouth, where they were poised to provide essential cover for a German response to the Normandy landings.

> I was a plotting officer by then, the projected flight of the enemy aircraft was plotted on a large table with a floating light underneath; it showed you the information coming from the radar that was fed into the predictor, so you could calculate the aircraft as it went from A to B.

She pauses. 'It's hard to explain, it was all linked up, it became more and more automatic.' Grace too had moved, from Wales down to Lizard Point, England's most southern tip. 'The guns were up on the cliffs, we'd shoot out to sea.' No longer on the height-finder, Grace was also in the plotting room. 'That's right, dear, I didn't have to wear my greatcoat at night, I was inside.' Equipped with earphones, a mouthpiece and a marker pen, Grace and a colleague stood around the glass-topped table covering a map. 'As the planes flew into our area we traced them. Radar sent images onto the table and we put a cross on every few seconds.' They were overseen by an officer,

Martha's equivalent, only in this instance a man. 'He would ring the next site once the aircraft had left your radius.' Poised and ready for action, every girl knew her bit of kit inside out, cogs in a giant wheel that put a 'roof over Britain' and right across the white-crested waters of England's south coast.

'It could be cold, mind, 'cos we were under canvas. There were four of us in a tent. I still remember my regulation blanket and boy, did we needed it.' If the latest technology was finally up and running, accommodation for thousands of girls on England's shoreline was less easy to find. In Suffolk, Barbara recalls 'very very primitive conditions. There was no running water and no flushing toilet, and we were in tents for four months. I didn't enjoy it.' Martha meanwhile was in 'an incomplete block of flats with no glass in the windows'. When girls were first conscripted into the ATS, assurances had been given about accommodation providing 'a higher level of comfort' for women; tents were prohibited, with the Markham Committee primly observing ATS girls 'are the wives and mothers of the future . . . no one desires to apply a wholesale hardening process to the young women who are serving their country effectively and well'. The Committee avoided the other reason for outlawing tents: those 'prowling, sex-starved men'.[3] That both these concerns were overridden to howls of derision from politicians and press alike is indicative of the pressure that AA Command was under in 1944, when the provision of air defence for the D-Day landings was complicated by a second, terrifying threat.

I remember the first time I saw one, it came over our field in Suffolk, making a funny noise like the putt-putt of a motorbike with flames coming out of it. It went on its merry way and that was that. I didn't think anything more about it until the next day; the major called a muster parade of the entire battery and said: 'Whatever you saw yesterday, you do not discuss with each other or with anybody. Understood?'

Barbara and her friends resorted to whispering. They'd just seen their first ever V-1 rocket. 'I presume it was meant for London and had gone off course.' Many of the early tranches of flying bombs didn't hit their targets; the very first exploded into furrowed farmland near Dartford a week after the D-Day landings. Barbara's sighting was in the early summer, when chiefs of staff were frantically hoping that it would amount to nothing more than 'experimental activity', but in fact they'd long known that the V-weapon threat was potentially devastating. Information on Germany's lethal programme began arriving in 1943 and identified two terrifying new devices that dominated the last eleven months of Britain's domestic war, a flying bomb and a long range rocket: the V-1 and V-2.[4] By March 1944 AA Command committed itself to a double mission: the Overlord/Diver Concurrent Plan required unprecedented air cover both along the south coast (Overlord) and on the south-eastern approaches to London (Diver), where V-1 flying bombs were anticipated. The Germans' desperate response to an Allied assault could not be allowed to disrupt D-Day planning.[5] If that meant girls in tents, so be it.

With launch pads in northern France deliberately targeting London and Kent, Grace never saw a 'doodlebug. That's what we called them. No dear, they didn't bother us.' On the Cornish coast, her battery had been tasked with providing cover for the flotilla of vessels sailing east to join the invasion of France. 'I watched them leave from high up on the cliff. No, I didn't know what they were for. We were in our own bubble.' Grace had a bird's-eye view, one that was remarkably undisturbed by German bombers. An extensive deception operation, code-named Operation Fortitude, led the Germans to believe that Overlord was not the real invasion, and their stretched air force failed to retaliate against the mass departure of troops and munitions from British shores. 'Never had AA Command moved so many guns . . . to so little purpose.'[6] Within weeks girls and guns were relocated once more to address the latest threat, V-1 flying bombs, with London and Bristol initially identified as prime targets. Grace was redeployed between Gloucester and Cheltenham and Martha's battery moved east to Southminster in Essex, 'diver belt' territory.

Doodlebugs 'were a miracle target'. Martha explains that, unlike planes, these pilotless aircraft 'flew at a constant speed and a constant height. All you needed was their bearing and elevation in order to hit them.' But early on extenuating factors got in the way of this fight against a brand-new enemy. She tuts. It still bothers her that under her watch as plotting officer one got away. Things are less clear now, who was doing what and how exactly it happened are hard to piece together, but the sentiment remains: disappointment. 'So when the fuse you have to set is ready, you say, "STAND BY, FIRE!" But you don't have very long, you've got to be very quick.' She taps her fingers together. Once the V-1 had been identified by the radar, the quartermaster, a man who was her senior, gave the wrong order, Martha's sure of this:

> I should have cleared his order but in those few seconds it was impossible to shoot it down, it was coming and coming and coming, we could see it, we were tracking it, but it was too low and the shrapnel coming down from our own shells would have hit the village.

Martha is still wrestling with her decision not to issue the command to fire. 'The flying bomb flew on to London,' she says, 'no longer in radar contact.' She sighs. Her commitment to the task was so all-encompassing that even today, aged ninety-nine, the repercussions of that split-second decision remain with her, no matter that her wartime track record was unimpeachable.

Martha's story is symptomatic of the teething problems associated with fighting a new enemy. If a flying bomb – an early cruise missile – made contact with its target, it wreaked havoc, and of those first V-1s, 1,270 reached London. Bletchley Park's ATS girl Betty was stunned when colleague Mark Glover discovered his wife and son had been wiped out by one. 'I shall never forget the look on that man's face. He came back on duty and said, "All I found was my boy's tie."'[7] Anti-aircraft defence had to quickly adapt to this new robotic threat and by August a decision to focus on the coastline afforded them the freedom of firing over water. By the end of that month AA Command was shooting down 74 per cent of all V-1s entering the diver belt. A perfect storm of events saw Pile's guns and searchlights enjoy their finest hour: 'The newspapers, the newsreels, and the letters that poured into us were full of praise.'[8] Once more Mary Churchill's gun-site stole the show when her father visited them in Kent to watch doodlebugs being knocked out of the sky.[9] There was cause to celebrate; by the autumn of 1944 the gunner's hit rate had reached 82 per cent of all V-1s coming into range, at a time when AA Command employed more women than men.[10]

*

But if Operation Diver was the gunners' 'hero' moment, in 1944 hero was still an exclusively male concept. By the end of August more than two million Allied men had landed in Northern France, of whom 226,386 were wounded or killed. Despite the odd news story about downing doodlebugs, hearts and minds were focused else-where. Martha has no extant letters from the latter half of that year. 'I think it's because the family were so shocked when my brother was injured, they probably didn't get around to keeping them.' Andrew, Martha's younger brother and the eldest son of Edward Bruce, 10th Earl of Elgin, was just nineteen when he was commissioned as second lieutenant in the 3rd Armoured Scots Guards. His war began and ended in Normandy. 'They were all trained in Yorkshire and then he was sent to France just after the landings.'

Martha is unsure about divulging her brother's story – 'he tells it much better than me' – but she's prepared to share the facts. It was during Operation Bluecoat, the Allies' breakout from Normandy in August 1944, that Andrew's tank was hit. Badly injured in the blast and minus his identity disc, the young officer was put on trans-port back to Britain. 'I don't know how he got across the

Channel, but they thought he was a lower rank, that he was telling a story, pretending he was an officer and the son of Lord Elgin.' In the army rank matters: unidentified Andrew was sent to Park Prewett, a mental hospital in Basingstoke. 'All the doctors and nurses thought he was delirious until one day he recognised the voice of 'Auntie Maudie', the Duchess of Wellington, who was being shown around her local hospital.' A family friend, she confirmed Andrew's identity and officer status and informed the Earl and Countess of Elgin that their eldest son was alive.

It was then that Martha received a call from her mother in Scotland. 'She gave me the address of his hospital. I was still on the south coast so I went to visit him.' Martha recalls finding her little brother in bed: 'His hair had grown, he looked much younger than his nineteen years.' Andrew was so badly injured that according to his sister Jean 'he probably should have had his leg removed'. He was eventually sent to the Princess Margaret Rose Orthopaedic Hospital in Edinburgh, where he spent another two years. Martha concedes 'his leg has bothered him his whole life' but she won't give in to sentiment. The question of what she felt sitting at the bedside of her injured younger brother is deflected:

We were surrounded with people who were wounded. A lot of his friends were wounded as well. It became a sort of normality. Part of the war, yes. Nowadays we have become very afraid of risk, but I suppose then you faced up to what could happen. I had known other people who were killed.

The details of the visit are obfuscated in a story about how Martha got stuck in her brother's padded cell in the hospital ('there was nowhere to put officers'), which led to her late return to the gun-site. Not acceptable – doodlebugs did not wait for absent gunners. But if a big-sister, stiff-upper-lip approach helped get Martha (and her brother) through those difficult initial days, that Andrew's lifelong injury had an impact on the family's narrative is in no doubt. Later to become the 11th Earl of Elgin, a Scottish peer and the Chief of the Clan Bruce, Andrew has led a revered life in his native Scotland, and to those who knew him as a young man, he's still a brave soldier who rarely complained about his war wound. In 2019, at the centennial celebrations for the Women's Royal Army Corps, Martha (the recipient of an OBE for services to Scotland's Territorial Army) was reacquainted with Her Majesty the Queen. A photograph of the two nonagenarians captures the moment in the grounds of Holyrood Palace. But the conversation between the two women did not concern their own years of service, nor shared childhood experiences, instead 'the Queen asked after my brother'. Andrew was the hero of the piece when he was injured, and nearly eighty years on, he still is.

PART THREE

FOREIGN WAR

25

Service Overseas

Maud wasn't prepared for the intensity of feeling that followed Charlie's departure. 'I was supposed to retake a shorthand test in London, it would have led to a promotion. I said I didn't want to go. I couldn't face it with the doodlebugs and that. I just couldn't face anything.' But she found enough energy to write to Charlie, first at his Commando training camp in Wrexham and then via the army post office in France. In July his response finally arrived.

France, July 1944

Hello, my dear,

By golly, I thought you had forgotten all about me and I was cursing the fickleness of all chickens when your letter arrived to shame me . . . I suppose you've heard in the papers what a nice time we are having . . . yes, you are right [Hollymoor] seems a different world right now, I suppose I was there, I must have been, for do I not receive letters from you?

You mention dancing, I know I'm bad but why bring that up at a time like this! I haven't seen my feet for days – I must look at them tonight. Well, Maud, I would give a lot to take you to the Hare & Hounds, don't get too browned off, you know, with all that work, I'm afraid you may get too tired to write me, and then think what would happen to the morale of the Commandos. When you go to bed tonight, just think of me. It must be lovely to have a bed, I will sleep for a week when I get back. Well, chick, keep a place for me in Hollymoor, ps, I mean as a patient.

Maud still has his letters bundled neatly into a keep-sake box, proof of Charlie's increased devotion to his girl back in Birmingham. No. 3 Commando had made it ashore on D-Day with relatively few losses, but what came next, the spearheading of a ground offensive against the onslaught of enemy fire, makes for difficult reading.[1] Boys on both sides were pitted against each other in a battle for their lives: snipers, grenades, attack and counter-attack, death and dirt. Charlie lived what Hollywood has spent the last seventy years recrafting into epic blockbusters,[2] but the reality was difficult to endure and came with no guaranteed happy ending. Charlie's refuge was dreaming of and writing to Maud.

I was thinking about you last night when I was on duty – a beautiful night, the moon smoothed out all the harsh angles of the farmhouse, gave them mysterious shadows and curves, filled the fields and the hedges with moon witchery. Not a cloud in the sky and the stars hung there like diamond drops, reminding me of the night I first saw the Southern Cross. Now and then a flare from a Jerry would shoot up into the sky and hang there quivering for a moment before dropping gracefully down to vanish behind the trees that stood against the skyline, black sentinels of a new world. You talk about your romantic moods, what of me thinking about you – I know that I had an intense longing to see you. Goodnight, your Charles.

Maud was Charlie's feminine idyll, and he her brave soldier. Across a war zone, between two countries, they fell in love. 'In one letter he mentioned my long eyelashes and I realised then that he must've paid attention!' By August No. 3 Commando had forced the Germans to withdraw, catching up with a rearguard and smashing ahead through local villages, but Charlie studiously avoids danger and death in his letters, they remain a safe, private space. If two months into the campaign his platoon were still just miles from the English Channel, at least momentum was on their side. But it wasn't military progress that informed Charlie's mood.

It made me happy to receive your letter this evening and the photo, golly, it's been the best day since I had your first letter at Wrexham, and believe me that was an exciting moment in my young life. And I'm not kidding. I sat and looked at you for quite a while and still I can't believe it. I keep taking you out to reassure myself you're there. Yes, it's you, and you're just as lovely as the picture I've been carrying around in my mind. For you know that you have been with me ever since that last moment outside the guardroom when we said goodbye. (I know it sounds trite but damn you, it's true.) How glad I was when you came along, I had been longing to see you all morning but had been afraid of making a pest of myself.

Finally, the Battle for France was over and after eighty-three days of continuous action the surviving troops from No. 3 Commando, including Charlie, were sent back to Britain on leave. 'I saw his green beret first, coming up towards Edward's Club. We met and walked together.' Shy suddenly after so much time and so many thoughts shared from a safe distance, in September 1944 Maud and

Charlie were at last reunited in Birmingham, a handsome couple in khaki, walking hand in hand. 'Over the bridge, on towards New Street Station. And there was a theatre showing *When We Are Married* by J. B. Priestley and Charlie said, "Oh, *When We Are Married*! What an idea, we'll do that."' And they kissed, 'a proper kiss it was, not just a peck. Charlie was so thrilled with that kiss he walked me all the way back to where I was stationed at Hollymoor.' Their future was sealed. Charlie just had to stay alive and they'd be married by Christmas.

Maud's and Charlie's is a beautiful story. He did survive and they were married on 23 December 1944.

All the other ATS girls were surprised when they saw it on Part One Order, that's a big notice board where they saw 'Private Florence Maud Chadwick 167954 has changed her name from Chadwick to Ward'. 'My God,' they all said, 'she's gone and married Charlie,' they couldn't believe it. Yes, I suppose he was a catch, he was older and good-looking.

Penny also married her Tom, another survivor of the Battle for Normandy, although they waited until 1947. 'We weren't demobbed till 1946 and he had to get it past his mother!' Like so many wartime love stories, Maud's and Penny's follow a distinctive, compelling pattern: the woman serving on the home front and the man, risking his life abroad, maintained by thoughts of his girl in a familiar setting. In both cases there was a happy ending. Maud details the build up to her wedding: the registrar's office, her brother demanding a church betrothal, her mother popping in daily to Lewis's department store to find sufficient meat, and the colourful chairs procured from a neighbour's house for guests. 'It was lovely, really. God's been good to me. I ought to try and put something back but I think I've left it too late.' She grins. Maud's time in the ATS was affirming, straightforward and by her own admission unadventurous. 'I could have applied to go abroad but I didn't. I should have, really.' But if Maud had gone overseas, what would Charlie have longed for? Who would he have returned home to? The defined gender spheres which saw most ATS women serve in supporting roles at home was a formula that suited the status quo and the hero-men fighting overseas, but by 1944 it was no longer sustainable.

*

In late 1944 Mary Churchill observed in her diary: *'Finally General Tremlett told the assembled ATS of 137 (Regiment) that we have been chosen for service in North West Europe. Wild excitement and enthusiasm. And lots of work preparing.'*[3] Girls were needed to support over two million men pushing across the Continent, including anti-aircraft defence and a large administrative staff. The ATS were ideally placed to fulfil this role but despite unprecedented female service, entrenched mindsets hadn't changed; there was a predictable outcry against the idea of sending girls overseas, with Mary Churchill once more the poster girl for recruitment efforts.

In a private letter, her father acknowledged a division between the girls whose response to the prospect of going abroad was *'not 'alf!'*, and the *'troubles'* many of them had convincing their *'papas and mamas'*.[4] Until the end of 1944 only those girls who volunteered could serve overseas, and they needed a written letter of permission from parents or a husband. These were rarely forthcoming. Maud concedes that the main brake on an application overseas was not her blossoming correspondence with Charlie but concerns about her ageing parents. Meanwhile Daphne, whose days as a searchlight teleplotter were numbered after D-Day, also shakes her head.

> The battery I was with was split up. I put my name down to retrain in Edinburgh and I passed all the tests and became a teleprinter operator for the 21st Army group, that's right, Monty's group. They were eventually sent to Egypt but Mother wouldn't let me go. Absolutely not. I stayed in Didcot, working on inventories. No, I never went abroad, not until much later, after the war.

Perhaps inevitably, the FANY was an exception. Class was one of the few distinctions that could trump gender, and their elite status saw them serve abroad throughout the war. In January 1944, six months before the mass recruitment of ATS girls overseas, code and cipher FANY Jean was given the option of going abroad, 'but I had a terrible time persuading Mummy'. Tanned and relaxed on her sister's sofa, she's amused at the memory of her former self: stubborn, entitled and determined to get her own way. 'I've always loved the idea of adventure and sun! But, you see, I needed written permission and Mummy was having a terrible time because Daddy was a prisoner of war in the Far East. She told me, "We don't know when we're going to see him again so no, Jean, you can't go abroad."' Jean was undeterred. 'I asked Grandboffin [Grandfather] to help. He had been around the world twice when he was a young man and knew exactly how an eighteen year old felt about a chance to travel. He backed me up.' Jean's persistence eventually won out, and in early January 1944 Mrs Owtram sent a letter of permission to FANY headquarters.

Prior to departure, Jean was armed with a new rank ('*I am an officer now with a pip (red) on each shoulder. I'm an ENSIGN (= 2nd Lieut). Coo!*' she gloated to younger brother Bob.)[5] By 1943 the FANYs resorted to early promotion for their overseas recruits. Standards had to be maintained and among the lightweight khakis that were issued came the instruction to bring an evening dress; 'Officer' Jean had to borrow her mother's.

'*I hate leaving you darling but it does seem rather a pity to miss seeing all the things I shall see, and doing all the things I shall do.*'[6] Jean's mounting anticipation is palpable and more reminiscent of a girl on a gap year than one going off to war. Her mood underscores the drab realities of life on the home front, so often contrasted with heroics overseas. Jean couldn't believe her luck; 'with her heart in her mouth' she travelled on a troop train to Liverpool, 'drank the worst cup of tea of my life' and boarded a requisitioned cruise liner, the MV *Stirling Castle*. On board there was an entertainment (ENSA) troupe and at sea a prowling U-boat that preoccupied the ship's destroyers. Jean was enthralled. Shedding their convoy as they slipped into the Mediterranean, the teenager marvelled first at Europe's dark bulk save a single light on the rock of Gibraltar, and then, to the south, a glittering North African coast with Tangier 'all lit up like a Christmas tree'.[7] FANY Jean was heading for Egypt.

*

'No, never.' Anne is very clear: she has never felt frustrated by her gender. Prior to the Normandy landings she'd been sent north to Inverness, where, like Penny's, work was top secret, 'typing up reports on the military manoeuvres taking place throughout the Highlands'. She 'never realised for a moment that the hush-hush military exercises going on were, in reality, preparations' for D-Day. By May that year, with Operation Overlord pending, priorities changed and ATS girls were invited to apply for overseas service. Along with several colleagues, Anne put her name down, but few made the final cut. 'Their parents stopped them. They wanted their daughters to be at home; safety was the main reason.' Anne, who had grown up in Burma, was an exception. 'I had to have parental consent, and to their eternal credit this was given without delay or hesitation.' She subsequently recounts how the nearest she came to being killed was a V-1 rocket attack in London. 'In June we'd congregated in the undercroft of an East End church for training prior to departure and it blew out all the building's windows.' Anne had just filled out the will form in her Army Book, lest she should 'come to a sticky end' on her first posting overseas.[8]

There were 200 'trade-tested and experienced ATS shorthand typists' selected to sail on the SS *Queen of Bermuda* in June 1944, a vessel where men vastly outnumbered women. Parental consent and clerical skills were not the only criteria required. Anne recalls, 'We had to go through a sort of health check, which included finding out about your views on relationships with men. Because they didn't want to send out people who are going to find men and male advances very difficult to cope with.' The girls were warned 'that working with the military abroad, the female sex would be very much in the minority'. Anne is certain most men, 'particularly the soldiery', were respectful. She emphasises this point several times but concedes that as she boarded the ship, 'I remember a couple of smirking soldiers . . . saying to each other, "It's no use looking at them, they only sleep with officers."'[9] Her experience provides context for the debate that preoccupied the government: the Allies needed girls to back up the army on the Continent, but they had to carry public opinion with them. 'Papas and mamas' were worried about more than enemy fire. Jean, en route to Egypt, was physically separated from the men on her ship; the entry into the Mediterranean via the Straits of Gibraltar was a rare occasion when the FANYs were allowed on deck with the troops. Meanwhile, Anne recalls a boat on the *Queen of Bermuda* where 'some of the more promiscuous girls were shut up if they had been found cuddling' servicemen. Once more the onus was on girls to behave and even to manage male expectations.

Like Jean, Anne keenly remembers halcyon days spent travelling to an (initially) unknown destination: the cabins and salons in a one-time passenger liner, and the camaraderie shared between 200 ATS girls and a 'large number of Lovat Scouts'. It feels unfair that the political focus was on untoward relations with the opposite sex when Anne, who 'played endless games of cards with the boys below deck' recalls many innocent friendships made during the two-week journey. She knew how to handle herself and loved the common experience of a voyage which they worked out was destined for Italy. The Lovat Scouts 'had been trained in ski warfare in the Rockies. We knew that Rome had just been liberated by the Allies and guessed that fighting would now be going on in the mountains further north.'[10]

But as in so many war stories, there is contradiction at the heart of Anne's tale. On the one hand her overseas war has an enviable sheen: buoyed up by exciting new friends, arriving in the 'beautiful bay of Naples', ferried to Caserta Palace, a behemoth of royal splendour built to rival Versailles, and working in rooms where 'golden cherubs cavorted among beautiful naked ladies on the richly decorated ceiling'. She was finally out of grey Britain, breathing sun-baked Continental air, bathing in Caserta's magnificent fountains, enjoying opera in her free time and operating from the heart of Allied headquarters with French, American and British troops. But the experience was not straightforward. Anne's arrival as a clerk in a legal department resulted in the removal of the 'existing male personnel, who were duly dispatched to the front to fight, and I remember feeling a bit upset about this'. Non-combat ATS girls settled down to work for 'Sergeant Major Batchelor. He is a bachelor and he hates women.'[11] But on the whole, Anne quickly discovered, women had it easy in a brutal war.

Prior to the launch of a second front through France, Churchill had keenly promoted a diversion through Italy as Europe's 'soft underbelly'. In July 1943, regiments were transferred from North Africa to Sicily, where the Italian campaign began. Italy capitulated in September, but their own civil war muddied a grim battle as the Allies tried to dig out the Germans. American General Mark Clark rebranded Churchill's 'soft underbelly' 'one tough gut' and headlines skirted around a bloody reality that cost nearly a million lives.[12] Before she left Britain, Anne heard the good news that 'the Allies had liberated Rome'. But in Italy the picture was very different. There was appalling poverty, desperately hungry children and, at the army head-quarters, inadequate hygiene. An outbreak of hepatitis saw Anne 'turn bright yellow', and recuperation with a slew of other very sick ATS girls ('several nearly died') involved a camp infested with rats.[13]

Italy was scorched from bottom to top. Shortly after Anne's arrival, she visited the same Lovat Scouts she'd travelled out with. 'It was really dreadful, as we found so many of them in pain, some with missing limbs, blinded or unable to hear.' Anne shifts in her seat; the visit to their military hospital was deeply shocking and remains with her today. 'I was absolutely horrified. Some were blind, some had lost their minds.' Just a few weeks earlier these soldiers, her friends, were young healthy men, now they were torn up and punctured like rag dolls. It was only then, Anne concedes, in the relentless Italian heat, that she fully understood the meaning of war.

Even on foreign soil, where ATS girls operated near the front line, dealing with casualty figures and court mar-tials, this was still a man's war. Women were servicing a conflict that belonged to the opposite sex. The girls' pres-ence was essential and therefore tolerated, but there were complications. Anne (reluctantly) returns to the subject of male–female relations. 'All over the place there were far more men than women. The men were pretty desperate for female friendship, quite apart from wanting sex.' Her recollections again resonate with high-level exchanges back in Britain. Earlier in 1944, the Secretary of State tried to argue that 'it is desirable to have as many British women as possible overseas', as the policy of non-fraternisation

between soldiers and civilians planned for German occupation was only going to be possible with the presence of
'British and Allied women'. However, these projections
were offset by fears that unsupervised girls overseas would
act 'immorally'.[14]

It was up to Anne to 'morally' assert herself against
male advances. 'After a dance or so forth, you'd be taken
home in a lorry and it was specially arranged so the girls
had to sit on the men's laps, there'd deliberately not be
enough room and men would love to explore your body so
you had to be very definite. I'd said, "I'm not having that."'
To which the response was often a wheedling 'please, I
haven't seen a woman for ages. Please.' Many of the men
in Italy had been fighting in North Africa; they hadn't
been home for months, sometimes even years. But Anne
did not relent; already a lance corporal with an officer
promotion pending, she knew her own mind. And she still
does, aged ninety-six. Against today's noisy world crowded
with feminist jargon and politicised gender relations, she
reiterates her concern about overstating wartime 'issues'
between men and women. 'I loved my time in the army.'
And she is protective of it and them – the soldiers she
fought with – in an era when men were expected to dodge
advancing bullets and women advancing men.

*

FANY Jean was initially stationed just outside Cairo, the
honeypot of the Middle East, armed with an evening
dress and plenty of pocket money to supplement her
modest pay. 'Darlingist mummy' was promptly informed of
her daughter's escapades: visiting pyramids in moonlight,
attending Anglican communion in the local cathedral and

feeling '*awfully lucky only meeting nice people and I am beginning to feel more sure of myself*'. The same teenage girl, with
officer status, was also shift leader in an office overlooking
the banks of the Nile.

Receiving messages from agents in mainland Greece
and Crete, Jean couldn't divulge her work in letters home.
Nearly eighty years on, she thinks she was communicating with underground agents tracking Greek communists
hoping to seize power from the exiled monarchy. By the
end of 1944 a revolt would break out in Athens, with
Churchill determined to succeed in Greece where he had
failed Poland, but Jean shakes her head. Much of what she
was relaying back to London was meaningless without a
wider context, and girls were rarely privy to context, but
she does repeat several times, 'It's extraordinary I was
given that much responsibility so young. Extraordinary.'

Good at what she did, Jean was transferred to Southern Italy by March 1944, which replaced Cairo as the
more proximate coordination point for Balkan resistance.
Like Anne, Jean was charmed by Italy; she found the
locals in Puglia friendly, loved the spontaneous operas and
was mesmerized by Italian wild flowers which were

> *just paradise. I spent my leisure hours . . . in an atmosphere
> of honey and buttercups and sun . . . I counted 14 different
> kinds of flowers up there yesterday. Cyclamens, crocii (yellow
> and mauve and tiny little ones), dog daisies, real daisies,
> buttercups, baby narcissae with a heavenly smell, dandelion-
> things and various little ones I don't know.*

But there's an unsettling quality to the many letters
Jean sent her older sister Pat, a Wren stationed back in
England. Here was a girl just out of school fending for

herself in a complex adult world. The traffic sent to Jean's office focused on supporting Josip Broz Tito's partisans in Yugoslavia (regarded by the Allies as the most effective anti-Axis resistance movement, no matter that they were communists). Early on Jean was promoted to team leader, which '*as I've only just joined this shift and am the youngest, is a bit of a strain, like being a prefect*'. She longs to tell her sister about the work ('*one can say so little in a letter*') and instead marvels over the few partisans she meets. '*A partisan officer saluted me once and it's what I always wanted to do to them, it was a little overwhelming . . . I do think these underground people are the most terrific thing ever.*' Jean's awe is a reminder of her tender years and her lonely war playing with codenames on a typewriter, a process that reduced the details of a country to machine guns and ammunition, medical supplies and food drops, where an agent was a person who might be killed at any moment. 'There were casualties and they had to be brought out in a hurry. It was often very tense. One dreaded hearing the worst.'

On the ground in Italy, as a girl Jean's job wasn't confined to codes and ciphers.

> *The other day the town major came round to the mess and asked for volunteers to search Italian women for things they were supposed to be stealing, so as there was no one else in Jean and I said OK and we had to make these . . . women undress completely in case they had hidden things in their clothes . . . it was so sordid and dreary I felt literally sick.*

In her free time she smoked and drank. '*2/6 for a bottle of Carlo Bianco and one has cognac and vermouth locally produced . . . I love whisky, there is a bottle in my wardrobe now.*'

Her missives to Pat are peppered with tremendous

highs: '*I'm on an up-wave at present*,' Jean admitted after a thirty hour party when '*we sang and talked . . . and no one got really sentimental or annoyingly inebriated*'. And there were crashing lows: '*Do you ever find for no reason at all you get pathetically depressed and everything is just grey and dreary and not even black?*' She cheered good news and watched the line on the unit's board edge slowly up the map of Italy, but she no longer believed her father, a Japanese prisoner of war, would return alive, and she hung out with boys in grave danger. British airman Wally went to a concert with her and two days later he was dead. '*His plane crashed and the crew were killed. He was so young and so sweet . . . it does turn one's insides over a bit when friends get killed like that, doesn't it?*'

There's a picture of Jean in a crumpled khaki shirt with wavy dark hair and strong, unapologetic features; she looks tired and much older than her eighteen years. Managing her own emotions and those of the men around her was draining. When she had downtime, Jean often went to dances, but '*the trouble with people here is they think they are entitled to kiss you after one dance and I don't agree. It comes of being out of England too long. People just out are quite different and so much nicer.*' She was surrounded by damaged men. Major Eric Galworthy was a constant presence; over twenty years her senior, he taught her to drive and dance, but the relationship was not straightforward. Jean discovered '*he has got a wife only they've separated . . . he was blown up just after El Alamein and was blind for three weeks and lost all his teeth and is still deaf in one ear*'. Initially she was sure they were just friends but later confessed to Pat: '*I'm getting molto tired of always going out with him . . . I think he's getting a wee bit too interested . . . But just how does one choke people off without injuring their feelings? Oh dear.*' Like Anne, Jean fended for herself and in doing so fulfilled the Establishment's presumption that FANYs were the sort of girls who could be trusted overseas. As she wearily explained to her sister, '*Everyone's morals just go by the board here if they are not careful. There is too much chance to do as you choose,*' before concluding, '*Public opinion and convention aren't such a bad idea really.*'

26

Conscription Overseas

Born and brought up in the small town of Soham, Joan couldn't wait to spread her wings. She'd been stationed for most of the war in nearby Cambridge, working for the Army Kinema Service, and brief training stints in Northampton (*'oh dear, it is so dull. The side streets are all red brick houses, doors opening straight on to the pavement'*) and Durham (*'the whole place is terribly dirty and squalid and half the shops seem to be closed down'*) were reminders of an England locked in war-mode. Joan was ready for adventure and, an accomplished clerk already promoted to corporal, ideal material for the British Liberation Army.

But like so many others, Joan's 'Ma and Pa' weren't keen on the prospect of their only daughter going abroad. By December 1944 just one in thirty girls had received parental permission to serve overseas, and they included Ena: with no extant parents to consult the twenty-six-year-old Jamaican was part of a 4,000-strong team of ATS volunteers sent into liberated north-west Europe. It wasn't enough. That winter was particularly dismal and the war dragged on: continental anti-aircraft sites and an army of two million men desperately needed more girl power.[1] It was not a demand the exhausted British public welcomed and by early 1945 the government once more resorted to conscription. Indignant parents lambasted MPs; in the words of one politician, they 'did not visualise their daughters being compulsorily sent overseas'.[2] 'Perhaps not,' chuckles Joan, 'but by that time I was twenty-five and could do what I liked!' Once again the law was on her side; overseas conscription (excluding married women and those aged nineteen or under) was introduced in February 1945. Allied tanks had rolled into Belgium, Holland and Luxembourg and de Gaulle was back in Paris, the new prime minister in a recently liberated France, but for many British girls this was just the beginning.

In March 1945, after '*parading and marching with full equipment – it weighs half a ton*', '*a sleepless night rocking about on the North Sea*' and an '*unspeakably awful train journey through war-ravaged countryside*,' Joan finally arrived in Prinz Albert Barracks, Brussels. In the death throes of the European conflict her wish to experience a different sort of war had come true, and proof of its impact lie in the seventy letters this dutiful daughter wrote home to her parents over the subsequent eighteen months. '*Yesterday we came here by road through dull uninteresting countryside, all the same, like in many ways Soham Fen! Much of the land is uncultivated and desolate.*' Joan had arrived in recently liberated Belgium, a country vulnerable and unsure after years of occupation.

The local populace . . . are getting used to seeing us here too, they speak to us in the streets, lift their hats and smile. But they do stare! Just as if they've never seen English girls in uniform before. Many a time I have had to slip into a shop doorway to check if I've lost my elastic or if my skirt is tucked up behind. They tell us quite a lot but still seem scared to give a lot of

information away; four years of not being able to speak their
minds freely have left their mark.

Anne and Jean were in Italy, a bloodied schizophrenic
land riddled with partisans and injured soldiers. Belgium
hadn't been exposed to frontline action in the same way,
but a four-year German occupation had left society dis-
torted and compromised. Once Joan acclimatised to wide
cobbled streets, the service club (marbled stairs and palm
trees) and her new job in the 'Legal Aid Office' (a *'great
disappointment'*), her letters hint at a growing awareness of
the cost of war in one of the many countries the Nazis
had controlled. Yvonne and Henriette, Belgian translators working in Joan's office, became firm friends; they
procured dinner dates for the English girl and opened
her eyes to their painful war. *'They weren't allowed any entertainment, no dances, no films except propaganda ones and food and
fuel were very short indeed. They took the men away to Germany.'*
Joan visited Henriette's tiny cramped flat, where she lived
with two small children and a husband who'd hidden in
the countryside for years to avoid German call-up. Their
friend's father had died in hiding, and his wife was taken
away. No, Henriette didn't know where to. There'd been
no word for years. Others were imprisoned and shot for
killing a German; one woman believed her four children
had escaped to England only to discover a tip-off had led
to their death before departure. *'Henriette is still most tearful
when talking about these incidents . . . she knew the people well.'*

Joan listened and learnt. She was polite and helpful and liked her hosts, they fed her delicious food and
finally they were all on the same side. But Belgium's war
underscored differences that perhaps no British soldier

could ever really understand.[3] The country's administrative system had quickly become a pliant tool in German hands, and the emergence of significant pro-fascist organisations left many unsure in which direction to turn. The Germans depended on collaboration, but the stakes were high. Joan '*saw an unveiling of a plaque on a wall where two patriots shot a Belgian collaborator*'.

In a small country where over half a million Belgians were taken to Germany as prisoners and conscripted labourers, the end of occupation and the Allies' arrival brought untold joy. There was

> *a parade of returned Belgian army prisoners complete with band. They get so hysterical on such occasions . . . one day a short parade of about three bands went along past the office and quite an hour before it was due the streets were so thick with people that the police had to clear the way for trams to pass.*

She marvels at Belgian emotion, admitting '*it's all very enlightening*'. But it was not her victory. War in Britain, a country never occupied or morally compromised in the same way, meant something very different. Joan admits to her parents: '*When all these things happen and everybody is wagging flags and bursting into tears and getting thoroughly het up, all the men in the office and Mary and I get all the more stolid and just look on with a solemn face, which must be annoying!*'

Joan was British, she waited eagerly for the continental edition of the *Daily Mail*, and even today, a wise, gentle woman of one hundred, she is unrepentant about the Germans. 'We hated them,' she hisses, 'in their awful grey uniforms.' Truckloads of German prisoners, many of whom would not see their prostate homeland for several more years, elicited no sympathy. Joan noted '*the reaction from the [local] population was frightening*'. In that moment, hatred was universal, but during the war, while Belgians had learnt to doubt each other and lie, Britain had enjoyed a high noon of patriotic fervour, men and women in the same uniform whistling the same tune. Perhaps these two very different national experiences explain why one country would later become synonymous with a collaborative European project and the other a persistent exceptionalism. But Joan, ever the soldier, will not be drawn. 'Let matters rest,' is her diplomatic reply.

*

In the spring of 1945, still working in Belgium, Joan was impatient for the end.

27 April 45
Isn't the news exciting? I wonder where Hitler is? But we feel the war should have ended properly by now, waiting each day for something spectacular to happen.

3 May 45
When IS this war going to end? Any minute now, we've said for the past three weeks, and it still hasn't come to a head.

In Italy, Jean was tired.

11 April 45
Isn't the news exhausting? I could sit down and howl with relief. I can hardly remember 'no war' but I suppose it is possible.

Anne, on an officer's training course in Palestine, was ecstatic.

23 April 1945

Today, St George's Day . . .

. . . the whole garrison town had a holiday and we watched horse jumping and shot at Hitlers and ate horrible ice cream and I spent rest of the day wandering around getting gloriously sunburnt.

Russians are fighting in the streets of Berlin, Bologna has really been taken at last, Mandalay has fallen and the real battle for Burma is about to begin – oh, how marvellous.

But back in Britain, for many girls whose transition into adulthood had been defined by uniform, routine, discipline and drill, the long-anticipated end of the war had a bittersweet quality. Grace missed her battery.

Sometime after the V-1 rockets started to die down our battery was split up. They didn't need gun-sites no more, so I was sent to Glasgow with another little Cockney girl called Lil. They had us working on tanks, they were sent back from abroad all damaged and needed repairs and so forth. It was in a big hangar and we were doing the cleaning, and some other lad did the spraying.

Fiddling about with tanks in the underside of Glasgow was an anticlimax after the camaraderie of AA Command but at least Grace had something to look forward to. 'You see, I'd got married to my Bob so we were waiting to be together.' With her mother long dead and an absent father, Grace had no home to return to; marriage made sense and Royal Artillery mechanic Bob loved her very much. 'He worshipped the ground I walked on.' Bob proposed and they were married by September 1944. 'I asked my father's permission, I wrote to him and he said, "You make your bed, you lie on it."'

The wedding took place a week after Grace's twentieth birthday in a small church in Shepherd's Bush. No, she doesn't have a photograph. 'We stayed with his sister, we went back to her house afterwards. What's that, dear? No, none of my family were there; I didn't know anyone. There was some finger food on a long table in the front room.' Grace had made the decision that Bob was the man for her and in a borrowed wedding dress ('it belonged to his niece') and a pop of red lipstick she committed herself to a brand-new family. 'Yes, the wedding night was in their house.' She stops mid-sentence, the memories suddenly overwhelming. She's back in the terraced house in West London fingering her most treasured possession; an ankle-length white nightie hand-sewn from the nylon of a German parachute. 'We'd shot down a plane and the next day all the girls on the gun-site were given a piece of material as a memento.'

On their wedding night Grace was sent upstairs by her sister-in-law. 'I got myself undressed and put the nightie on. Oh, it was a special nightie; no, I wouldn't've worn it in the barracks. I lay down and pulled the sheets right up to my chin.' Eventually Bob came upstairs. He was nervous and so was Grace. She watched his manly shadow slip into a pair of pyjamas before he got into bed beside her. 'No, we didn't.' She suppresses a giggle. 'We didn't even hug, no. Eventually I turned around and fell asleep.' But at least they were married. 'He was sent away after that 'cos married couples couldn't be on the same gun-site.' Grace starts to laugh. 'I think we had a bit of leave to get to know each other, if you know what I mean!' But that was it. Sent away to Glasgow, soon she was miles from her man. 'It was very flat; I wasn't sure what I was going to do after the war but I knew I would be demobbed early 'cos I was married.'

Only one category got demobbed faster than married women and that was pregnant married women. 'But they didn't write down the word "pregnant". You were discharged for "family reasons".' Maud was surprised (disappointed even) when she discovered she was pregnant. 'It happened so quickly. After our wedding Charlie was back serving in Europe with the Commandos and I was at a concert, Handel's *Messiah* in Birmingham Town Hall, and I felt something wasn't right. I remember it very vividly because I was sitting next to an American woman. She wasn't Black exactly but she was a nice colour, mixed race I suppose you'd say. Yes, she was an American in service dress.' Maud's memory matches the dates exactly. The 6888th Central Postal Directory Battalion, a unit of more than 800 girls serving in the Women's Army Corps (WAC), was the only Black female American unit permitted to serve overseas. They arrived in Birmingham in February 1945 tasked with sorting through a backlog of American service mail.

The two girls started talking. The American was staying in a hostel with her battalion. She looked at Maud, taking in her pale face and blue eyes and said, 'You can't think what it means to be able to sit with you like this, it's lovely. Because, you know, we're not allowed to.' Maud moved in her seat, it was difficult to fathom even then. 'I remember thinking how awful it was to be separate and it wasn't that long ago, you know.' The American girl offered her a cigarette and Maud accepted. 'We had a smoke and I remember feeling odd, my uniform felt tight. I can see it all now very clearly.' That first flush of pregnancy hormone, Maude's heightened awareness of her body, her surroundings and the Black American woman's gratitude.

She reported in to sick parade and was checked out at Birmingham's Queen Elizabeth Hospital. Maud was pregnant with her first child. 'My discharge date was 11 May 1945.'

27

Bittersweet Victory

Where was peace? That's what Joan wanted to know. So
did a full House of Commons which expected Churchill
to deliver a victory announcement on 1 May. Instead he
told MPs he had 'no special statement to make about the
war position in Europe, except that it is definitely more
satisfactory than it was this time five years ago'.[1] Just
the day before Adolf Hitler had committed suicide but
it wasn't until 7 May that Germany finally surrendered
at the Rheims headquarters of the Allied Expeditionary
Force. In Britain, war officially ended at midnight on Tues-
day 8 May and the day was declared a bank holiday. The
Daily Mail captured the moment in the heart of London:
'Draped in crimson, fringed in gold, the great royal balcony slashed the grey front of Buckingham Palace like a
flame.'[2] Hundreds of thousands of people turned out to
roar at their wartime leader and royal family. Appearing
almost every hour, standing next to her father, George VI,
was ATS girl and heir to the throne Subaltern Princess
Elizabeth. The crowds looked up at her and cheered
and she looked down at the heaving mass of humanity
and begged to be allowed to join them. Permission was
granted. As Queen, Elizabeth recalled 'lines of unknown
people linking arms and walking down Whitehall, all of

us just swept along on a tide of happiness and relief'.
8 May 1945 was one of the most memorable days of her
young life.[3]

Joan's letter home from Brussels suggests her VE Day
also matched the best of them.

> *At 3 o'clock we heard Mr Churchill speak through a loud
> speaker . . . what a thrill it was and what excitements took
> place . . . In the main square was a loudspeaker playing
> all the national anthems . . . we were pelted with flowers,
> confetti, slapped on the back and cheered, and it was a most
> embarrassing experience . . . Cars are going around the city,
> jeeps, three-tonner private cars, all full to bursting with cheer-
> ing and waving people . . . about one o' clock we staggered
> back to barracks, hot, tired, and still excited by it all.*

But Joan wanted to be where the future Queen was –
on the streets of London: '*What a time it's been, although
I should have loved to have been at home. I think everyone I have
spoken to has said, "I wish I had been at home or in London."
I guess it has been simply wonderful in London.*' FANY Jean stationed in Italy felt the same. '*I wish I had been in London, it
must have been colossal.*' Churchill's words rang in her ears:
'Advance Britannia! Long live the cause of freedom! God
save the King!' Like Joan, longing for home heightened
Jean's emotional response to peace. '*Oh honey, it's glorious,
isn't it? No more organised murder in all of Europe.*' She listened
to the Prime Minister's speech on the wireless, read the
Union Jack special edition (a British services newssheet) and

> *we danced and everyone looked a bit dazed and you could feel
> the excitement all over the room . . . every ship in the port
> was sounding its siren and all the flags were out and people*

*were letting off revolvers into the air all around! It was very
impressive and as usual I wanted to cry.*

There was plenty to cry about; a continent on its knees,
the Far East still fighting, Jean's father a prisoner of war
and Jean unsure about what came next. The end of the
war was euphoric – 'in all our long history we have never
seen a greater day than this' – but there was no point in
pretending the transition to peace would be easy. Churchill
could reassure the country 'everyone, man or woman,
has done their share' but for a generation who'd grown
up at war, conscripted to eat, work, drill, drink and live
together, the 'task' that lay ahead – 'rebuilding our hearths
and homes'[4] – would require considerable adjustment.
Perhaps no generation felt that change as acutely as young
service girls.

Jean's prolific letters from Italy reveal a distinct anxiety
about the future. Service with the FANYs had lit a touch
paper: within the space of a year she'd deciphered codes,
talked shop, led shifts and fended for herself and the prospect of it coming to an abrupt end worried her greatly.
On the one hand she dreamt of returning to Britain and
marrying a Scottish laird, living the '*rest of life shooting and
fishing and going down to the village and even doing the washing
up!*' As the daughter of minor rural gentry, a good marriage was expected, but despite lots of FANY weddings in
Italy, Jean wasn't tempted by early nuptials and she hadn't
found a suitable man. Alternative options were hardly
more appealing; '*being a FANY in England after this would be
grim*' but likewise '*to sit in an office or in a bank or somewhere
would be hell*'. Secretly harbouring hopes of becoming a
writer, towards the end of the war Jean sent off poems to

several publications, including *Country Life* and *Chambers.* '*Oh dear. I just got a refusal from Country Life magazine yesterday couched in such glowing terms I feel as if I was the world's greatest success instead of owning the largest ever collection of refusal chits.*'

Jean's creative ambition was complicated by her conventional upbringing. A visit to an Italian palm reader predicted '*a happy married life which would be so pleasantly restful however I have a strong career line too, to my horror. I do dislike women with a purpose.*' With the exception of Russia, Britain had mobilised more women than any other belligerent, but in the 1940s ambition remained decidedly unfeminine, even bourgeois. It was her father's return from a Japanese prisoner-of-war camp that prompted Jean's return to Lancashire, where the Owtram family reunion was caught on camera. FANY Jean is reliably standing to attention in her uniform but beneath the impressive display of service and survival there were tensions in Newland Hall that autumn. Colonel Owtram was obliged to adjust to a civilian world where his forthright daughters expected to have their say and drink whisky; meanwhile, Jean and Pat quickly discovered no one was interested in their war. 'It was so very flat.' Jean shakes her head. As she had predicted, life back in England proved 'hell'. By 1947 she had secured a return to post-war Italy working as a clerk with the Allied Commission, 'to help the country get back on its feet'.

Even girls who never left Britain were in for a shock. 'I didn't feel happy. I missed the army life. I had a good home with Mother and Father but I felt like a fish out of water.' Pregnant Maud wasn't ready for what came next. Clement Attlee's new Labour Government did not stretch to sex equality, quite the reverse. A girl's reward for her effort in the war focused on her return to the private sphere and the opportunity to perfect the art of domesticity. The Beveridge Report was unequivocal: 'housewives and mothers' must be supported in their 'vital work' of 'ensuring the adequate continuance of the British race'.[5] Married and pregnant in May 1945, Maud was a frontrunner in this revamped game of 'home and hearth', but 'I missed all my friends in the army. It's a big organisation, like a blanket over you and when you come out from under the blanket you don't feel quite right. It took me a long time to get used to looking after and changing a baby. I didn't enjoy it.'

No matter what Maud thought, the War Office anticipated releasing 135,000 women from military service by the end of 1945. Churchill had wanted to go further faster; he argued 'all women should be free to retire as soon as possible from the services' and believed that 'those who like to stay will be sufficient to do the necessary jobs'.[6] But Grace wasn't given a choice; within six weeks of VE Day married women were demobbed. 'My Bob went into the British Liberation Army in Germany and I found myself back in London. To begin with I had about three jobs. I was selling tickets at the King's Theatre in Hammersmith. I don't remember celebrating the end of the war.' Grace smiles. 'You see, when you're in the army you really look forward to coming out and when you get to Civvy Street you wished you'd stayed in.' Still, she had 'things to be getting on with. I wanted to get a job with the General Post Office and I was getting a home ready. I found a couple of rooms and bought some utility furniture.'

*

Churchill was certain that women who wanted to carry on serving would, and Martha proved him right. 'At the end of the war I was on the list but I just missed out by one day on promotion to junior commander. Mary Churchill was already a commander.' Martha was born to lead, the failed promotion was irksome, but in May 1945 there was still plenty of opportunity to prove herself.

The ATS had been both ordered to downsize and tasked with maintaining the Allied occupation across Europe. 'I said, "Ma'am I'm not trained in administration, but I'll do my best."' On the edge of Green Park in central London, in a street of requisitioned houses, Martha readied herself to receive 'squads of girls prior to demob. I went from working on a gun-site to this place full of girls who had to be sorted. The War Office wanted the ones who could type, and the others needed written testimonials and a final payment.' Martha was organising chaos; one girl broke down in tears because she didn't give her an 'exemplary reference' ('she made such a fuss I had to get permission to change it'), others were simply glad army life was over. Martha procured a pay clerk from Regent's Park Barracks and felt calmer. She liked order, she still does. 'I told our battery commander I also needed to borrow a corporal.' There were legions of girls to get through.

Most women have proudly held onto their service testimonials, often the only reference they ever received, irrespective of who wrote them. Diana, who was still cooking for the ATS when it was rebranded the Women's Royal Army Corps in 1949, and didn't leave the military until she got married in 1951, proudly pushes her service book across the table. '*She is an extremely pleasant woman who is at all times willing, cheerful and conscientious and very easy to work with.*

She is very honest, likeable and trustworthy.' A glowing reference, but one that is notable for its failure to cite Diana's ability to run a mess or feed hundreds of men. Post-war, professional expectations for most women remained narrow: apparently, after years of army cooking, Diana could be *'recommended to take a job where children are involved or in any private household'*. Today, aged ninety-seven, she laughs, 'I ended up running a large hotel kitchen and catered for busloads of people!'

Cornish-born Vera, no.1 on a predictor in AA Command, before working as an orderly in Leicester prior to demob, has a testimonial that reads much like Diana's: '*This auxiliary is an excellent worker, is absolutely trustworthy and has a cheerful disposition . . . she can be relied upon to carry out her duties without supervision.*' In fact, she never worked again full time. 'I was a school cleaner for a bit but I didn't need a reference for that.' Private Vera Waddington had got married before she was even demobilised. Like so many girls, she met a soldier, Len, during the war and for the best part of four years their relationship was confined to letters. 'Ha,' she laughs:

> He surprised me with his return from the Far East; there he was sitting in his grandma's house in Leicester. We weighed each other up and afterwards he walked me to the bus and took me in his arms and kissed me and the conductor announced, 'I brought this young man down from London Road Station with his kitbag on. After four years he deserves a kiss like that!'

Vera turned around to a chorus of 'Oooh, give him another!' They were married four months later in St Nicholas's Church back in her Cornish village, Saltash.

Post-war, the average age for nuptials tumbled to twenty-two. Girls hardly knew the boys they were marrying. *Good Housekeeping* recommended reading to help women understand the needs of their men, who'd 'probably be very difficult to get along with and very unhappy in himself'.[7] Vera shakes her head. 'He'd been out in the Far East but he never talked about the war. Mind you, we hadn't been married long when he used to get up out of bed and say, "Let me out! Let me out!" Next morning I'd say to him, "What was all that about?" But he wouldn't talk about it.' No one was spared the effects of war, but few looked back. 'We were fed up of it by then.' Vera and Len were fortunate; theirs was a long and happy union. 'Mind you, I didn't like his tattoos. I'd never seen him undressed until our wedding night, I had no idea and one was of a woman!' As for Len, he was onto a winner; according to Vera's ATS testimonial her '*appearance*' was '*pleasing*'.

*

Traditional thinking, which placed a premium on femininity, hadn't gone away. Historian Lucy Noakes observes that the 1944 Manpower Debate, which focused on demobilisation, visualised 'the returning soldier as male'. However when it came to the subject of dress, women were singled out. Instead of being given a standard demobilisation suit, women were issued with an extra £12.10s to buy their own clothes. Apparently the coupons would afford girls 'the means of becoming once again adequately and gracefully dressed'.[8]

Grace relished the prospect of going clothes shopping.

I liked my clothes, the best bit about being back on Civvy Street was wearing nice clothes. I remember my new look outfit, it had a long black costume skirt and was nipped in at the waist with a lovely little jacket. My figure weren't bad, you see, and I suited the more feminine look.

Daphne still has a photograph of herself in 'demob' clothes. 'Look at my nice shapely legs and nice shoes! I think this was outside Newcastle Station.' With narrow ankles and comely calves supporting a green belted tea-dress, Daphne, standing arm in arm with a former ATS colleague, cuts a dash against the grey of post-war Britain. Comrades in war and now on Civvy Street, the girls look great. Daphne had supplemented her demob coupons to the tune of £28 and offset the outfit with a luxurious coat in brown boucle that matched her chestnut waves. This was a girl who knew how to reclaim feminine. 'I bought that coat in Ridley's in Ipswich . . . It was £40 for the whole look; I could afford it because I was working by then in the Ipswich GPO – the General Post Office.' No expense was spared. Not released until 1946, for Daphne the end of the war had been a while coming, but it was worth it. A switchboard and teleprinter operator thanks to the ATS, this one-time shop assistant from Norwich had skills that were prioritised in a country obsessed with reconstruction.

The army looked after us. I remember before demob we were sent to educational classes and the sergeant who was taking them pleaded with me to stay on and become a trainer. But I wanted to come out. I wanted to work for the General Post Office or Shell-Mex, as they were the only two companies with teleprinters at the time.

Daphne is sure that female service in World War II has made a difference to the rest of her life. So is Grace. Within months of leaving the ATS both women targeted the GPO; it was a boom time for telecommunications and the state-owned company with decent remuneration was a popular choice. The girls applied, did the training, passed the tests and got the jobs, just as they'd done in the ATS. Compulsory service had taught women their worth and despite the post-war pay differentials and marriage bars, it was a genie that could never fully be put back in the bottle.

Martha saw that when she was writing testimonials near Hyde Park just after VE Day. Returning men were the heroes but women expected a good write-up. And for many service girls, including Martha, the story wasn't over. Just four days before peace was declared, Churchill confided to his wife, Clementine: 'I scarcely need tell you that beneath these triumphs lie poisonous politics and deadly international rivalries.'[9] If Britain wanted a say in a post-war world dominated by two emerging super-powers, then full military retrenchment was not an option. Post-May 1945, millions of Allied servicemen were in Germany, Austria, Italy and the Middle East and fighting in the Far East, supported by thousands of women, and at last Subaltern Martha Bruce was due to join them. 'I had spent all war serving in Britain and I wanted my turn abroad. I was posted first to Italy, then Austria.' Her clothing coupons would have to wait.

28

Germany and Beyond

We crossed the Rhine just as it was getting dark and that was particularly thrilling. It's a colossal river with a very swift current and made us wonder how on earth they could possibly have put a bridge over it . . . it was very thrilling and I wouldn't have missed it. But fancy crossing the Rhine about four months too late and in a railway train. So prosaic!

Initially flown from Brussels to her new German posting in June 1945, Joan was returning from leave that September when she finally crossed the Rhine, nearly six months after Churchill followed his army across Germany's giant river. It had been an event anxiously anticipated by his military staff; he liked to be where the action was and the press followed. George VI noted, Churchill 'is very restless nowadays and cannot bear to be out of things'.[1] The sentiment wasn't restricted to prime ministers, or indeed to men. Travelling in a nineteen-carriage train chock full of army, navy, air force and ATS girls, wide-eyed Joan was heading back into British-occupied north-west Germany. Her letters home provide a vivid portrait of a ruined country. '*All along the railway tracks were little graves with wooden crosses, some of them had steel helmets on them.*' Five million Germans had died in the war, 400,000 in Allied bombing.

The stench of rotting matter hung fetid in the air. '*The whole place looks like a rubbish dump and the smell is something fearful. I expect if the truth were known there are still some remains underneath all the rubble.*' Having spent years as an ATS clerk in south-east England, Joan was catapulted into what war looked like for losers.

> *There is something different somehow about bombed English towns and German ones. In England the places still seem full of life and everybody carrying on much as usual, but here there is a horrible air of deadness, very eerie . . . there can't be a single undamaged building in Bielefeld and by damage I don't mean just broken windows and ceilings but entire walls out and floors fallen.*

Numerous Allied victory parades deliberately reinforced Germany's defeat and denazification of the country was prioritised; over 100,000 civilian suspects were rounded up and war criminals were vigorously pursued. Joan marvelled: '*It's a strange thing, or is it, no one has ever admitted to being or having known a NAZI!*'

The maelstrom of angry homeless humanity in the immediate aftermath of Germany's devastating war saw radical measures introduced to prevent anarchy and violence. Joan could not leave the British '*compound*' and '*go to the other side of the barbed wire*' unless she was in a party of six ATS girls, accompanied by an armed guard. Nowhere and no one was deemed safe, and yet Joan and her ATS colleagues were not allowed to carry guns. As restrictions were gradually lifted she noted: '*It's strange the men have to be armed to go out but the ATS are allowed out in pairs with no arms and no escorts.*'

Morbid fears persisted about possible German retaliations and dangerous displaced persons. Grace's new husband, Bob, was also stationed in occupied Germany. 'It's funny,' she muses 'he got through the whole of the war without an injury and there he was in Germany walking back to barracks and this man jumped him and stabbed him. He came home cut all down his chin and under his arm. You can see it in the pictures there.' Tensions ran dangerously high and yet rigid British military thinking clung tenaciously to the idea of women as non-combatants. Like Bob, Joan and her female colleagues wore the British military khaki of an occupying force but unlike Bob they were unarmed. Self-defence was not an option.

The ATS was part of the 800,000-strong British Army of the Rhine (BAOR), assisted by the Allied Control Council in Berlin, which employed a combination of civil servants and military staff. With headquarters in Bad Oeynhausen in North Rhine-Westphalia, BAOR requisitioned scarce housing from local Germans to accommodate their troops, Joan included. Acquisitions didn't stop at housing. *'It's really quite disturbing to see the stuff the men out here have acquired – beautiful wireless sets, electric heaters, jewellery, crockery, all kinds of things'*, they are *'all living in luxury'*. The atmosphere between the British soldiers and the Germans was unpleasant: 'They hated us and we hated them.' She told her parents *'The civilians give us filthy looks and won't get off the pavement to let us past so we have to walk in the gutter which no doubt pleases them.'*

Joan alternated between fear, revulsion and compassion.

We went into one of the empty houses in the compound one evening. It was eerie, just as the German family had left it when they had been turned out. The kitchen was in utter chaos, the bedrooms the same. Most of the beds were on the ground floor, Herford has had several bad air raids. It was so creepy one could imagine a German in one of those horrible helmets (the sight of which still gives me the jitters) lurking in a dark corner.

Conversations with children were permitted. They were '*very blonde, very pretty, it is noticeable that there are so many of them*'. The fruits of Nazi breeding programmes were visible on the streets.

One of them, a fascinatingly pretty child of about twelve . . . said, 'This used to be our school, do you like it?' Then she said, 'We have no school now.' She asked if she could visit her old home, which her family had been turned out of and is now within the compound. We got permission for her to do so and she was very happy. It is now full of British officers.

British men were strictly banned from 'fraternising' with 'local German girls' and petite brunette Joan had to work hard to keep her male colleagues at bay. '*Apparently the ratio of girls to men out here is one to a couple of thousand . . . Remember I told you about that AWFUL man . . . I wish he would go to Burma, he really is sickening. And what could be worse than a sickening solicitor? I'd like to have the opportunity of wringing his neck.*' Stuck in the Legal Aid department, where Joan was subjected to lurid details of adultery ('although sometimes the information was deemed inappropriate for innocent creatures and I wasn't allowed to type it up!'), she was often bothered by men, and one man in particular. An army lawyer, he left roses on her desk, followed her around, tried to kiss her, got in contact with her parents and moved his leave to match hers. Joan's forbearance was admirable, but his constant attentions depressed her. In a letter home she wrote: '*I'm sick of parties and men. Especially the latter. I begin to wish I wasn't so pleasant to them.*' Now aged one hundred Joan laughs heartily. 'They were an absolute pest, especially that one. I should have been much firmer if it were today!'

Much of the war had been spent trying to reduce contact between the opposite sexes but (initial) determination to keep British men away from German women saw the ATS's presence in Germany actively encouraged. However, Joan was quick to point out that even the most lecherous male would have struggled to gain full access. '*We're kept inside barbed wire, and bossed about by an eagle-eyed old battleaxe, all our acquaintances checked, misdemeanours punished and we have to be in at 10.30.*' She was twenty-five years old.

Due to a shortfall in ATS girls, clerical staff eventually had their numbers boosted by civilians. The resulting influx was not popular. '*We've just had some more civvies arrive from England working with the Control Commission. They don't go down very well with us, they look upon it as a holiday . . . when we were told we had to "pamper them" because they hadn't been used to roughing it, we nearly blew the roof off.*' Joan and her colleagues keenly asserted their difference. '*We do polish our medals!*' By the end of 1945 Joan was a proud soldier; she enjoyed the discipline, the camaraderie, the routine, and even relations with the local Germans gradually improved. Joan visited a German family in early 1946 and '*I phoned up the ATS officer . . . and said we wanted to get rid of the cooks and have the Germans working for us instead*'. There was a week of leave spent in Paris, moonlit rides on a horse called Monsoon and winter ice-skating with friends.

In December 1945 she '*went for an interview about getting a testimonial and things for demob*' and came away having signed up for a further six months' service. '*Are you mad?*' her friends laughed, '*are you going to see a psychiatrist?*' But Joan knew what she was doing. She was part of a mission that was morphing from occupation into collaboration. Relations with the Soviets hardened (by March 1948 Russia would withdraw from the Allied Control Council) and as the Cold War hotted up West Germany's status shifted from foe to friend; Joan was in on the beginning of something remarkable and at the same time she was also building and developing herself. The army provided German lessons and French lessons, even photography lessons – all part of her preparation for a return to civilian life.

21 Jul, 1946
Nine more days to go. Anybody would think I was count-ing the days and anxious to leave the place. The nearer it gets, the more I think twice about it. However, it's got to be done some time, so let's get on with it.

*

'It was dreadful, I felt like a fish out of water.' Joan arrived back in Soham, Cambridgeshire, with a bump. Over-night she lost her rank, her pay and her purpose. She had mooted the idea of staying on longer, but nothing lasts for ever and Joan was a practical woman; entering the job market in a flattened British economy was better done sooner rather than later. Before she arrived home she'd already turned down two prospective jobs in her local village; seeing 'Ma and Pa' again was one thing, living with them quite another. A corporal in an army of occupation one day, a twenty-six-year-old daughter back in her childhood bedroom the next, Joan lasted six weeks in Soham before she procured lodgings and a secretarial job in Cambridge. 'I became a shorthand typist in the chemistry department of Chivers the jam people and I stayed there until I got married.'

It was hardly her dream job. A year earlier Joan had peevishly written home stating that she didn't want to work in an office, '*certainly not shorthand and typing. But I don't know what I could do. Don't reckon I am cut out for school teaching or nursing or anything vital.*' The letter deftly summed up the (lack of) options for girls in post-war Britain. Joan's ATS job was clerical but it had come with an all-encompassing way of life: travel, companionship, a common mission and a keen sense of belonging. Even today, seventy-five years later, the disappointment is palpable. Joan missed service life, briefly it had blown her out of a small corner of England into a much bigger world where she'd excelled, before she was dropped back into a Britain that was trying to convince itself the war had been a wonderful training ground for prospective wives and mothers.

Re-entry into civilian life wasn't easy for ambitious girls, especially not in a country that prioritised professional options for men. At the helm of a Bedford army truck, Yorkshire-born Barbara had learnt a lot in war. After Victory in Europe she made selection and was posted to No. 2 Driving School Wales, where she acquired advance driving skills and was promoted to lance corporal. But despite these sterling credentials, post-demobilisation Barbara was 'out of work from September 1946 until the following January, when I got a job as a taxi driver in Rotherham'. By July 1947 piecemeal driving had been replaced by marriage to airman Stan. 'Both our fathers were policemen and after the war Stan also joined the constabulary.' Barbara became a full time housewife and mother. 'I had four children and I was very methodical. In the day I did the cooking and was with my four children. Once they were in bed at six o' clock I did the cleaning.' It was fortunate she enjoyed domesticity because 'as a policeman's wife you weren't allowed to work, not until the 1960s'.

*

The experiences of women returning from overseas service suggest that readjustment was harder for those who'd endured (and enjoyed) a foreign war. Barbara had less to reacclimatise to than Joan, who had been on the Continent for eighteen months, or vicar's daughter Anne, who likewise had spent most of her war in Italy. Just twenty years old in early 1945, based at Caserta Palace, 'we really felt proud to be making a small contribution to [the victory], especially when Field Marshal Alexander became Commander in Chief of the Mediterranean Forces, with his offices in the very same building as ourselves'.[2] Talk to Anne today and that pride is still tangible; here was a young British woman serving her country in its finest hour.

Despite her tender age, backbone and ambition saw Anne spend the end of the war on an officer's training course in Palestine. 'Six of us flew from Naples to Cairo in a Dakota, which was for all of us our very first flight in a plane (and very exciting!).' During their stop-over in Egypt conditions were rough (unacceptably so), but Anne, a keen Guider, excelled. Her letters home burst with enthusiasm.

I'm so lucky to have a whole two months in which to learn and not bother about working. Oh dear, oh dear! How marvellous. People continue to be as nice as ever. I'm terribly happy. Thank you for everything.

With a commission under her belt, she returned to Italy and was appointed second-in-command of a transit centre receiving British service girls arriving on the Continent in the aftermath of war.

It's just one wonderful rush from dawn till night and sometimes in the night as well. I love this place and job as I've never loved anything in the army before and now a new officer has arrived . . . she has brought me a very wonderful thing. I am now a full subaltern and supposed to be in charge here . . .

Engagement, status, pride: the comedown from Anne's war was always going to be hard. Just as Britain adjusted to a new socialist government, rebuilding homes and redistributing wealth, Anne was discovering new ways of being and new ways of feeling and by the end of 1945 she'd run the full gamut of emotions.

'It was one of the worst days of my whole life.' Granted leave in September, Officer Anne, in charge of a group of ATS girls, had endured a terrifying flight to England 'sitting on the converted bomb rack of a Liberator'. Four weeks later she flew back to Italy, having successfully challenged the War Office's request for her early return. 'On arrival in Naples, I found myself surrounded by senior male army officers demanding to know what had happened to the other girls.' She quickly discovered they'd set off for Italy a fortnight earlier but that their Lancaster had 'disappeared mid-flight'. The shock was appalling, it still is. She shakes her head. Anne felt sick; her female colleagues were dead. Two weeks earlier, on 4 October 1945, their plane had fallen out of the sky but 'there had been no mention of it in the papers'. And there wasn't, until 16 November, when the mother of missing ATS girl Jessica Ellen Semark sent a letter to the *Express*. 'It told for the first time of a plane which left England one night 6 weeks ago with 17 ATS girls on board and vanished.'[3] The aircraft was never found.

One of the greatest tragedies in the history of the ATS – seventeen girls caught in a storm flying across the Mediterranean and never seen again – and it was a grieving mother who alerted the media. The Air Ministry defended their silence, insisting, 'Until recently it was not the Ministry's policy to issue reports of crashed aircraft.'[4] With thousands of young women directed overseas, the news was potentially devastating and the government's silence sinister. The Air Ministry felt compelled to make a second statement, explaining, 'we made no announcement in conformity with war security regulations' (six months after the end of war in Europe), and promised that 'as from today announcements would not be delayed'.[5] Anne, meanwhile, struggled with survivor's guilt: if she hadn't challenged the early return and instead 'done her duty' and flown back to Italy with the other girls, she too would probably be dead.

It wasn't the end of Anne's war story. In 1946 she was a junior commander running an ATS transit centre in occupied Austria, 'coping with all sorts of people including mothers with babies who our soldiers had married' but the Lancaster's disappearance was a defining moment.

That the war was over exacerbated the shock and pain behind such a great loss. Today she flaps her arms against her thighs, an involuntary gesture that captures the impotence she felt, then and now. The girls were gone and there was nothing Anne could do about it.

Back in Britain the muted response to the accident was symptomatic of a country keen to discover a new normal, where women no longer needed to be heroes, albeit unarmed ones. 'It was lovely to be home' but Anne concedes, 'there was an intensity that was missing. Britain was very different after the war and it wasn't easy emotionally.' Even with a confirmed place at nearby Bristol University, life in the vicarage required a new form of endurance. 'There was a calibre of friendship that we had in service which didn't really exist in the outside world.' Anne missed it, and seventy-five years later, in 2020, doing her duty and isolating alone, she still does.

29

Remembering the War

'I had a motto: 'Orderly management.'

'Oh, I'm not orderly or well managed.'

'I know. I've noticed. I'm glad you weren't in my regiment, Tessa, you would've been a handful.'

Ninety-nine-year-old Martha has called me out, correctly too. It's hardly surprising when you discover that she's spent her whole life leading women; Subaltern in the ATS was just the beginning. Next came twenty years service in the Territorial Army, for which she was awarded an OBE, and as we talk she frequently drifts into her second career, when she was assistant governor, then governor of two Scottish prisons. 'Greenock was the first one, yes, always women.' Martha, small, hugely accomplished and kind beneath a brusque exterior, learnt her craft in wartime service. As she puts it: 'After the war I had experience, I knew how to handle myself.'

In 1946, after a stint in occupied Europe, she returned to Scotland in need of a job. 'It was entirely fortuitous that almost in my back garden the Territorial Army were setting up a MHAA regiment.' Entrenched relations with Russia eventually saw the British military relent and introduce national service in 1949 (for men only), but in the meantime volunteers were expected to meet the shortfall, and Martha, capable of commanding both sexes, was a godsend. 'Early on I managed to talk the male gunners down from munity and persuade them to fire their guns.' Quickly she climbed the ranks; the commander role which proved elusive during the war was soon hers and by the time she left the service Martha was a lieutenant colonel.

The distinctions were all hard-earned. After mixed anti-aircraft sites were disbanded she focused on the military recruitment and training of young women. There was cross-fertilisation between the ATS's successor organisation, the Women's Royal Army Corps, and the TA, with Martha taking the very first group of volunteer girls across the Channel under the umbrella of the Highland Division. They returned to Saint-Valery-sur-Somme, where the 51st Highland Division had surrendered to the Germans in June 1940. The tartan-clad regiment marched through the centre of the town: the mayor greeted them, locals dusted off their wartime flags and Martha gave a spontaneous speech in schoolgirl French. Back in Scotland, they were welcomed by a piper at Perth Station; it was the first of many overseas trips for the girls of Highland Division.

Martha has always been unconventionally conventional, breaking patterns and transforming lives within rigid hierarchies. That she never entered the institution of marriage gave her a freer hand elsewhere. 'It didn't bother me being different; I suppose you get to a certain stage and you don't think any more that you might've been married.' Of all the individuals in this book, Martha is the lifelong flagbearer for women in the military. World War II was an era of obligatory service when many girls were thrown into uniforms who otherwise would never have served, and post-war most opted for civilian life and marriage. Martha was one of the few who continued to serve the army at a time when girls still occupied supporting roles and non-combat status. From a titled family, she dedicated decades to an organisation renowned for its traditional conservatism. Where do women fit into this world of entitlement and rank?

'What do you mean?'

'Are you a feminist, Martha?'

'You've asked me that before.'

'I know, and you haven't answered.'

She pauses, refusing to be jumped into a hasty reply. 'Well, I'm not a "lock 'em to the railings" sort of feminist, no. But do I believe that women should be given an equal chance? Yes, I do.'

Much later in her career Martha the conservative feminist would push for girls to be given opportunities and fair pay that didn't exist in her day. 'Early on I accepted my lot, but later I had experience, I was in the position to effect change.' Martha has lived a century. There was no female army when she was born; it had been disbanded after World War I, when women in military uniform were not deemed appropriate for peacetime. One hundred years later we are back in peacetime and again there is no separate women's service; nowadays they fight alongside men, irrespective of their sex. There is no part of the army that individuals identifying as female cannot enter. Martha gives a small nod. 'I am too far removed from events these days to comment, but yes, so it seems, women can do anything these days provided they are the right height and weight.'

*

Martha is sure that 'the Second World War helped women in the army'. Certainly post-1945 the utility of female military service could not be negated; on 20 November 1946 a parliamentary announcement confirmed that women's auxiliary corps had become a permanent feature of the armed forces and by 1949 the WRAC had replaced the ATS. However, old tropes and traditional thinking quickly resurfaced (they had never gone away). There was no question of integrating the WRAC with higher status male units; they remained a separate and 'strictly non-combatant service'.[1] British society slowly acknowledged inequality but hard-baked ideas surrounding the 'weaker sex' and femininity saw section 85(40) of the Sex Discrimination Act (introduced in 1975) permit the continued exclusion of women from combat roles. By 1980 women were allowed to train with small arms for self-defence, but even when females were absorbed into the army proper* they were still largely restricted to support and medical roles.

As late as 2002, the Ministry of Defence concluded that women in ground combat could adversely affect 'unit cohesion'. Former ATS driver Barbara laughs. 'But in the Second World War we improved morale on the gun-sites. The male-only ones were very stuffy! And the women directing guns were technically combatants anyway.' Matter of fact, she dismantles decades of hesitancy and sexism in one sentence, and delivers a bold reminder of just how groundbreaking women's military service was in World War II. Another seventy-seven years after girls

---

*   In 1992 the WRAC was finally disbanded and women were
     absorbed into the regular army.

first appeared on anti-aircraft gun-sites would pass before the British Defence Secretary Gavin Williamson finally announced in 2018 that all combat roles were open to women, including infantry and special forces units.[2]

It was a hard-fought victory for equality, but to focus on the narrowest definition of military action – combat – is to overlook perhaps the greatest contribution women offer the army, and that is their humanising presence. We know from her letters it was to Joan that blonde homeless children turned in Germany, not her male counterparts, and it was Joan who was invited to dine with the army's Belgian translators and subsequently became their friends. Anne talks of the great pride she felt belonging to the British military in World War II, but when I read her letters, it is Anne I feel proud of, just twenty years old, miles from home, visiting injured soldiers, helping displaced persons and reminding men to behave themselves. Joan, Jean, Anne and Martha were the females in an occupying army, often meeting and dealing with humanity at its most vulnerable. Today, ask any soldier who it was that civilians (especially women and children) turned to first on the ground in Kosovo, Afghanistan, Iraq, and they will tell you it is the female soldier almost every time. In World War II the government and the public constantly worried about girls' demoralising, feminising impact on the army and the army's defeminising, sexualising impact on girls; meanwhile the benefits (beyond additional 'manpower') were rarely considered.

Back in Britain, General Dwight Eisenhower was so impressed with AA Command's mixed batteries that the Americans imitated the British model and discovered they had 'high unit cohesion and bonding, performing better than all-male units'.[3] Martha is sure that her brand of 'orderly management' was more effectively executed by a woman, and during the war it was acknowledged that girls mastered Morse faster and more effectively than their older male counterparts. Integration has not been without problems (the harassment and bullying of female service staff is an ongoing issue and one that has been belatedly recognised[4]) but nowadays it's widely accepted that women improve the performance and image of the British army. The seeds of that sea change in military thinking began in World War II; never before had so many girls served in khaki and covered such a wide range of jobs. The women in this book were game changers who, for almost a lifetime, have been hiding in plain sight.

'Yes, I do have a sense of pride. It is not a swanky pride but I am proud.' Over the last twenty years Barbara has been a devoted member of her local York Royal Artillery Association and is an active ambassador for the British Legion, but it was not always thus. After the war her husband, airman Stan, didn't want his wife (or himself) to belong to any wartime associations. 'We had been regimented for so long.' Nor was there much encouragement elsewhere. Post-war, an insecure Britain, shedding its Empire and slipping down the world's pecking order, compensated by remembering its heroic efforts in World War II. The conflict was deliberately cast as a brave man's war with a plethora of celebratory masculine films and books. Women and their unprecedented role were airbrushed out of the story.

'It was fifty-six years after the war when the Royal Artillery Association finally issued an apology.' Barbara, a stickler for detail, remembers the occasion well. 'It was at one of our ATS reunions and Major General Michael Steele, a former Royal Artillery officer, told us women we'd been treated very badly. "Welcome home," he said. "At last you can call yourself gunners." The women of AA Command long had, but they always knew the colloquialism 'gunner girl' was just that. Nearly six decades passed before they were given equivalent status with the men. Many were already dead. Widowed Barbara decided to join her local artillery group and found the all-male meeting polite but distant. 'I'm not going again,' she thought, 'but then I changed my mind. I realised many members hadn't even been in the war, they'd just done national service.' In comparison, Barbara was the real deal; aged ninety-five, she's now president of the York Royal Artillery Association and the only member who saw active service in World War II. Remembering the war and being remembered has changed her life.

It was May 2015 and the final tweaks were being made to the VE Day anniversary line-up in Westminster Abbey. 'There were four of us, standing not far from the tomb of the unknown soldier; it was me and three men. I was going to be last but then they moved me up to the front so I met the Queen first.' Seventy years after the end of the war, an exchange between two female veterans, former Lance Corporal Barbara Weatherill and former Junior Commander HM Queen Elizabeth II, led royal proceedings. Almost exact contemporaries and both drivers in the ATS, Barbara has always felt close to her queen, and on 8 May 2015 they finally talked. 'But you know, I've no clue what she said to me! Apparently that happens a lot when you meet the Queen.'

FOREIGN WAR

More important than their pleasantries was their presence: women, millions of them, served in World War II; their role was vital and life-changing but because men were dying on the front line they were all too easily forgotten. In Westminster Abbey six years ago, Barbara and Elizabeth II reminded the watching world that in war as in peace, men need women. After the Queen, it was the Duke of Edinburgh's turn to meet Barbara. 'Gosh,' he said, eyeing the numerous medals on both sides of her blazer, 'you've been busy!' She shot back: 'I'm wearing my late husband's medals too.' Barbara is one of the last veterans standing; nowadays she represents her generation, male and female, and their service for our nation.

Epilogue

Dear Tessa,

I am Yvette, Norma's daughter . . . sadly Mum passed away at the weekend, on Saturday 1 August 2020 . . . she was a wonderful mum and highly respected.

In 2020 Norma Best was one of the very few (perhaps the only) extant West Indian ATS veterans living in Britain. She travelled from British Honduras (now Belize), via America to Scotland in 1944. She said of the war: 'Serving in the armed forces was wonderful, it was one of the best experiences I've ever had.' I can't tell you much more than that as I never met Norma; I'd just started researching *Army Girls* when I received Yvette's email. Her mother's death was a poignant reminder that I was working with the most precious people sitting on the very edge of their long lives, a situation aggravated by a pandemic that was potentially fatal for the women I wanted to talk to. Often I reached out to veterans who no longer existed. Letters were returned and books bounced back. I quickly discovered that 'recipient no longer lives here' was code for 'recipient no longer lives'.

The WRAC Association worked tirelessly to help find extant veterans willing to share their stories before it was too late. Jamaican Ena deserves a bigger role in this book, but coronavirus ruled out international travel and Zoom calls are hard work when you are one hundred and three. Her wartime service was just the beginning of an extraordinary career; Ena returned to the West Indies after studying law in London and became a groundbreaking judge in Jamaica, as well as bringing up three children. 'Don't limit yourself because you are woman' is a hallmark message from her exceptional long life.

I last saw Penny leaning keenly out of her window, waving goodbye, one sunlit September afternoon. Covid-19 restrictions had been briefly lifted and she fed me warm snacks and cake in her Hampshire flat. Penny talked through her young life; she had a rich sense of humour, a beautiful dancer's poise and shared her stories with uninhibited panache. I looked forward to seeing her again. Then, just before Christmas, she stopped answering the telephone. I panicked and rang the reception of her sheltered accommodation. There was no reply, it was the weekend. On Monday a woman called and explained Penny had suddenly been taken ill and died in hospital two days later. She reassured me of her wonderful life and good health until the very end but in that moment I didn't want reassurance, I wanted Penny back. She was ninety-nine and three-quarters but she was also one of my newest friends and a very important part of *Army Girls*. If you are reading this and wondering why Penny didn't feature more, it is because I didn't get all her story; aged ninety-nine she died too soon. When I close my eyes I can still see her waving from the window.

I started writing this book in July 2020 with a cast of seventeen extant women; in April 2021 there are just fifteen. ATS PT instructor and dance teacher Beryl died in January 2021. Like Penny, she was ninety-nine and again the news came as a shock. The women telling me their war stories were very old but the lives that I was writing about and imagining were very young. In my head and on the page Beryl and Penny are just girls, casting out into a life defined by war. I received an email from Beryl's dear friend Diana informing me of her death.

> She rarely complained and she didn't give up, but sadly, her last year was more like imprisonment since she was unable to see her friends thanks to coronavirus.

Neither Penny nor Beryl died of Covid-19 but the new rules introduced to marshal the virus's impact defined the final furlong of their lives, restricted their movements and perhaps even hastened their deaths. I watched Beryl's funeral on a small plasma screen and was struck by how loved she was in Norwich. Dance teacher Miss Manthorp commanded respect throughout the city, just as she had in war, when she imposed obligatory exercise on her reluctant ATS charges.

Both then, in the maelstrom of war, and now, amidst the uncertainty of a pandemic, *Army Girls* is a story about belonging. Wartime service helped bind a generation together, diminishing well-worn differences of geography and gender, class and colour. Some eighty years later that military effort has provided a rainbow of unexpected contacts, projects and assistance for many of the women in this book. Joan in Norwich was a friend of Beryl's; she too watched her funeral on a small screen. They met through their local ATS Association; Joan became the branch secretary and explains how 'a whole new world opened up' in old age. 'I got the chance to attend a Buckingham Palace garden party.'

The Queen remains an important symbol for these women. She served, albeit briefly, alongside them and her milestones through later life – marriage, children, public service and now widowhood – often mirrored theirs. The army thrives on uniform, hierarchy, display and discipline, and across the last eight decades Her Majesty has consistently embodied those qualities. I realised the book wouldn't be complete without the inclusion of Britain's most famous army girl and wrote to Buckingham Palace. I received a reply within two weeks from Windsor Castle; the Queen sent me her 'warmest good wishes' but was unable to contribute. Instead the National Army Museum's archive of her service and the high regard every woman in this book has for their monarch as a fellow time traveller and ATS girl speak for the Queen. Like them, Her Majesty's continued presence ties us back to a unique period in British history when belonging and national service defined a generation of young lives.

This book began with Daphne. Born in 1923 she grew up in Norfolk and during the war served as an ATS teleplotter and teleprinter operator, work that set her up for a career in the GPO. Daphne subsequently defined her old age and widowhood through service to others, working as a volunteer at Chelmsford's Broom Hospital until well into her nineties. But time takes its toll; when we eventually met in mid-2020 the outlook was dicey; aged ninety-seven, Daphne had a broken hip and then a bout of coronavirus. 'But I'm not ready to go yet. I want to make sure your book is how I think a book about war should be.' Daphne, who still likes to starch her tablecloths and iron her napkins, does not tolerate half measures. It's Easter weekend 2021 and the light is flashing once more on my answer phone.

> I do hope that I will be able to see you, dear, I will do my best to get well. I have had all sorts of problems, it's the waterworks at the moment. But don't worry about me. If I can be of any help, give me a ring, I think a lot about you, dear, if there is anything more you want to know for your book, give me a ring. Love you. Daphne.

I need to go now and call Daphne back – the war ended seventy-six years ago but standards remain high.

Notes

Introduction

1 Unless otherwise stated all the quotations from the veterans featured in this book are taken from interviews (in person, on the telephone, via email) with the author between July 2020 and April 2021.

2 The rose replaced the star that the WAAC was prohibited from using by the War Office, Dame Helen Gwynne-Vaughan, *Service with the Army*, London, Hutchinson, 1941, pp.16–17

3 Quotations in italics are extracts from the women's wartime letters. In this case Joan was writing to her parents in England from occupied Germany in 1945.

4 Martha to Countess of Elgin, 7 Sep 1943, Lady Martha Bruce's personal papers

5 https://www.atlasobscura.com/places/memorial-to-the-women-of-world-war-ii

1. Olivia's Drôle de Guerre

1 Julian Jackson, *France: The Dark Years, 1940–44*, Oxford, Oxford University Press, 2001, p. 117

2 Much of Olivia's story, including this comment, comes from handwritten notes, memoirs and documents in her personal archive. Letters are cited in italics.

3 Andrew Roberts, *Churchill: Walking with Destiny*, London, Penguin Books, 2018, p. 495

4 Ibid., p. 528

5 Jackson, *France*, p. 120

6 Ibid., pp. 120–21

Notes

2. 'Flowers for the mess room'

1 Gwynne Vaughan, *Service with the Army*, p. 122
2 *Daily Telegraph*, 24 Feb 1940
3 Gwynne Vaughan, *Service with the Army*, p. 124
4 Juliette Pattinson, *Women of War: Gender, Modernity, and the First Aid Nursing Yeomanry*, Manchester University Press, 2020, p. 263
5 Hugh Popham, *The FANY in Peace and War: The Story of the First Aid Nursing Yeomanry 1907–2003*, Barnsley, Lee Cooper, 2003, p. 62
6 Ibid., p. 67
7 Ibid.
8 Anne Carter, *What a Life!*, unpublished memoir, p. 15
9 Ibid.
10 Ibid.
11 1938 press cutting, File 9802-47, National Army Museum Archive (NAM), London
12 Lucy Noakes, *Women in the British Army: War and the Gentle Sex, 1907–48*, London, Routledge, 2006, p. 101
13 Gwynne Vaughan, *Service with the Army*, p. 59
14 Daniel Todman, *Britain's War: Into Battle, 1937–1941*, London, Allen Lane, 2016, ebook, p. 27
15 Noakes, *Women in the British Army*, pp. 25–6
16 Helena Vlasto in '1939 – That was the Season that was', *London Portrait Magazine*, April 1984

3. Escape to England

1 For a good summary of the fall of France from Churchill's point of view, see Roberts, *Churchill*, ch. 21, pp. 517–61
2 Julian Jackson, *Charles de Gaulle*, London, Haus, 2003, p. 1
3 Ibid.

4. 'We are standing at our posts'

1 Noakes, *Women in the British Army*, p. 105
2 Todman, *Britain's War*, p.264
3 Noakes, *Women in the British Army*, pp. 106–7; Gwynne Vaughan, *Service with the Army*, p. 94
4 14 Oct 1939, *Woman's Own*

5 Colin Dobinson, *AA Command, Britain's Anti-aircraft Defences of World War II*, Methuen, 2001, p. xiv

6 Ibid., p. 88

7 General Sir Frederick Pile, *Ack-Ack, Britain's Defence against Air Attack During the Second World War*, London, George G. Harrap and Co, 1949, p. 115

8 Dobinson, *AA Command*, p. 307

9 18 June 1940, Churchill's 'Finest Hour' speech to the House of Commons

5. *Olivia's Croix de Guerre*

1 Interview between Chris Grace and Olivia Jordan, July 2008

2 Charles de Gaulle, *The War Memoirs of Charles de Gaulle, Vol. 1: The Call to Honour, 1940–1942*, translated by Richard Howard, London, Weidenfeld and Nicolson, 1955, pp. 88–9

3 Jackson, *Charles de Gaulle*, p. 14

4 Ibid., p. 15

5 Ibid., pp. 14, 17–18

6 Certificate in Olivia Jordan's private papers

7 *Sevenoaks News*, 2 Jan 1941

6. *Bombing Girls*

1 Frank Hurd, London fireman, private papers, Imperial War Museum, https://www.iwm.org.uk/history/fireman-frank-hurds-account-of-the-london-blitz

2 Roberts, *Churchill*, p.595

3 Ibid., p. 576

4 Penny Summerfield, *Women Workers in the Second World War: Production and Patriarchy in Conflict*, Routledge, 2014, p. 3

5 Roberts, *Churchill*, p. 579

6 Gwynne Vaughan, *Service with the Army*, p. 128

7 *Daily Telegraph*, 10 Jan 1941

8 Noakes, *Women in the British Army*, p. 112

7. *Steel Helmets and Lipstick*

1 Gwynne Vaughan, *Service with the Army*, p. 138

2 Noakes, *Women in the British Army*, p. 110

3 Naomi Games, *Abram Games: His Wartime Work*, Amberley, 2019, p. 28

4 Ibid., pp. 28–31

5 Noakes, *Women in the British Army*, p. 104

6 Games, *Abram Games*, p. 32

7 Ibid., pp. 34–5

8. Recruiting Gunner Girls

1 Dobinson, *AA Command*, p. 311

2 Ibid., p. xiv

3 Ibid., p. 309

4 Ibid., pp. 308–9, 314

5 Eileen Bigland, *Britain's Other Army: The Story of the ATS*, Nicolson and Watson, 1946, p. 76; Gerard J. DeGroot, 'Whose Finger on the Trigger? Mixed Anti-aircraft Batteries and the Female Combat Taboo', *War in History*, Vol. 4, No. 4, Nov 1997, p. 439

6 Mary Soames, *A Daughter's Tale: The Memoir of Winston and Clemetine Churchill's Youngest Child*, London, Doubleday, 2012, pp. 198–9

7 Ibid., pp. 207–8

8 Noakes, *Women in the British Army*, p. 119

9 Dobinson, *AA Command*, p. 307

10 Ibid., p. 314

9. 'YOU are wanted too!'

1 Noakes, *Women in the British Army*, p. 117

2 His most recent biographer Andrew Roberts doesn't mention conscription for women (Roberts, *Churchill*, 2018). Nor is there any mention in Roy Jenkins, *Churchill*, London, Macmillan, 2001

3 *Daily Telegraph*, 18 Oct 1941

4 Noakes, *Women in the British Army*, p. 115

5 2 Dec 1941, 'Maximum National Effort', *Hansard* Vol. 376, https://hansard.parliament.uk/Commons/1941-12-02/debates/1856d9fd-c45e-468a-bf96-ec34f492ef0d/MaximumNationalEffort

6 Noakes, *Women in the British Army*, p. 117

7 *The Auxiliary Territorial Service*, compiled by J. M. Cooper, War Office, 1949, p. 216
8 Roberts, *Churchill*, p. 722
9 Lecture notes from No. 1 ATS OCTU, Edinburgh, 1942/43, 9710-157, NAM

10. 'The girl behind the gunner'

1 1939 WWII Ministry of Information *ACK ACK* film, https://www.youtube.com/watch?v=_M10k-t73-s
2 'Maximum National Effort', *Hansard*, https://hansard.parliament.uk/Commons/1941-12-02/debates/1856d9fd-c45e-468a-bf96-ec34f492ef0d/MaximumNationalEffort
3 *Guardian*, 26 Jan 1942
4 *The Times*, 21 Apr 1942
5 Dobinson, *AA Command*, pp.115–6
6 *Predictions While You Wait!* (1939), British Pathé, https://www.britishpathe.com/video/predictions-while-you-wait/
7 https://www.feltwell.net/feltwell2/times/aliferemembered.htm
8 Dobinson, *AA Command*, p. 356–7

11. 'Top Ack!'

1 The problem was neatly summed up post-45. 'On the one hand the ATS was established as a woman's service, to be directed by women. On the other hand the men maintained that it was impossible to expect them to employ in important positions women over whom they had no control.' *The Auxiliary Territorial Service*, p. 25
2 Noakes, *Women in the British Army*, p. 120
3 *The Auxiliary Territorial Service*, p. 21
4 Dobinson, *AA Command*, p. 313
5 Svetlana Alexievich, *The Unwomanly Face of War*, translated by Richard Pevear and Larissa Volokhonsky, London, Penguin, ebook, pp. vii, 62, 105
6 Dobinson, *AA Command*, p. 313
7 'Maximum National Effort', *Hansard*, https://hansard.parliament.uk/Commons/1941-12-02/debates/1856d9fd-c45e-468a-bf96-ec34f492ef0d/MaximumNationalEffort

8 Bigland, *Britain's Other Army*, p. 76
9 Gwynne Vaughan, *Service with the Army*, pp. 28, 45
10 Noakes, *Women in the British Army*, p. 114
11 *Report of the Committee on Amenities and Welfare Conditions in the Three Women's Services*, London, HMSO, 1942, p. 28
12 Beryl F. Manthorp, *Towards Ballet, Dance Training for the Very Young*, London, Dance, 1988
13 Beryl F. Manthorp, *A Mobile PTI*, unpublished memoir

12. 'Come into the army, Maud'

1 *The Times*, 12 Dec 1941; *New Statesman and Nation*, 6 Dec 1941
2 Summerfield, *Women Workers in the Second World War*, p. 34
3 *Daily Telegraph*, 11 Dec 1941
4 Noakes, *Women in the British Army*, p. 122
5 *Report of the Committee on Amenities and Welfare Conditions in the Three Women's Services*, p. 5

13. 'Rumours derogatory to the service'

1 *The Auxiliary Territorial Service*, p. 227
2 Ibid.
3 Ibid.
4 Ibid.
5 *Report of the Committee on Amenities and Welfare Conditions in the Three Women's Services*, pp. 49–52
6 DeGroot, 'Whose Finger on the Trigger?', p. 438
7 Ibid.
8 *Report of the Committee on Amenities and Welfare Conditions in the Three Women's Services*, p. 49

14. Figureheads and Secret Work

1 Gywnne Vaughan, *Service with the Army*, p. 56
2 Ibid., p. 100
3 Soames, *A Daughter's Tale*, p. 207
4 She was well known for her style – Mary Churchill described Knox as 'glamorous', ibid; ATS statistic from *The Auxiliary Territorial Service*, p. 47

5 *Report of the Committee on Amenities and Welfare Conditions in the Three Women's Services*, p. 16

6 *National Geographic*, May 2020

7 Tessa Dunlop, *The Bletchley Girls*, London, Hodder and Stoughton, 2015, pp. 84–5

8 Ibid., pp. 41–2

9 Charlotte Webb, *Secret Postings: Bletchley Park to the Pentagon*, Redditch, BookTower Publishing, 2011, p.29

10 Ibid., p.32; Dunlop, *Bletchley Girls*, pp. 94, 101, 104

11 Dunlop, *Bletchley Girls*, pp. 108–9

12 Sinclair McKay, *The Secret Life of Bletchley Park: The WWII Codebreaking Centre and the Men and Women Who Worked There*, London, Aurum Press, 2011, p.159

13 Dunlop, *Bletchley Girls*, pp. 166, 185

15. A Reluctant Recruit

1 Summerfield, *Women Workers in the Second World War*, p. 44

2 'Maximum National Effort', *Hansard*, https://hansard. parliament.uk/Commons/1941-12-02/debates/1856d9fd-c45e-468a-bf96-ec34f492ef0d/MaximumNationalEffort

3 *The Auxiliary Territorial Service*, p. 61

4 Dunlop, *The Bletchley Girls*, p. 111

5 Ibid., pp. 103–4

16. The Cookhouse – 'a woman's natural home'

1 *The Auxiliary Territorial Service*, p. 167

2 Gywnne Vaughan, *Service with the Army*, pp. 129–30

3 Roberts, *Churchill*, p. 594

4 DeGroot, 'Whose Finger on the Trigger?', p.437

5 Extract from 'Ours is Not to Reason Why', Andrew Sinclair (ed.), *The War Decade: An Anthology*, London, Hamilton, 1989, p. 43

6 Gwynne Vaughan, *Service with the Army*, p. 130

7 Lecture Notes from No.1 ATS OCTU Edinburgh, 1942/43, 9710-157, NAM

8 Soames, *A Daughter's Tale*, pp. 207, 223

9 Roberts, *Churchill*, p. 594

10 Lecture Notes from No.1 ATS OCTU Edinburgh, 1942/43, 9710-157, NAM

17. Driving like a Princess

1 Robert Lacey, *Majesty: Elizabeth II and the House of Windsor*, New York and London, Harcourt Brace Jovanovich, 1977, pp. 27–35; Kate Williams, *Young Elizabeth: The Making of Our Queen*, London, Weidenfeld and Nicolson, 2012, p. 149

2 Williams, *Young Elizabeth*, pp.170, 172

3 Ibid., p. 164

4 Ibid., p. 177; Elizabeth Longford, *Elizabeth R*, London, Weidenfeld and Nicolson, 1983, p. 95

5 Report of interview with Her Majesty the Queen, 30 Nov 1944; Maud L. Maclellan to Director Whateley, 6 Dec 1944, Lady Katherine Seymour to Whateley, 10 Dec 1944, Whateley to Seymour, 10 Feb 1945, File 9802-70, NAM; http://www.helensburgh-heritage.co.uk/index.php?option=com_content&view=article&id=868:i-taught-the-queen-to-drive&catid=72:reminiscences&Itemid=493

6 Report of interview with Her Majesty the Queen, 30 Nov 1944, ibid.

7 Ibid.

8 Director Whateley to Lady Katherine Seymour, 6 Apr 1945, Seymour to Whateley, 7 Apr 1945, Senior Controller Baxter Ellis to Seymour, 10 Apr 1945, ibid

9 Her Royal Highness the Princess Elizabeth, questionnaire with suggested answers, ibid

10 Popham, *The FANY in Peace and War*, p. 71

11 Director Whateley to Katherine Seymour, 14 Feb 1945, Maud Maclellan, Chief Commander No.1 MTTC to the Director ATS, 13 Mar 1945, ibid.

12 *Daily Telegraph*, 12 Apr 1945; *Guardian*, 12 Apr 1945

13 *Guardian*, 12 Apr 1945

14 http://www.helensburgh-heritage.co.uk/index.php?option=com_content&view=article&id=868:i-taught-the-queen-to-drive&catid=72:reminiscences&Itemid=493

15 Williams, *Young Elizabeth*, p. 189

16 Elizabeth Longford wrongly concludes that with the exception

of sleeping at Windsor Elizabeth was 'treated like any other girl in this women's organisation', Longford, *Elizabeth R*, p. 97

17   Williams, *Young Elizabeth*, p. 188; Syllabus and Programme for NCOS Cadre Course, No. 1 MTTC, ATS, File 9802-70, NAM

18   http://www.helensburgh-heritage.co.uk/index. php?option=com_content&view=article&id=868:i-taught-the-queen-to-drive&catid=72:reminiscences&Itemid=493

18. Gun-site Life

1   The King consented to his daughter's 1946 engagement to Philip on the condition it remained a secret until after the Windsor's tour of South Africa in the spring of 1947. Even then George VI required further persuading, with the engagement announcement finally made on 7 July 1947, Robert Lacey, *The Crown: The Inside History*, London, Blink Publishing, 2017, pp. 10–17; Lacey, *Majesty*, pp. 125–30; Longford, *Elizabeth R*, pp. 108–9

2   DeGroot, 'Whose Finger on the Trigger?', p. 443

3   Pile, *Ack-Ack*, pp. 190–91

4   DeGroot, 'Whose Finger on the Trigger?', pp. 443–4

19. Becoming a FANY

1   Patricia and Jean Owtram, *Codebreaking Sisters: Our Secret War*, London, Mirror Books, 2020, ebook, p. 34

2   Ibid, p. 57

3   Popham, *The FANY in War and Peace*, pp. 67–9

4   Roy Terry, 'Gamwell, (Antonia) Marian (1891–1977), volunteer ambulance driver and commanding officer of the FANY', 2011, *Oxford Dictionary of National Biography*. Retrieved 30 Apr. 2021, from https://www-oxforddnb-com.lonlib.idm. oclc.org/view/10.1093/ref:odnb/9780198614128.001.0001/ odnb-9780198614128-e-67668.

20. Deadly Parlour Games

1   For a biography of Violette Szabo, see Susan Ottway, *Violette Szabo: The Life That I Have*, Barnsley, Pen & Sword, 2003

2 For an accessible recent biography of Krystyna Sharbek, see Clare Mulley, *The Spy Who Loved: The Secrets and Lives of One of Britain's Bravest Wartime Heroines*, London, Macmillan, 2012

3 Ottway, *Violette Szabo*, pp. 53–60

4 Mulley, *The Spy Who Loved*, ebook, pp. 150, 174

5 Ibid., p. 151

6 Owtrams, *Codebreaking Sisters*, pp. 71–3

7 Ibid., pp. 73–4

8 Leo Marks, *Between Silk and Cyanide: A Code Maker's War 1941–45*, The History Press, 2007, pp.22–3

9 Ibid., p. 12, 14

10 Ibid., p. 15

11 Owtrams, *Codebreaking Sisters*, pp.75–6

12 Marks, *Between Silk and Cyanide*, p. 420

21. Multi-racial War

1 Manthorp, *A Mobile PTI*, unpublished memoir

2 Angus Calder, *The People's War: Britain 1939–1945*, London, Vintage, 1971, p. 308

3 Estimates put the number of Black and mixed-race citizens of African, Caribbean, American and British backgrounds in the UK when war was declared at about 15,000, although some have argued the figure could have been as high as 40,000, Stephen Bourne, *Mother Country: Britain's Black Community on the Home Front, 1939–45*, Stroud, History Press, 2010, p. 11

4 Hugh Robert Hill (ed.), *The International Geography, by Seventy Authors*, London, Macmillan, 1911, pp. 103–8

5 Manthorp, *A Mobile PTI*

6 Hill (ed.), *The International Geography*, pp. 103–8

7 Carter, *What a Life!*, p. 17

8 Noakes, *Women in the British Army*, pp.125–6

9 Zoom interview recorded with Ena Collymore-Woodstock, her daughter Marguerite Woodstock-Riley and Curious PR, 13 Oct 2020

10 Notes, Curious PR interview with Ena Collymore-Woodstock

11 Noakes, *British Women in the Army*, p. 125

12 Curious PR interview with Ena Collymore-Woodstock

13 Photograph 60, 9407-283, NAM
14 Notes, Curious PR interview with Ena Collymore-Woodstock

22. 'One can look but one must not touch!'

1 In the 616-page contemporary study *Logistical Support of the Armies* that covers this period the women's services are not mentioned. Roland G. Ruppenthal, *Logistical Support of the Armies, V1: May, 1941 to September, 1944*, Washington DC, Department of the Army,1953
2 Jane Waller, *Women in Wartime: The Role of Women's Magazines, 1939–45*, London, Macdonald Optima, 1987
3 Carter, *What a Life!*, p. 18
4 Ibid.
5 *Report of the Committee on Amenities and Welfare Conditions in the Three Women's Services*, p. 31

23. Boys, Girls and D-Day Landings

1 Roberts, *Churchill*, pp. 822–3

24. Operation Diver

1 Over 1,000 heavy and 500 light anti-aircraft weapons were moved, Dobinson, *AA Command*, p. 429
2 Ibid., p. 423
3 *Report of the Committee on Amenities and Welfare Conditions in the Three Women's Services*, p. 8; DeGroot, 'Whose Finger on the Trigger?', p. 443
4 Air defence against the much deadlier V-2 rocket, operating at a range of 150–200 miles at speeds of 3,000 mph, proved elusive although radar detection rates had improved by March 1945, Dobinson, *AA Command*, pp. 442–51
5 Ibid., pp. 421–38
6 Ibid., p. 429
7 Dunlop, *The Bletchley Girls*, p. 215
8 Dobinson, *AA Command*, p. 438
9 Soames, *A Daughter's Tale*, picture plate, pp. 300–301; 1 Jul 1944, *The Times*
10 Dobinson, *AA Command*, pp. 437–8

25. Service Overseas

1 Gripping recent accounts of the D-Day Landing and the Battle for Normandy include Antony Beevor, *D-Day: The Battle for Normandy*, London, Penguin, 2010; James Holland, *Normandy '44: D-Day and the Epic 77-Battle for France*, Atlantic Monthly Press, 2019

2 Films such as *The Longest Day* (1962), *Overlord* (1975), *Saving Private Ryan* (1998), *D-Day: Battle of Omaha Beach* (2019).

3 Soames, *A Daughter's Tale*, p. 322

4 Ibid., p. 323

5 Owtrams, *Codebreaking Sisters*, pp. 76, 79

6 Ibid., p. 79

7 Ibid., pp. 80–81

8 Carter, *What a Life!*, p. 19

9 Ibid.

10 Ibid., p. 20

11 Ibid.

12 For an engaging read on Italy's war, see James Holland, *Italy's Sorrow 1944–45*, London, Harper Press, 2008

13 Carter, *What a Life!*, p. 21

14 Noakes, *Women in the British Army*, p. 127

26. Conscription Overseas

1 Noakes, *Women in the British Army*, p. 128

2 *The Times*, 24 Jan 1945

3 For more on post-war Europe see Keith Lowe, *Savage Continent: Europe in the Aftermath of World War II*, London, Penguin, 2012

27. Bittersweet Victory

1 Roberts, *Churchill*, p. 873

2 *Daily Mail*, 9 May 1945

3 HM Queen Elizabeth talking in *The Way We Were*, BBC documentary, 1985

4 Churchill's VE Day speech, https://www.bbc.com/historyofthebbc/anniversaries/may/ve-day-broadcasts#:~:text=Winston%20Churchill%20announced%20the%20end,and%20efforts%20that%20lie%20ahead%22

5 Angela Holdsworth, *Out of the Doll's House: The Story of Women in the Twentieth Century*, London, BBC Books, 1988, p. 26
6 Noakes, *Women in the British Army*, p. 138
7 Ibid., pp. 140–41
8 Ibid., p. 137
9 Roberts, *Churchill*, p. 874

28. Germany and Beyond

1 Roberts, *Churchill*, p. 867
2 Carter, *What a Life!*, p. 22
3 *Daily Express*, 16 Nov 1945
4 Ibid.
5 *The Star*, 16 Nov 1945

29. Remembering the War

1 Noakes, *Women in the British Army*, p. 147
2 Visit the National Army Museum website for a concise timeline of women in the British Army, https://www.nam.ac.uk/explore/timeline-women-army
3 DeGroot, 'Whose Finger on the Trigger?', p. 440
4 In July 2020 a raft of measures were introduced to tackle 'unacceptable levels' of discrimination and bullying in the armed forces and in December 2020 the Defence Committee launched an inquiry on Women in the Armed Forces. See https://www.bbc.co.uk/news/uk-53365517; https://committees.parliament.uk/committee/24/defence-committee/news/136800/defence-committee-launch-inquiry-on-women-in-the-armed-forces/

Bibliography

Unless otherwise cited in the footnotes, all references concerning the veterans and their family and friends were taken from face-to-face interviews, email exchanges, letters, Zoom calls and telephone conversations throughout the course of 2020 and 2021. *Army Girls* has also benefited hugely from access the women gave me to their personal wartime correspondence, photographs and unpublished memoirs, for which I am extremely grateful.

These documents were particularly valuable in a book predominantly written during a pandemic when the vast majority of archives and libraries were closed and access to primary and secondary sources limited. Historians always stand on the shoulders of those who have come before them but, operating under Covid-19-restricted conditions, certain books really did become my 'bibles' and Lucy Noakes's meticulous *Women in the British Army* deserves a special mention, likewise Colin Dobinson's thoroughly researched *AA Command* for its portrayal of anti-aircraft gun-sites during World War II.

Below is by no means a comprehensive list of all the materials that fed into *Army Girls* – those have been accrued over a lifetime. Rather it is a list of the specific texts which I have consulted in the last eighteen months; needless to say, courtesy of three lockdowns, my personal 'library' has grown somewhat!

ARCHIVES

National Army Museum Archive, London

BOOKS

Kate Adie, *Corsets to Camouflage: Women and War*, London, Hodder & Stoughton, 2003

Svetlana Alexievich, *The Unwomanly Face of War*, translated by Richard Pevear and Larissa Volokhonsky, London, Penguin, 2018

Antony Beevor, *D-Day: The Battle for Normandy*, London, Penguin, 2010

Eileen Bigland, *Britain's Other Army: The Story of the ATS*, Nicolson and Watson, 1946

Stephen Bourne, *Mother Country: Britain's Black Community on the Home Front, 1939–45*, Stroud, The History Press, 2010

Dorothy Brewer Kerr, *The Girls behind the Guns: With the ATS in World War II*, London, Robert Hale, 1990

Mike Brown, *The Day Peace Broke Out: The VE-Day Experience*, Stroud, Sutton Publishing, 2005

John Buckley, *Monty's Men: The British Army and the Liberation of Europe*, New Haven, Yale University Press, 2014

Angus Calder, *The People's War: Britain 1939–1945*, London, Vintage, 1971

The Auxiliary Territorial Service, compiled by J. M. Cooper, War Office, 1949

Charles de Gaulle, *The War Memoirs of Charles de Gaulle, Vol. 1: The Call to Honour, 1940–1942*, translated by Richard Howard, London, Weidenfeld and Nicolson, 1955

Colin Dobinson, *AA Command: Britain's Anti-aircraft Defences of World War II*, London, Methuen, 2001

Colin Dobinson, *Operation Diver: Guns, V1 Flying Bombs and Landscapes of Defence, 1944–45*, Swindon, Historic England, 2019

Tessa Dunlop, *The Bletchley Girls*, London, Hodder and Stoughton, 2015

Tessa Dunlop, *The Century Girls*, London, Simon and Schuster, 2018

Beryl E. Escott, *The Heroines of SOE: F Section, Britain's Secret Women in France*, Stroud, The History Press, 2010

Naomi Games, *Abram Games: His Wartime Work*, Stroud, Amberley, 2019

Dame Helen Gwynne-Vaughan, *Service with the Army*, London, Hutchinson, 1941

Carol Harris, *Women at War 1939–1945: The Home Front*, Stroud, The History Press, 2010

M. Michaela Hampf, *Release a Man for Combat: The Women's Army Corps during World War II*, Weimar, Wien, Böhlau Verlag, 2010

Desmond Hawkins (ed.), *War Report: From D-Day to Berlin AS IT HAPPENED*, London, BBC Books, 2019

Hugh Robert Hill (ed.) *The International Geography, by Seventy Authors*, London, Macmillan, 1911

Anglea Holdsworth, *Out of the Doll's House: The Story of Women in the Twentieth Century*, London, BBC Books, 1988

James Holland, *Italy's Sorrow 1944–45*, London, Harper Press, 2008

James Holland, *Normandy '44: D-Day and the Epic 77-Battle for France*, Atlantic Monthly Press, 2019

Bibliography

Julian Jackson, *Charles de Gaulle*, London, Haus, 2003

Julian Jackson, *France: The Dark Years, 1940–44*, Oxford,
　　　Oxford University Press, 2001

Roy Jenkins, *Churchill*, London, Macmillan, 2001

Tony Judt, *Postwar: A History of Europe since 1945*, London,
　　　Vintage Books, 2010

Robert Lacey, *Majesty: Elizabeth II and the House of Windsor*,
　　　New York and London, Harcourt Brace Jovanovich,
　　　1977

Robert Lacey, *The Crown: The Inside History*, London, Blink
　　　Publishing, 2017

Elizabeth Longford, *Elizabeth R*, London, Weidenfeld and
　　　Nicolson, 1983

Keith Lowe, *Savage Continent: Europe in the Aftermath of World
　　　War II*, London, Penguin, 2012

Beryl F. Manthorp, *Towards Ballet: Dance Training for the Very
　　　Young*, London, Dance, 1988

Leo Marks, *Between Silk and Cyanide: A Code Maker's War
　　　1941–45*, The History Press, 2007

Sinclair McKay, *The Secret Life of Bletchley Park: The WWII
　　　Codebreaking Centre and the Men and Women Who Worked
　　　There*, London, Aurum Press, 2011

Clare Mulley, *The Spy Who Loved: The Secrets and Lives of
　　　One of Britain's Bravest Wartime Heroines*, London,
　　　Macmillan, 2012

Lucy Noakes, *Women in the British Army: War and the Gentle
　　　Sex, 1907–48*, London, Routledge, 2006

Susan Ottway, *Violette Szabo, The Life That I Have*, Barnsley,
　　　Pen & Sword, 2003

Colonel Cary Outram, OBE, *1000 Days on the River
　　　Kwai: The Secret Diary of a British Camp Commandant*,
　　　Barnsley, Pen & Sword, 2017

Patricia and Jean Owtram, *Codebreaking Sisters: Our Secret War*, London, Mirror Books, 2020

Tanya-Jayne Park (ed.), *100 Wonderful Women: 100 Stories of Women's Service in the British Army since 1917*, Women's Royal Army Corps Association, 2019

Juliette Pattinson, *Women of War: Gender, Modernity, and the First Aid Nursing Yeomanry*, Manchester University Press, 2020

General Sir Frederick Pile, *Ack-Ack: Britain's Defence against Air Attack During the Second World War*, London, George G. Harrap and Co, 1949

Hugh Popham, *The FANY in Peace and War: The Story of the First Aid Nursing Yeomanry 1907–2003*, Barnsley, Lee Cooper, 2003

Report of the Committee on Amenities and Welfare Conditions in the Three Women's Services, London, HMSO, 1942

Andrew Roberts, *Churchill: Walking with Destiny*, London, Penguin Books, 2018

Vee Robinson, *Sisters in Arms: How Female Gunners Defended Britain against the Luftwaffe*, London, Harper Collins, 1996

Paul Roland, *Nazi Women of the Third Reich: Serving the Swastika*, Arcturus, 2018

Steward Ross, *Rationing: At Home in World War Two*, London, Evans Brothers Ltd, 2007

Roland G. Ruppenthal, *Logistical Support of the Armies, Vol. VI: May, 1941 to September, 1944*, Department of the Army, Washington DC, 1953

Virginia Scharff, *Taking the Wheel: Women and the Coming of the Motor Age*, Albuquerque, University of New Mexico Press, 1992

Andrew Sinclair (ed.), *The War Decade: An Anthology*, London, Hamilton, 1989

Mary Soames, *A Daughter's Tale: The Memoir of Winston and Clemetine Churchill's Youngest Child*, London, Doubleday, 2012

Penny Summerfield, *Women Workers in the Second World War: Production and Patriarchy in Conflict*, Abingdon, Routledge, 2014

Daniel Todman, *Britain's War, Vol I: Into Battle, 1937–1941*, London, Allen Lane, 2016

Daniel Todman, *Britain's War, Vol II: A New World, 1942–47*, London, Allen Lane, 2016

Richard Vinen, *National Service, Conscription in Britain, 1945–63*, London, Allen Lane, 2014

Jane Waller, *Women in Wartime: The Role of Women's Magazines, 1939–45*, London, Macdonald Optima, 1987

Arthur Wauters, *Eve in Overalls*, London, Imperial War Museum, 2017

Charlotte Webb, *Secret Postings: Bletchley Park to the Pentagon*, Redditch, Book Tower Publishing, 2011

Leslie Whateley, *As Thoughts Survive*, London, Hutchinson & Co, 1949

Brian Williams, *Britain at War, 1939–45*, Norwich, Pitkin, 2005

Kate Williams, *Young Elizabeth, The Making of Our Queen*, London, Weidenfeld and Nicolson, 2012

ARTICLES

Gerard J. DeGroot, 'Whose Finger on the Trigger? Mixed Anti-aircraft Batteries and the Female Combat Taboo', *War in History*, Vol. 4, No. 4, Nov 1997

Bibliography

Tessa Stone, 'Creating a (Gendered?) Military Identity: The Women's Auxiliary Air-force in Great Britain in the Second World War', *Women's History Review*, 1999

Newspapers/Magazines/Journals

Daily Express
Daily Mail
Daily Telegraph
Guardian
London Illustrated News
London Portrait Magazine
National Geographic
Punch
Sevenoaks News
Star
New Statesman and Nation
The Times
Woman's Own

Websites

www.bbc.com
www.britishpathe.com
https://committees.parliament.uk
www.feltwell.net
https://hansard.parliament.uk
www.helensburgh-heritage.co.uk
www.iwm.org.uk
www.nam.ac.uk
www.oxforddnb.com
www.youtube.com

Acknowledgements

When you write a book that's heartbeat is the lives of others, it's hard to know where to start in terms of acknowledgements. That is especially the case with *Army Girls*, a story that made demands of our very oldest and most precious women at a time when they were contained and imperilled by Covid-19 and its accompanying restrictions. Alongside my remarkable cast of seventeen, I would like to thank their carers, family members and friends, who helped facilitate my visits and field my questions. Special mention is needed for Olivia's nephew Charles Grace and his sterling work linking me up with his aunt and her abundant archive. Thanks also to Grace's mainstay and dear friend Lorriane Singleton, for keeping us connected via WhatsApp, and to Martha's sister, Lady Jean Wemyss, and niece, Lady Georgina Bruce, for additional interviews and information.

It was Lyn Wyer, former physical training instructor for the Women's Royal Army Corps, who introduced me to her coterie of ATS veterans in the Norwich area. Lyn is a member of the Women's Royal Army Corps Association, without which I could not have written this book. The organisation helps maintain contact between former servicewomen, and in the case of *Army Girls* they surpassed themselves. A very special thank you to the Association's Julia Doig, who helped me find Britain's final few female veterans when the book was still a figment of my imagination – her enthusiasm for the subject and the veterans helped drive the project across the line. Ditto Colonel (retired) Alison Brown, OBE, the association's former president; it was hearing her extraordinary service story that motivated me to explore the history of women in the military.

The 80th anniversary of female conscription and the great age of the *Army Girls* featured here explains the World War II focus of this book, but Alison made me realise that this is just the tip of the iceberg. Since 1945, women have been on an extraordinary military journey that has finally seen them incorporated into every area of the British army. The road hasn't been a smooth one: as I write these acknowledgements the Defence Committee has just published a damning indictment against the current procedures designed to protect women from bullying and harassment in the armed forces. The veterans featured on these pages were trailblazers and catalysts for change in a different era, but there is still more, much more, to be done.

Researching and writing in lockdown comes with its own set of unique problems (and perks). More than ever I've relied on the knowledge and assistance of others. Simon Robinson, a dear friend who shares my passion for oral history, dug deep into his collection of memorabilia, names and addresses, without which this book would not have the magic touch of Daphne and Joyce. His unstinting enthusiasm for both the subject and the women was an essential pick-me-up on dark winter days.

At the height of the pandemic, when almost everything was closed, staff at the London Library kept the postal service fully occupied with my military requests, and at the National Army Museum, Claire Blackshaw and Nicola Aryton were consistent champions of this project, which was greatly facilitated by access to the NAM archive; thank you, Rob Fleming, for being the generous gatekeeper to such an amazing collection.

I am grateful to Emeritus Professor Bruce Collins for fielding my endless military and historical questions and for fact-checking the manuscript, and my pubilsher Iain MacGregor at Headline for taking the plunge with me for a second time and understanding the demands and time constraints involved when working with the extremely elderly. His able accomplice editorial assistant Holly Purdham has been brilliant at managing my many queries and talking down my anxieties! Likewise publicist Emily Patience, who has more than lived up to her name. There are, of course, plenty of others behind the scenes at Headline and beyond who I've not met, courtesy of Covid-19, but who've played a part in getting this book out to a tight November 2021 deadline. Thank you all.

Thank you to my agent Robert Kirby for standing by my desire to write a final 'Girls' title; the trilogy is complete! Thanks to John Murphy for coming on (another) road trip and magically transforming what I tried to capture on these pages into a Radio 4 half hour (set to air in December 2021). To Daniel Fagerson and Dan Jones, you both made me see clearly that this was the right book at the right time. To Kate Williams, Rebecca Rideal and Helen Carr, you in particular have helped me feel included in an online history community that's become part of the publishing game. Hilary Murray at Arlington Enterprises is always top of my thank you list, likewise my long-suffering mother, Anthea, and daughter, Mara, both of whom listened and listened again. It was very much a female affair. Appropriately, husband Dan was in the kitchen earning his stripes when I was once more delayed with visits, deadlines, decisions and rewrites. Oh yes, and that old chestnut: procrastination.

Finally, all my love and thanks go to the women in this book. I have never been good at professional boundaries and I know you are very old, but to those that remain, really and truly, I wish you could live for ever.

South London
July 2021

Olivia

Joyce

Anne

Martha

Daphne

Diana

Barbara

Penny

Vera

Grace

Joan

Beryl

Maud

Betty

Nanza

Jean

Ena

PLATE SECTION PICTURE CREDITS

page 1   top: NAM.1995-01-48; courtesy of the National Army Museum, London

bottom: Courtesy of Olivia Jordan

page 2   top: Tessa Dunlop

bottom: NAM.1994-07-291-24: courtesy of the National Army Museum, London

page 3   top: Poster by Abram Games/Imperial War Museum via Getty Images

bottom: NAM.1994-07-291-239: courtesy of the National Army Museum, London

page 4   top: NAM.1994-07-277-15; courtesy of the National Army Museum, London

bottom: Tessa Dunlop

page 5   top: Courtesy of Joyce Wilding

bottom: Courtesy of Anne Carter

page 6   top: Courtesy of Barbara Weatherill

bottom: NAM.1994-07-291-70; courtesy of the National Army Museum, London

page 7   top: NAM.1994-07-283-60; courtesy of the National Army Museum, London

bottom: Courtesy of Martha Bruce

page 8   top: Courtesy of Anne Carter

bottom: Courtesy of Daphne Attridge

Index

AA (Anti-Aircraft) Command
    xv–xvi, 41, 91, 116, 299–300
  allows employment of women
    75–7
  casualties 99–100, 102–5
  expansion of 42
  female accommodation 188
  first female casualty 99–100
  first mixed gun-site 75–6, 77
  gender division 112–4
  numbers of women serving 183
  Operation Diver 241
  quality of recruits 42, 79–80
  recruitment 99
  routine 184
  solves manpower problem 73–5
  training 77, 77–8, 81–2, 97
Abdication Crisis 174
abortions 228–9
accommodation 188
ack-ack guns. *see* antiaircraft guns
administrative remit 113
Aeroplane and Armament
    Experimental Establishment,
    Boscombe Down 85
Afghanistan 299
air defence, expansion of 42
Air Ministry 35, 293
Air Raid Precautions Act 54
air raids
  the Blitz 53–4, 54–6, 58–61, 61,
    73–4, 108

  casualties 57, 60
  incendiary 58–9
  Liverpool 102
  Manchester 103–4
  mass psychological trauma 55
  and morale 55, 61
  Plymouth 57–8, 106–9
  purpose 55
  V1 attacks 239–43, 256
air raids shelters 54
Anglesey 97–8
Anne, Princess 176–7
antiaircraft guns 40–1, 98
  40mm Bofors 183
  effectiveness 41–2, 107
  finest hour 242–3
  fire 106, 107–8
  Germany 115
  gun-laying equipment 110–1,
    237–8
  gun-sites 184–5
  height-finder readings 100–2
  placement 107
  routine 184
  Russian 115
  shells 113–4
  technical training 110–2
  women's role 99
anxiety 232
aptitude testing 79, 103
Arcachon 28
Ardennes, the 8

Argles, Jean (nee Owtram) xiii, xxi
    anxiety about the future 276–7
    creative ambition 276–7
    Egypt posting 260–1
    father missing 196
    fathers return 277
    impatient for the end 269
    Italy posting 261–4
    joins FANYs 195–7
    overseas service authorised 254–5
    pre-war existence 195–6
    promotion to ensign 255
    promotion to team leader 262
    signs Official Secrets Act 207
    SOE service 206–10
    VE Day 275–6
    voyage to Egypt 255, 257
aristocracy, the, pre-war existence
    22–6
Army Act 70, 118
ARP 53–4, 54–5
Astor, Nancy 127
Attlee, Clement 7, 277–8
Attridge, Daphne, (nee Williams)
    ix–x, xii, xx, 306–7
    attitude to ATS 85
    and Battle of Britain 43–4
    cousin William 38–40
    death of cousin William 39–40
    and death of Dorothy Lemmon.
        102–3
    demobilization 282
    desire to join war effort 61–3
    duties 105–6
    family background 37–8
    joins ATS 87–8
    and male desire 135–7
    memory of ack-ack guns 40–1
    and overseas service 254
    post-war life 282–3
    pre-war existence 36–40
    resistance to idea of equality xi
    and sexual health 224–5
    strong women around 38
    training 88–9
Austria 294
Auxiliary Fire Service 54

Auxiliary Territorial Service x,
        xvii–xviii
    accommodation 239
    bad start 34–5
    BEF service 13–4
    British West Indies recruits
        216–20
    casualties 100n
    clerk ratio 128–9
    Dame Helen appointed first
        director 21
    downsizing 279
    Elizabeth II joins 174, 176
    establishment 19–20
    evacuation from Dunkirk 13
    expansion 142
    FANY status within 16–7, 70, 198
    first woman to be recruited 18, 19
    flaws 79
    image overhauled 70–2
    image problem xiii, 13–4, 62–3,
        85, 122, 123, 126
    included in Army Act 69–70
    instruction school 17
    lack of popularity 34–5
    Lancaster flight crash 293–4
    lipstick advert 70–2
    loss of recruits 34, 35, 36
    main problem 159
    Mary, the Princess Royal as
        controller commandant
        140–2, 176
    medicals 91–3, 216
    oldest known living veteran 217
    overseas service authorised 253–4
    rebranded 279
    recruitment 19–21, 123, 215–6
    recruitment campaign 69
    recruits 71–2, 132
    rumours derogatory to the service
        132–9
    shortage of volunteers xiv, 35
    special problem 132–4
    strength 142
    talent identification 237
    training 77–8, 127, 128, 145–6,
        219

uniform 70, 90
unpopularity 62–3
West Indian veterans 303

Baiely, Tom 222–3, 230–1, 235, 252
Bailey, Penny (nee Daysh) xx,
    129–30
  ARP job 53–4, 54–5, 68
  D-Day landings 235
  death of 304, 305
  death of boyfriend 68–9
  family background 53
  father 54
  marries Tom 252
  meets Princess Anne 176–7
  naivety 133
  relationship with Tom 222–3,
    230–1, 235
  service book 222
  York posting 221–3
Baldwin, Stanley 42
Bar-de-Luc 9
barter 167
Battle of Britain 42–4, 53
Bayonne 28
BBC, de Gaulle's first broadcast
  47–8
Beaton, Cecil 78
Belgian army prisoners 268
Belgium 265, 265–9
Best, Norma 303
Beveridge report 278
Bevin, Ernest 61–2, 72, 126
Bexhill 107
Bill, Eddie 67–8
Bingham, Phyllis 198, 199–200
Bird, Harry 4
Birmingham 122, 124–5, 132, 158,
  252, 272
  Hollymoor hospital 232–4
Black Lives Matter 214
Black troops 212–4, 272–3
Bletchley Park x, 144–50
  card index 148
  discipline 150
  distractions 148–9
  Japanese section 149

Labour Review 156
lodgings 149
Madrigal Club 149
recruitment interview 147
sanitary arrangements 150
signals interception 151
staff 145
Station X 145
Y-station listeners 151
Blitz, the 53–4, 54–6, 58–61, 61,
  73–4, 108
Blitzkrieg 8
Booth, Mrs 162–3
Bordeaux 11, 27–8
Boris, Georges 50
Bot, Kathy 108, 227
Bournemouth 213
Boy Scouts 24, 54
Brentwood 66–7
Briggens House 14
Brighton 107
Bristol Evening Post (newspaper) 20
British Army of the Rhine 286–9
British Expeditionary Force xi, 13–4,
  34
British legation, Bordeaux 27–9
British Legion 300
British Liberation Army xi, xv,
  264–9, 278
British values xiv
British West Indies, ATS recruits
  from 216–20
Bruce, Andrew 23
Bruce, Jean 25
Bruce, Lady Martha, OBE xix,
  21–2, 82, 130, 138–9, 167, 215
  asked to join ATS 26
  brother injured 243–5
  contribution 300
  demobilization work 279
  determination to join ATS 74
  drill 117–8
  education 23–4
  fatigue duty 117
  feminism 297
  and food 161–2, 167
  on gender division 113

Bruce, Lady Martha (*cont.*)
   Girl Guides Association
     involvement 24
   joins AA (Anti-Aircraft) Command
     75–7
   and Mary, the Princess Royal 140,
     141–2
   motto 117
   officer training 142–4
   Operation Diver 238, 239, 241–2
   overseas service 283
   parents 22–3, 75, 76–7
   posting 79–80
   post-war life 295–7
   presented at Court 25–6
   pre-war existence 22–6
   promotion to Bombardier 111
   refuses officer training 80
   social network 167
   technical aptitude 111
   technical training 110–2
   Territorial Army service 295–6
   Top Ack performance 121
   as trainer 111–2
   training 77–8
   V1 flying bombs 241–2
Brussels 265–9, 275
Buckingham Palace 24
Burma xi, 18, 24, 215, 232

Calder, Angus 212
camaraderie 138, 181
Cambridge 91
camp followers, term dropped 70
Canadian troops 211
Carter, Anne (nee Garrad) xiii, xv,
    xvi, xix
   arrival in Italy 258
   Austria posting 294
   British identity xi–xii
   catches hepatitis 259
   and declaration of war 18
   impatient for the end 269–70
   Inverness posting 256
   joins ATS 18, 215–6
   Lancaster ATS flight crash 293–4
   mother joins ATS 19

   officer training 269, 291–2
   overseas service 256–60
   policing duties 225–6
   pre-war existence 18–20
   pride 291, 299
   promotion 226
   survives V1 attack 256
   survivor's guilt 293
   Training Centre posting 226–7
   upbringing xi
Cassin, Rene 50
Castle, Barbara 180
casualties 293–4
   AA (Anti-Aircraft) Command
     99–100, 102–5
   air raids 57, 60
   ATS 100n
   BEF 34
   civilian 27, 29, 166, 242
   D-Day 236–7
   dog 191
   Eastern Front 115
   first female anti-aircraft 99–100
   German 284–5
   Italy 262, 263
   Normandy 243
   SOE 202
   V1 attacks 242
Caveney, Nora 99–100
Cazalet-Keir, Thelma 71
Chamberlain, Neville 7, 19
chastity, national obsession with
    223–4
chemical warfare, threat of 94–5
Chequers 76
Churchill, Clementine 195
Churchill, Mary. *See* Soames, Mary
   (nee Churchill)
Churchill, Winston 7–8, 27, 28, 31,
    44, 45, 47, 55, 60–1, 73, 76,
    86–7, 94–5, 99, 115–6, 161,
    168, 234, 243, 261, 274, 275–6,
    283, 284
cigarettes 154
Clark, General Mark 258
class system 20
Clermont-Ferrand 10–1

Index

code breaking 144–50, 156
code of conduct 116
coding methods 206–8
Cold War 289
collaboration 268
Collymore-Woodstock, Ena, OD,
    MBE (nee Collymore) xxii,
    217–8, 304
  becomes radar operator 237, 238
  joins ATS 219
  medals and awards 217–8
  overseas service 264
  pre-war existence 218
  reception in Britain 219–20
  training 219
Colonial Office 216, 218–9
colour bar 216
combat roles, opened to women 299
Comite National Francaise 192
Commandos 233, 250–1
commemoration xvi–xviii, 301-2
Committee for Imperial Defence
  16–7
Commonwealth Graves Commission
  100n
communal living 94, 133
companionship 108
conscription xiv–xv, 39, 123
  AA (Anti-Aircraft) Command 42
  age lowered 175
  call up 151–3
  introduction of 86–8, 125
  overseas 265
conservatism 123
contraception 227
contribution 299
cookhouse, mechanisation 164
cooks 164–7
  dry swill 167
  promotion to tradeswoman
    168–9
  recipes 164
  scale of production 164
  shortage of 159–61
  training 164, 169
  and waste food 166–7
  wet swill 167

cosmetics 71
Covid-19 ix–x, xii–xiii, xviii, 96,
  153, 303, 304, 305
Crete 86, 261
Croix de Guerre 51–2
Crowe, Lillian 108, 227

Daily Mail (newspaper) 56–7, 268,
  274
daily routine 116–8
Daily Telegraph (newspaper) 62–3
dances 121
dancing 66–7
Dartford 239–40
Daysh, Ronald 54
D-Day
  air cover 236–43
  casualties 236–7
  deception operation 241
  first wounded return 236–7
  fuel deliveries 125
  landings 234–5, 250
  preparations 221–2, 224, 256
  Sword beach 234
  troop build-up 211–4
  troops concentrated 230–4
de Gaulle, Charles
  back in Paris 265
  Churchill's support 45, 47
  dependence on Britain 51
  English language skill 47
  first broadcast 31, 47–8
  first followers 50
  lack of trust in 45
  leaves France 27–8
  mission 46
  offices 45
  OJ lends car 46
  OJ on 50, 51
  OJ stops working for 192
  OJ visits offices 46
  recognised as head of Free French
    31
  temperament 51
Deal 107
Defence Committee 86–7
de-lousing 226–7

demobilization 272–3, 278–83,
     289–91
democracy 22
de-nazification 285
Devizes 110–2, 138–9
dirty old men xv, 138
discharge 272–3, 278
discipline 77, 81, 116–8, 150
discretion 231
disease 95–6
domesticity, return to 278–81, 291
Doney, Linda 157–8
Douglas 154–5
Downey, Nanza (nee Hughes) xxi
     Bletchley Park service 151
     and BW 151
     call up 151–3
     earmarked for Special Operator
          Training 153–4
     Harrogate signals interception
          posting 155–7
     indiscretion 157
     marriage 157–8
     parents 152–3
     post-war life 157–8
     training 153, 153–5, 156
Downey, Tom 157–8
Downham School 23–4, 26
drill 117–8
drinking 262
drivers 170–82
     camaraderie 181
     mechanics training 179–80
     relationship with vehicle 184
     title 170–1
     training 172, 177–8, 178–9
dry swill 167
Dunkirk, evacuation from 10, 13
Durham 264
duty xiii

Eastern Front 114–5, 116, 166
Eddystone lighthouse 32
Edwards, Dorothy 57
Egypt 255, 260–1
Eisenhower, Dwight 299–300

Elgin, Andrew Bruce, 11th Earl of
     243–5
Elgin, Edward Bruce, 10th Earl of
     22–3, 130
Elgin, Katherine Bruce, Countess of
     22, 23, 25–6, 121, 244
Elizabeth, Queen 141, 174
Elizabeth II, Queen xvii, 24, 190,
     244, 274–5, 306
     ATS service xiii
     driver training 170, 172, 177–8,
          178–9
     end of service 181–2
     first wireless address 174
     Honorary Colonel of the
          Grenadier Guards 175
     honorary rank 177
     joins ATS 174, 176
     mechanics training 179–80
     meets Prince Philip 187–8
     passes out 181
     pre-war existence 174–5
     security arrangements 176–7
     service symbolic 180–1
     special status 177
     VE Day anniversary, 2015 301–2
emotions, managing 263
enemy aliens 154–5
Enigma machines 144
ENSA 255
entertainment 120–1
equality 21, 298–9
     resistance to idea of xi
     reversed 277–8
euphemisms 118
evacuation 54
exercise 118, 119, 119–20, 190–1

fatigue duty 117, 159
fear 58
Feltwell 36, 37, 39, 103–5
female compulsion 61–3
female war work 61–3
femininity, 281
     preservation of 114
feminism 21, 297
Fillingham, Colonel 149

Index

First Aid Nursing Yeomanry x
  bravery 15
  elite reputation 194
  and the Fall of France 15–6
  formation 14
  identity 16–7
  individualism 198
  interviews 198, 206–10
  Motor Companies 198
  overseas service 254–5, 261–4
  recruitment 197–9
  references 197–8
  reputation 15
  service life 194–200
  as SOE cover 201–2, 208
  status within ATS 16–7, 70, 198
  strength 15, 197
  training 199–200
  uniforms 198–9
  in World War I 14–5
food 78, 159, 160, 161–2, 164,
  167–9
food waste 166–7
Foreign Office 23, 47–8
Four Weddings and Funeral (film) 169
France
  Battle for 249–51
  de Gaulle leaves 27–8
  escape from 27–30, 193–4
  Fall of 8–12, 13–4, 15–6
  OJ on 47–8
  Polish troops escape 30
  refugees 10
  surrender 11–2
Free French 31, 46–51
free time 108–9
freedom 59
friendship 294
Fulford Barracks 127, 129, 221–3

Galworthy, Major Eric 263
Games, Abram 70–2
Gamwell, Marian 198, 199
Garrad, Marjory 19, 34, 215
gas training 95
gender division 55–6, 60–1, 104,
  112–4, 253

gendered rigidity 30
General Post Office 88, 282–3
Gentle Sex, The (ATS recruitment film)
  160–1, 215
George VI, King 174, 175, 176,
  180, 188, 274, 284
Germany 115, 274, 284–9
Gibraltar 255
Girl Guides Association 24
glamour 71–2
Glasgow 151–3, 270, 272
Glen Parva barracks 81, 97
Glover, Mark 242
Gobowen Orthopaedic Hospital
  120
gonorrhoea 224
Good Housekeeping (magazine) 281
gossip 134
Granville, Christine 202
gratitude xvi
Greece 86, 261
Greenwood, Joan 161
Gubbins, Brigadier Colin 199–200,
  206
Guildford 163–4
Gun Operations Room 105
gun-laying equipment 110–1
gun-sites 184–5
Gwynne-Vaughan, Dame Helen 13,
  16–7, 20, 21–2, 35, 62, 70, 77,
  141, 142, 198

Halifax 128–9
Hambro, Ruth 210
Hamburg, bombing of 166
Hardie, Agnes 62–3, 86
Harrogate 155–7
Haslett, Caroline 74–5
Hastings 107
health checks 96
Heligoland 37
Henriette (Belgian translator) 267
Herring, General 5, 6
Hitler, Adolf 4, 5, 55, 61, 274
Hitler Youth 147
holidays 113
Holland 265

hospital, Birmingham 232–4
home, sanctity of 85
homosexuality 132–4
Howard, Leslie 160–1, 215

impotence, feeling of 68–9
incendiary bombs 58–9
injuries 165
inspections 112
instruction school, Auxiliary
    Territorial Service 17
intel 155–7
Intelligence Corps 72
Inter Service Research Bureau 208
invasion threat 48
Inverness 256
Iraq 299
Isle of Man 154–5
Italy 215
    arrival in 258
    capitulation 258
    casualties 262, 263
    conditions 259
    entry into the war 68
    liberation of Rome 257–8, 259
    overseas service in 256–60
    partisans 262
    unsettling quality of 261–4
    VE Day 275–6

Johnson, Ken 'Snakehips' 60
Jordan, Olivia (nee Matthews) xvi,
    xviii, xix, 3–12, 129
    on the ATS 13–4
    the Blitz 58–61, 73
    bombed 60
    in Bordeaux 27–8
    condemned to death *in absentia* 50
    Croix de Guerre 51–2
    on de Gaulle 50, 51
    and de Gaulle's first broadcast
        47–8
    driving skill 48–50
    escape from France 27–30, 193–4
    and the Fall of France 8–12
    family background 3–4

    on France 47–8
    freedom 59
    great achievements 193
    has to return car 48–9
    health checks 95–6
    hero status 51–2
    joins SSAF 5–6
    language skills 47
    leaves for France 3
    lends de Gaulle car 46
    meets Duchess of Windsor 7
    memory 46–7
    nurses German prisoners 9
    philosophy 3
    the Phoney War 5
    pre-war existence 17
    on RAF morale 41
    return to Britain 31–3
    return to London 32–3
    riding accident 6
    sees Hitler 4
    self-deprecation 47
    sends Fortnum & Mason hamper
        to Poles 33
    sights Eddystone lighthouse 32
    stops working for de Gaulle 192
    and surrender of France 11–2
    training 5–7
    twenty-first birthday 3
    uniform 6
    upbringing 4
    vaccinations 96
    visits de Gaulle' offices 45–6
    vulnerability 27
    war dismissed 33
    wedding 192–3
    work for Free French 46–51
Jordan, Peter 192–3

Keel, Gladys 100
Knox, Jean 70, 142, 218
Kosovo 299

Lancaster ATS flight crash 293–4
Lancastria, SS 29, 33
Le Mans 13

leadership 142
Legal Aid department 287–8
Leicester 56
Lemmon, Dorothy 87
   death of 102–5
lesbianism 132–4
Lidstone, Diana (nee Scott) xx, 167
   as cook 164–7, 168–9
   injuries 165
   joins ATS 163–4
   leaves service 279–80
   Old Harlow posting 165
   post-war life 169
   pre-war existence 44, 162–3
   promotion to Lance Corporal
      169
   references 279–80
   relationship with food 169
   service book 279–80
Liphook 169
Liverpool 41, 102
London 140
   the Blitz 53–4, 54–6, 58–61, 73–4
   Café de Paris 60
   Claridges Hotel 192–3
   Devonshire House 147
   evacuation 54
   Fortnum & Mason 33
   Mayfair Hotel 73
   Park Lane Hotel 32–3
   the Ritz 60
   St Stephen's House 46
   V1 attacks 240, 242, 256
   VE Day 274–6
London Underground 118
Lovat Scouts, the 257, 259
Luftwaffe 9–10, 41, 42–4, 43, 107
Luxembourg 265

Malaya 196
male desire 135–9
Malta 68
Manchester 41, 103–4
Mangotsfield 143
manning up 110
Manpower Debate, 1944 281

manpower problems 61
Manthorp, Beryl xxi
   and Black troops 212–4
   dance performances 120, 121
   death of 305
   funeral 305–6
   joins ATS 119
   link with Trinidad 214
   NCO training 119
   pre-war existence 119
   promotion to sergeant 211
   PT instruction 119–20, 211–2
   training 119
marching 129–30
Margaret, Princess 175
Markham, Violet 127–8
Markham Committee 127–8,
      132–3, 134–5, 139, 142, 223–4,
      228, 239
Marks, Leo 207–8, 209–10
Mary, Queen 140
Mary, the Princess Royal 140, 176,
      219
masculinity, preservation of 114
Matthews, Trevor 33
meals 161–2, 168
Meccano 173
mechanisation, cookhouse 164
medals and awards xi, xviii, 51–2,
      150, 217–8, 302
medicals 91–3, 216
Megève 5
Melton Mowbray 88–9
menstruation 118, 150
mental editing 93
Middlesborough 189–90
military status, women granted 70
Mills, John xvii
Ministry of Defence 298
Ministry of Information 31–2, 98
Mitford girls, the 4
modesty 91–2
Montagu, Judy 75–6
Montecassino 156
morale 9, 41, 55, 61, 71
morality question 132–9

Index

Motor Transport Training Company 172–3
Munich 4
Munich Crisis 20
Muselier, Emile 50
Music and Drama Society 120

NAAFI 117
National Army Museum 306
National Geographic (magazine) 144
national service 295
National Service (No.2) Act xiv, 87–8, 90, 91, 122
Navy Army and Airforce Institutes 117
New Statesman (magazine) 19–21, 122
New Zealand forces 211
Newbattle Abbey 76–7, 78
Newcastle 282
Nightingale, Florence 15
Noakes, Lucy 281
Normandy
    breakout from 243–4
    casualties 243
North Africa 68, 86, 215, 260
North Rhine-Westphalia xv, 286–9
Northampton 264
Northfield experiments 232
Norton-on-Tees 183–4
Norway 7
nostalgia xvi

Officer Cadet Training Unit 168–9
officer training 142–4, 269, 291–2
officers 129
    appointment 77
    female 113
    food 169
    quality 78, 143
    youth 155
Official Secrets Act 148, 156, 207
Old Harlow 165
Operation Aerial 29–30
Operation Bluecoat 243–4
Operation Bolero 212
Operation Diver 236–43

Operation Fortitude 241
Operation Gomarrah 166
Operation Overlord 165
Operation Torch 107
operational duties, ban lifted 72
Oswestry 120
overseas conscription 265
overseas service
    authorised 253–4
    in Egypt 260–1
    in Italy 256–60
    male-female relations 259–60
    need for female 259–60
    parental permission 253–5, 264
    return from 291–4
Overthorpe Park 206–8
Owtram, Colonel Carey 196

parades 112
Paragraph 11 227
Paris 5, 265, 289
partisans 262
Pathé news 69
patriotism 21
Pearl Harbour, attack on 86
perfume 108–9
periods 118, 150
Pétain, Marshall Philippe 11, 48
Philip, Prince, Duke of Edinburgh 187–8, 302
Phoney War, the 5, 40–1
physical training 118, 119, 119–20, 190–1
Pile, Sir Frederick 'Tim' Alfred 42, 74–5, 76, 79, 113, 114, 135–9, 189
Pluto project, the 125
Plymouth 31, 56, 99
    air raids 57–8, 106–9
poison gas 94–5
Poland, invasion of 5
policing duties 225–6
Poole 64
Poole Royal Artillery Association 97
Post Traumatic Stress Disorder 232
predictors 79, 100–2, 237

pregnancies xiii, 85, 224, 227,
227–9, 272–3
Pre-Officer Cadet Training Unit
143–4
pride xii, xiii, 299, 300
prisoners of war 44, 196
German 268–9
return 277
privacy, lack of 133
promiscuity xv, 132–9, 223–4, 226–
7, 227–9, 257
promotion 77, 111, 112, 112–3,
143, 146, 149, 169, 226, 254–5,
262, 264
protocol 129–30
psychiatric treatment 232–3

Queen Charlotte's Ball 25–6
Queen of Bermuda, SS 256–7

race relations 212–4, 216–20
radar 110, 237, 238, 238–9
radio location girls 120
RAF 35, 41, 42–4
rank, badges of xi
ranks, not allowed to use 112–3
Rathbone, Eleanor 90
Ravensbruck concentration camp
202
recruitment xiv–xv, 19–21, 99, 123,
197-9, 215-6
Redcar 190–1
references 279–80
refugees 10, 27
Registration for Employment Order
61–2
remembrance 301–2
replacement ratios 113–4
reputations 37–8
respect 118, 130
Reynaud, Paul 8, 11
Rise Park 135–6
Rogers, Peter 163
Rolls Honour 104
romance 186
Rome, liberation of 257–8, 259

Rommel, General Erwin 8
Royal Artillery 72, 75, 97, 100, 110,
112–3, 183
Royal Artillery Association 172, 183,
300–1
Royal Corps of Signals 72, 153–4
Royal Electrical and Mechanical
Engineers 165
royals, and military service 140–2
ruling class nexus 76
Russia 277, 289
Russian Vera 115
Rye 107

Saint-Exupéry, Antoine de 10
Saint-Jean-de-Luz, evacuation from
29
St Nazaire 29, 30
Saint-Valery-sur-Somme 296
Saltash 56–8
salutes 129, 130
sanitary towels 118, 150
sanitation 10–1
Sartre, Jean Paul 3
Scotland 21, 22–4
searchlight companies 88–9, 105–6,
188–90
Sections Sanitaires Automobiles
Féminines (SSAF) 5–7, 8–12
segregation 212–4, 218
Semark, Jessica Ellen 293
service books 221–3, 279–80
service life, lack of glamour 94
Sevenoaks, Kent 3
Sex Discrimination Act 298
sexism 123
sexual health 224–5
sexualised language 227
Seymour, Lady Katherine 176
Sharbek, Krystyna 202, 204, 205–6
shoes 94
shorthand 128–9
Sicily 258
signals interception 155–7
Singapore, fall of 196
singing 184–5

smoking 154, 262
snobbery 123
Soames, Mary (nee Churchill) xiii,
    55, 60–1, 74, 75–6, 77–8, 141,
    168, 195, 243, 253–4
Spain 28
Special Operations Executive xi
    agent training 203–4, 205–6
    Baker Street headquarters 208–10
    casualties 202
    codenames 208
    coding methods 206–8, 208–9
    female agents 201–2
    poem-code system 208–9, 210
    service life 201–10
    Thame Park Special Training
        School 201–5, 202
    training 199–200, 206–8
    transmitter hut attendants 201,
        202–3
special problem, the 132–4
Sprugeon, Lance Bombardier Jack
    120
Stalingrad 115
statue xvii
Steele, Major General Michael 301
Stirling Castle, MV 255
Stittle, Joan (nee Awbery) xiii, xv,
    xvi, xx–xxi, 305–6
    Belgium posting 265–9
    contribution 299
    daily routine 130
    decision to join up 89–90
    demobilization 289–90
    and food 168
    Germany posting 284–9
    impatient for the end 269, 274
    joins ATS 91
    medals and awards xi
    medical 91–2
    overseas service 264–9, 284–9
    pre-war existence 90–1
    promotion to corporal 264
    training 92–6
    VE Day 275
survivor's guilt 293
syphilis 224

Szabo, Violette 201–2, 204, 205,
    210
Talavera Training Camp 92–3,
    95–6, 103, 130
talent identification 237
taxation 22
Taylor, Bob 185–6, 270–2, 286
Taylor, Grace (nee Clarke) xv–xvi,
    xx, 116, 127, 159
    dancing 66–7
    death of mother 64–5
    demobilization 278, 281–2
    and end of the war 270
    family background 64–5
    father 64–5
    first boyfriend 67–8
    free time 108–9
    German parachute nightie 271
    on gun-laying equipment 110
    joins ATS 64, 69
    and Kathy's unfortunate
        disposition 227–8
    lies about age 81
    marries Bob 270–2
    meets Bob 185–6
    Operation Diver 238–9, 240–1
    opinion on the war 66
    perfume 108–9
    periods 118
    Plymouth posting 106–9
    posting 97–9
    post-war life 283
    pre-war existence 64–7
    response to lipstick advert 71
    on singing 184–5
    stepmother 65
    training 81–2, 97
Telegraph, The (newspaper) 178
teleplotters 88–9, 106–9
Terrington St Clements 136–7
Territorial Army 21, 295–6
Tester, Ralph 145
Thame Park Special Training School
    201–5, 202, 228–9
Thorne, General Andrew 76–7
Thorne, Pansy 76–7, 80
The Times (newspaper) 100

Top Ack performance 121
training 5–7, 77, 77–8, 81–2, 88–9,
    92–6, 97, 103, 110–2, 119,
    145–6
  cooks 164, 169
  drivers 172, 177–8, 178–9
  FANY 199–200
  mechanics 179–80
  officer 142–4, 269, 291–2
  signals interception 153–5, 156
  SOE 199–200, 206–8
transferable skills 128–9
Turing, Alan 145
typing 128–9

Ultra 156
uniforms 6, 70, 90, 94, 135, 153,
    198–9
US Army
  Black troops 212–4
  over-sexed 222
  troop numbers 224

V1 flying bombs 239–43, 256
V2 240
vaccinations 95–6
Valentina (Russian anti-aircraft
    artillery commander) 115
VE Day 274–6
VE Day anniversary, 2015 301–2
venereal disease 224–5, 228
Versailles 6
veteran duties 172
Vichy France 28, 48, 50
Vickers Wellington 37
victory parades 285
*Violet Markham Committee on Amenities
    and Welfare in the Three Women's
    Services* 127–8
vulnerability 27

WAAF (Women's Auxiliary Air
    Force) xiii–xiv, 35
Waddington, Vera (nee Edwards) xx,
    91–2, 95
  bombed 57–8
  father 56–7

on food 161
on gender division 113–4
Liverpool posting 102, 106
marriage 280–1
medical 92–3
mother 57
posting 100–1
predictor use 100–2, 237
pre-war existence 56–7
references 280, 281
wages xv, 113, 160, 188
war
  declaration of 5, 18
  German surrender 274
  impatient for the end 269–70
War Office 61, 75, 216, 217, 218,
    219, 279
Ward, Charlie 231–4, 249–52, 272
Ward, Florence Maud (nee
    Chadwick) xxi, 277–8
  and Charlie 231–4
  Charlie's letters 249–51
  D-Day landings 234
  experience of men 126–7
  joins ATS 123, 126, 231–2
  marries Charlie 252, 252–3
  and overseas service 254
  posting 128–9
  pre-war existence 122, 124–5
  pregnancy 272–3
  training 127, 128, 132
Warrington 164
weapons xv, 116, 285
Weatherill, Barbara (nee Crorken)
    xvii, xx, 159–60, 298
  association membership 300–1
  camaraderie 181
  demobilization 290–1
  desire to be driver 170–1
  driver training 172, 177, 178–9
  and driving 49
  on FANYs 194
  joins up 171–2, 173–4, 176
  marriage 291
  mechanics training 179–80
  medals and awards 302
  meets Stan 186–7

Weatherill, Barbara (*cont.*)
    Norton-on-Tees posting 183–4
    Operation Diver 236–7, 239
    parents 171, 173–4
    post-war life 300–1
    pre-war existence 173
    pride 170–1, 300
    promotion to lance corporal 290
    Redcar posting 190–1
    relationship with her vehicle 184
    as searchlight operator 188–90
    sees V1 239–40
    service life 188–91
    VE Day anniversary, 2015
        301–2
    veteran duties 172
    wages 188
Weatherill, Stan 186–7, 291
Webb, Betty MBE (nee Vine-Stevens)
        xxi, 159
    Bletchley Park service 144–50
    language skills 146–7
    medals and awards 150
    mother 145–6
    and ND 151
    periods 150
    posting to Bletchley Park 147–8
    promotion 146, 149
    signs Official Secrets Act 148
    training 145–6
    V1 attacks 242
Wellington, Maud, Duchess of 244
Welwyn Garden City 38, 39–40
West Germany 289
West Indian veterans 303
Westminster Abbey, VE Day
        anniversary, 2015 301–2
wet swill 167
Weygand, Maxime 51
Whateley, Leslie 70

Wilding, Joyce (nee Chamberlain)
        xix, 14, 16, 211
    dog 204
    driving experience 195
    horse 204
    joins FANYs 194–5, 197–200
    on pregnancies 228–9
    pre-war existence 17, 195
    SOE service 201–5
    SOE training 200
Williams, Annie 37–8
Williamson, Gavin 299
Windsor, Edward, Duke of 7
Windsor, Wallis Duchess of 7
wireless 17, 44
Woman's Own (magazine) 36, 71
women, granted military status 70
Women Royal Auxiliary Corp 140
Women's Army Corps 272
Women's Auxiliary Army Corps 16
Women's Auxiliary Corps of India
        217
Women's Consultative Committee
        153
Women's Royal Army Corps 141,
        279, 296, 298, 303
Women's Royal Army Corps
        Association 244
World War I 14–5, 23, 91, 95, 140,
        170
Wrexham 146, 226–7
WRNS (Women's Royal Naval
        Service) xiii–xiv, 34–5, 85

York 221–3
York Royal Artillery Association
        300, 301
Yorkshire Post (newspaper) 172
Yugoslavia 262
Yvonne (Belgian translator) 267